# FEMINIST VIEWS FROM SOMEWHERE

*Feminist Views from Somewhere: Post-Jungian Themes in Feminist Theory* explores what and how Jungian thought contributes to feminist thinking. Broadly speaking, feminist thinking, or thinking by and about women as autonomous, intelligent and independent agents, has opened up scholarship through insightful, reflective critique and practice. This is the starting point of this collection from a range of theorists, interested in the multiple concerns of Jungian and analytical psychology.

The contributors take a unique approach to Jungian thinking. Rather than focusing on its mythological aspects, the authors develop alternative, feminist approaches that enhance the appreciation of the possibilities for Jungian and post-Jungian studies.

With a primarily theoretical orientation, the rigorous, critical approaches in the collection highlight the possibilities of imaginative Jungian theory. Divided into three parts, 'Viewing Earth', 'Clinical Perspectives' and 'Literary Landscapes', the chapters cover themes including embodiment, intersubjectivity, individuation and narrative. The contributors vividly reflect the range and diversity of opinions amongst women influenced by Jungian thought. *Feminist Views from Somewhere* is essential reading for academics and students of Jungian and post-Jungian studies, women's studies and gender studies, as well as analytical psychologists in practice and in training.

**Leslie Gardner** is director of Artellus Ltd, an international literary agency, and Visiting Fellow at the Centre for Psychoanalytic Studies at University of Essex, UK. Her previous publications include *Rhetorical Investigations: G. B. Vico and C. G. Jung* and *House: The Wounded Healer on Television* (co-edited with Luke Hockley).

**Frances Gray** is Honorary Senior Research Fellow in the School of Historical and Philosophical Inquiry at the University of Queensland, Australia. She is the author of the Routledge titles *Jung, Irigaray, Individuation: Philosophy, Analytical Psychology and the Question of the Feminine, Cartesian Philosophy and the Flesh: Reflections on Incarnation in Analytical Psychology* and *Jung and Levinas: An Ethics of Mediation*.

# FEMINIST VIEWS FROM SOMEWHERE

Post-Jungian Themes in Feminist Theory

Edited by Leslie Gardner and Frances Gray

LONDON AND NEW YORK

First published 2017
by Routledge
2 Park Square, Milton Park, Abingdon, Oxon OX14 4RN

and by Routledge
711 Third Avenue, New York, NY 10017

*Routledge is an imprint of the Taylor & Francis Group, an informa business*

© 2017 selection and editorial matter, L. Gardner and F. Gray; individual chapters, the contributors.

The right of the editors to be identified as the authors of the editorial material, and of the authors for their individual chapters, has been asserted in accordance with sections 77 and 78 of the Copyright, Designs and Patents Act 1988.

All rights reserved. No part of this book may be reprinted or reproduced or utilised in any form or by any electronic, mechanical, or other means, now known or hereafter invented, including photocopying and recording, or in any information storage or retrieval system, without permission in writing from the publishers.

*Trademark notice*: Product or corporate names may be trademarks or registered trademarks, and are used only for identification and explanation without intent to infringe.

*British Library Cataloguing in Publication Data*
A catalogue record for this book is available from the British Library

*Library of Congress Cataloging in Publication Data*
Names: Gardner, Leslie, 1949- editor. | Gray, Frances, 1949- editor.
Title: Post-Jungian themes in feminist theory : feminist views from somewhere / edited by Leslie Gardner and Frances Gray.
Description: Milton Park, Abingdon ; New York, NY : Routledge, 2017. | Includes bibliographical references. Identifiers: LCCN 2016029194 | ISBN 9781138897830 (hbk : alk. paper) | ISBN 9781138897823 (pbk. : alk. paper) | ISBN 9781315708973 (ebk)Subjects: | MESH: Jungian Theory | Feminism | Literature, Modern | Body Image Classification: LCC BF173.J85 | NLM WM 460.5.J9 | DDC 150.19/54--dc23LC record available at https://lccn.loc.gov/2016029194]

ISBN: 978-1-138-89783-0 (hbk)
ISBN: 978-1-138-89782-3 (pbk)
ISBN: 978-1-315-70897-3 (ebk)

Typeset in Bembo
by Cenveo Publisher Services

# CONTENTS

| | |
|---|---|
| *Acknowledgements* | *vii* |
| *Notes on contributors* | *ix* |
| *Background* | *xiii* |
| LESLIE GARDNER AND FRANCES GRAY | |
| *Introduction: Feminist views from somewhere?* | *xvii* |
| FRANCES GRAY | |

## PART I
## Theme: Viewing Earth                                          1

| | | |
|---|---|---|
| 1 | Women and land: reflections on physicality<br>*Lyn Cowan* | 3 |
| 2 | Becoming human<br>*Amanda Dowd* | 9 |
| 3 | Medial women: views of a feminist epistemologist<br>*Susan Wyatt* | 25 |

## PART II
## Theme: Clinical Perspectives                               39

| | | |
|---|---|---|
| 4 | Working with a woman with binge eating disorder<br>*Sue Austin* | 41 |

**vi** Contents

5    Emma Jung's pen: Jung, feminism and the body       56
     *Cheryl L. Fuller*

6    In search of the heroine       70
     *Coline Covington*

**PART III**
**Theme: Literary Landscapes**       **81**

7    Feminism, Jung and transdisciplinarity: a novel approach       83
     *Susan Rowland*

8    Fierce young women in popular fiction and an unpopular war       99
     *Elizabeth Eowyn Nelson*

9    Explorations in the poetics of the feminine pronoun       118
     *Leslie Gardner*

*Appendix: Voices from the IAJS forum October – December 2013*       132
*Index*       148

# ACKNOWLEDGEMENTS

We thank our contributors, each and every one of you, for your resilience, for your patience and for your generous cooperation during the creative phase of this cornucopia of women's ideas, always from somewhere.

Thank you to Lucy Huskinson and Craig Stephenson for your encouragement, and to Luke Hockley for your creative inspiration.

Thank you, Michael Glock, for your archival skills and encouragement in the production of the 'Voices' appendix.

We thank the International Association for Jungian Studies (IAJS) for hosting the online seminar which was the origin of this project.

Thank you Andrew Samuels for your support for our collection and on-going promotion of Jungian and post-Jungian studies.

Thank you Susannah Frearson, our warm and encouraging editor at Routledge, for your patience, good will and support throughout the development of this collection.

The authors acknowledge permission to use previously published material:

Amanda Dowd 'Becoming human':

*Sonnets to Orpheus*, II,4, from *The Selected Poetry of Rainer Maria Rilke* published originally by Random House and found in the Picador Classics edition published by Pan Books in 1987. Translation © 1987 by Stephen Mitchell. Used by permission.

Lyn Cowan:

Lyn Cowan, 'Women and the Land' in *Tracking the White Rabbit*. London: Routledge. pp. 36–41. Used by permission.

# NOTES ON CONTRIBUTORS

**Sue Austin** trained with the Australian and New Zealand Society of Jungian Analysts. Her private practice comprises general analytic work and clinical supervision and she also specializes in working with eating disordered adults and supervising clinicians who work in the eating disorders field. Sue has run numerous clinical workshops and seminars in Australia, New Zealand, the UK, Europe and the USA. She has also published several clinical and theoretical papers and a book.

**Coline Covington** has worked as a Jungian analyst for over 25 years in private practice in London. She is former Chair of the British Psychoanalytic Council and a training analyst and supervisor of the Society of Analytical Psychology and the British Psychotherapy Foundation. She is a fellow of International Dialogue Initiative (IDI), a group formed by Professor Dr Vamik Volkan, Lord Alderdice and Dr Robi Friedman to apply psychoanalytic concepts in understanding political conflict and the effects of trauma on political behaviour.

Coline has co-edited *Terrorism and War: Unconscious Dynamics of Political Violence* (Karnac, 2002) and *Sabina Spielrein: Forgotten Pioneer of Psychoanalysis*, 2nd Edition (Routledge, 2015). Her books are *Shrinking the News: Headline Stories on the Couch* (Karnac, 2014) and *Everyday Evils: A Psychoanalytic View of Evil and Destructiveness* (Routledge, forthcoming).

**Lyn Cowan** has been a practicing Jungian analyst since 1980, Director of Training for the Inter-Regional Society of Jungian Analysts for six years and past President of the Society. She held a professorship for ten years in the doctoral programme in clinical psychology at Argosy University (Minneapolis) and five years in the Jungian Studies doctoral programme at Saybrook University. She is the author of three books: *Portrait of the Blue Lady: The Character of Melancholy* (Spring Journal, 2004), *Tracking the White Rabbit: A Subversive View of Modern Culture* (Routledge, 2002) and

**x** Notes on contributors

*Masochism: A Jungian View* (Spring Publications, 1982). A memoir, *Loyalties: Memoir Stories from the 1950s*, is moving slowly toward completion.

**Amanda Dowd** is a Jungian psychoanalyst, training analyst, psychoanalytic psychotherapist and clinical supervisor who has been in private practice in Sydney for over 20 years. She is a senior professional member of The Australian and New Zealand Society of Jungian Analysts (ANZSJA) and also a member of the International Association of Analytical Psychology (IAAP). Her theoretical orientation is developmental and relational, and her particular interests are trauma, the formation of mind, self, identity and cultural identity, the relationship between self and place, migration and displacement. She has lectured and published widely on these themes both in Australia and internationally. Amanda is co-editor, along with Craig San Roque and David Tacey, of *Placing Psyche, Exploring Cultural Complexes in Australia* (Spring Journal Books, 2011).

**Cheryl L. Fuller** is a Jungian psychotherapist and writer in private practice in Belfast, Maine. She has written and taught about Medea and feminism. For the last seven years she has written a blog, Jung-At-Heart.com. Her current academic research lies in the intersection of fat studies and analytical psychology. She is currently working on a book exploring stigma and anti-fat bias and their effects on the lived experience of fat women in and out of the consulting room.

**Leslie Gardner** is an American, based for 30 years in the UK. Her book *Rhetorical Investigations G B Vico and C G Jung* (Routledge, 2013) was an overhaul of her PhD dissertation; chapters have been published in *Psyche and the Arts* (ed. Susan Rowland, Routledge, 2008), and in other volumes, most recently *Jung and the Question of Science* (ed. Raya Jones, Routledge, 2013). She co-edited with Luke Hockley *House: the wounded healer on television* (Routledge 2010), published also in Hungarian. Reviews have appeared in *Journal of Analytical Psychology* and *IJJS*. She is director of an international literary agency, Artellus Ltd, and serves various functions for the International Association of Jungian Studies (www.jungianstudies. org). She is a Fellow in the Centre for Psychoanalytic Studies at the University of Essex, UK.

**Frances Gray** holds a PhD in Philosophy and Women's Studies from the Australian National University. She is Honorary Senior Research Fellow in the School of Historical and Philosophical Inquiry at the University of Queensland, St Lucia, Queensland, Australia. She is the author of *Jung, Irigaray, Individuation: Analytical Psychology and the Question of the Feminine* (2007), *Cartesian Philosophy and the Flesh: Reflections on Incarnation in Analytical Psychology* (2012) and *Jung and Levinas: An Ethics of Mediation* (2015) all published by Routledge UK. Her recent work revolved around ethics and professional conversations in mediation and psychotherapeutic practice. Her current work is dedicated to the relationship between hybrid forms of yoga and ecology.

**Elizabeth Eowyn Nelson** is core faculty and Dissertation Policy Director at Pacifica Graduate Institute near Santa Barbara, California where she teaches a broad range of courses in research process, methodology, and dissertation development along with courses in dream, imagery and cultural studies. Her own research interests include personal and cultural expressions of the shadow, gender and power, with a particular fascination with how we construct, encounter and understand evil and the monstrous. Elizabeth is the author of two books, *The Art of Inquiry: A Depth Psychological Perspective* (Spring Publications, 2005, coauthored with Joseph Coppin) and *Psyche's Knife: Archetypal Explorations of Love and Power* (Chiron, 2012). A professional writer and editor for nearly 30 years consulting in technology, health and finance, she now coaches aspiring authors across a variety of genres and styles.

**Susan Rowland** is Chair of MA Engaged Humanities and the Creative Life at Pacifica Graduate Institute, California. As writer on Jung, literary theory, gender and the arts, she published *Jung: A Feminist Revision* (Routledge, 2002) and other books including *Jung as a Writer* (Routledge, 2005) and *The Ecocritical Psyche: Literature, Complexity Evolution and Jung* (Routledge, 2012). She was founding Chair of the International Association for Jungian Studies 2003–6 and now teaches Shakespeare, gender theory, The Red Book, ecocriticism and Jung. Recent projects include a book on goddesses in mystery fiction and another on literary theory in James Hillman and Jung.

**Susan Wyatt**'s first career was as an engineer and manager of technical projects. Her ideas of feminist epistemologies developed in the context of resistance to the dominant paradigms of these fields. She teaches research in the Organization Management programme at Antioch University Los Angeles, focusing on topics such as systems and critical thinking, journaling, primary data collection methods, and collaborative and action research. She is a student of tai chi and qigong and has published 'Embodying the Tension between Opposites in Qigong' (*Conversations in the Field*) as well as articles and presentations on change agency, appreciative inquiry and the mythology of research.

# BACKGROUND

*Leslie Gardner and Frances Gray*

'Feminism' is considered by some theorists to be central in contemporary considerations about the self, personality and psyche. Feminist thought, developed from the early work of Mary Wollstonecraft, through that of Harriet Taylor and then the suffragettes to Betty Friedan and beyond in the anglophone world, and from Simone de Beauvoir in the francophone, has seen clearly different emphases and different orientations. The womanist movements and the lesbian/queer theorists of the eighties and nineties into the present day have contributed to a proliferation of views that now have histories, either 'fashionable' or out-moded. Across academic disciplines, psychologists, literary theorists, philosophers, political theorists, theologians and sociologists have alternately dismissed and ridiculed or subjected 'feminism' to paradoxical and obfuscating discussion; or else they have lauded the work of feminists who see an opportunity for women to have a voice, and to develop socio-political and personal autonomy. Hence sometimes, 'feminism' emerges as one of the most plausible critiques and practices of recent times. This is the starting point of this volume of essays by a range of theorists, broadly interested in the concerns of Jungian and analytical psychology.

Jungian and analytical reflections on feminist matters have so often been buried in woolly talk of mythological figures and goddesses. In this volume, we propose to take a different approach, framing our essays with the question, 'Just what, if anything, can Jungian thought contribute to feminist thinking?' This question will build on our contributors' engagement with the problem of developing a meaningful understanding and interpretation of exactly what feminist thought is. Of course, given the Jungian orientation of many of our contributors, one may find a smattering of loosely called 'archetypal' terminology. However, our orientation is primarily theoretical so we are aiming to rehabilitate previous Jungian thinking in more rigorous, critical terms.

**xiv** Background

Speaking very broadly, Jungian studies purports to enter legitimately into the discourses of philosophy, theology, mythology and psychology with a set of terms more or less systematically articulated through C. G. Jung's work. Quite often, the tropes of Jungian discourses revolve around allegedly binary terms like appearance and reality, interior and exterior, anima and animus, collective and personal unconscious. The binary divisions, at least as they are understood as such, are usually articulated as an intricate part of Jung's compelling concept of individuation. Implicit in this concept is the struggle of the individual to overcome her/his enmeshment in the collective, both conscious and unconscious. From a feminist perspective there is perhaps no greater contribution that Jungian thought can make than to embrace this profound idea: that as women, the path to individuation is treacherous, paved as it has been by the masculine paternal attitudes and values of mainstream (masculinist) Jungianism and analytical psychology.

There are many aspects of the feminist discussion that do not sit well in considerations of Carl Jung in his twentieth-century womanising and sexism, despite his aspirations to the contrary. His relationship with Emma, at once a collaborator and mother of his children, has been seen as problematic within the context of feminist thinking. Emma was expected to tolerate Jung's close and intimate relations with several other women – not only Toni Wolf whose work is considered in one essay in this volume, but also Sabrina Spielrein. It is alleged that he abused his personal relationships with female analysands and early smitten mediums he studied for his work, deceiving them in order to investigate and thereafter promulgate his theories (we think of 'Mrs Miller' and Helene Prestiwck). What we consider to be his antiquated and harmful ideas of what it meant to be female and his creation of the rigid concepts of anima and animus have been roundly criticized, notwithstanding the claim that these concepts are intrinsic to the ideal of transformation that is core to Jungian thought. This is part of what we seek to address in this volume.

Early women in the Jungian field like Marie-Louise von Franz persisted in an area generally not seen as women's work – in her case, physics. Yet she and others set the stage for some of the conversations in Jungian terms. In this light, Nancy Chodorow, Ginette Paris and numerous other women have brought their clinical experience with women analysands to bear fruitfully in past discussions. Hence there has been important recent work in the direction we are proposing to highlight in this book: Susan Rowland (*Jung, A Feminist Revision*, Routledge, 2002), Sue Austin (*Women's Aggressive Fantasies: An Exploration of Self-Hatred, Love and Agency*, Routledge, 2005) and Frances Gray's own recent work on Franco/Belgian feminist Luce Irigaray in Jungian contexts (*Jung, Irigaray, Individuation*, Routledge, 2007) among others.

## Why this book, now?

Irked by the animus/anima binary (among other themes on how women should live in Jung's writings), we recently nudged the members of the International Association for Jungian Studies to think of how to bring important Jungian notions up to date, eschewing the anima/animus opposition – or bringing its values to bear. How essential, we wondered, is that construct to Jungian thought? Using our questions as the basis of a seminar, we asked a group of women to develop short essays, and respond to each other. Those essays were mounted as an online seminar on the website of the *International Journal of Jungian Studies* (IAJS). They were thoughtful and born of individual experience and a grappling with complex theoretical positions. The response from both women and men members of the organization to the essays was sophisticated and lengthy, but often enough we found a re-iteration of ideas we have found problematic.

In this collection of essays some of the authors in the IAJS discussion, together with invited authors, have expanded and developed their views. The essays aim to explicate where we are now in feminist theory as it interweaves with Jung's ideas, and how this has significance in the broader discussion.

# INTRODUCTION

## Feminist views from somewhere?

*Frances Gray*

Proem: I have a friend who is a geneticist. His version of Darwinian/Social Darwinist philosophy commits him to natural selection and survival of the fittest. In his world, selection and survival are the *telos* of nature, of existing and being in the world. Species select the best characteristics to ensure their survival in the worlds in which they live. Sexual and natural selection determine species order. Selection and survival are principally the concern of the male of the species. In my friend's view, and indeed the view of some other scientists, various factors interplay in the competitive, survival stakes: socio-biology, genetic and psycho-social theories all expound the intricacies and fascination of survival on earth. For example, some might hold that peacocks grow beautiful tails to attract willing peahens so that the best progeny can be produced. The peahens blindly follow the seductive beauty of the peacock's tail, make no decisions and are passive rather than active in the procreative process.

We can think of my geneticist friend's view as a 'view from nowhere'. It is a view held traditionally by other scientists who understand and believe that a scientific perspective says something about the world that would be 'true no matter what'. There is an 'objectively real world' independent of human knowledge, but knowable nonetheless, and the job of science is to uncover and to report on that world in language that is value free, clear and rather minimalist. The personal subjectivity and values of the scientist are allegedly bracketed, so that only scientific data produced in the scientist's observations and experiments count as valid knowledge. Yet we can argue that this version of what constitutes a scientific programme of research relies on un-bracketable conditions that persist no-matter-what. Hence the peacock and peahen example above instantiates assumptions found in the philosophy of Aristotle – male/active, female/passive, the male provides the form, the female the matter of procreation. This view, we can argue, is embedded in a specific, gendered, view of the world. It is, in truth, a 'view from somewhere', a view that assumes consciousness had by someone who will always be existentially and socially located: Aristotle as the originator of the assumptions and 'modern' scientists as protagonists of his view albeit unconsciously in some cases. This critique argues that existential and social location inform both the conscious and the unconscious, influencing our opinions, beliefs, preferences, desires and the world views peculiar to each one of us.

That said, our world views are unique only in so far as they are manifested in each body: our locatedness manifests and ensures a shared, communal dimension to our being. We are both more and less ourselves, depending on the point from which we describe a circumference around ourselves. We might refer to each of these perspectives as, respectively, the subjective and the objective.

★★★

The title of this volume, *Feminist Views from Somewhere*, takes its inspiration from debates about objectivity and subjectivity and the importance of acknowledging located-ness or situated-ness as sex/gendered individuals in a plurality of overlapping social contexts. These debates have occurred over the past half century and the above vignette captures some of their important elements, for example, that my friend does not locate his views in a specific, scientific, male culture that creates a perspective bias that has an immediate effect on the theory he espouses. The volume aims to present views from women theorists and practitioners who have been influenced by the analytical psychology of C. G. Jung and subsequent depth psychologies. We understand these views to be 'feminist' because their authors, as women, take seriously the idea that women, as women, need to be listened to and to be heard if there is to be social transformation that involves liberating women from the desires and primacy of the masculine symbolic in which we all live. A social transformation such as is envisaged here includes ideas around equality in all spheres of our lived experience, and acknowledgement of the specificities of women's experience that cannot be theorized under the umbrella of 'male' or 'neutral' theory or practice. It assumes that women's voices are not listened to or heard by men as a whole social practice, that women's voices are still, in 2015, trivialized and discounted. We aim, in this volume to address implicitly that assumption. It takes as a given that we all have different perspectives on the influence and importance of C. G. Jung and analytical psychology in general. In order to establish the importance of having a view from somewhere, we need, however, to contextualize the somewhere-ness of the title.

If it is the case that we all have a view from somewhere, we might begin to wonder how human existence is possible as collective, and individual, experience. We might ask if there is a world or worlds to which we are not privy, and we might ask about the nature and possibility of there being anything outside our experience. We might ask if there can be a view from a somewhere which is not mediated? Is that an oxymoron? If so, what would that view be like, and how would it be realized? There are several issues at stake. What, then, are some of the elements in our title 'feminist views from somewhere'? That there are feminist views, or any other views: class views or 'racial' views or masculinist views or party-specific views for instance, we take to be the case. That it is the case is not based on assumptions about essences or particular properties or qualities; rather, as we shall see, we appeal to difference and similarity as they meet, separate, and come back together reformed and rethought, and then reenact those disintegrative and integrative processes again and again. We state our case by contrasting the ideas of subjectivity and objectivity, so central to the development of Anglophone feminist theory in the late twentieth and early twenty-first centuries.

C. G. Jung was familiar with, and used in a philosophically unproblematic way, an important idea with which we shall be concerned: objectivity (for example, the objectivity of the collective unconscious). Now 'objectivity', even as used by Carl Jung, has several ontological and epistemic connotations and implications. It can, and usually does, refer to the idea that a world or worlds exist independently of the human senses (think of expressions like 'objectively real' or 'external reality'); if such a world does exist, then, one might wonder, how can it be known? Relatedly, issues about the nature of *knowing about*, and *being acquainted* with, and *how we might know*, have been raised. Carl Jung held that the collective unconscious had an objective reality that was external to the human mind, but which simultaneously was available as an important factor in structuring our waking and sleeping experience. His evidence for its objective (and independent) character could be found, he claimed, in the universality of images and symbols, across cultures, often with meanings that were also shared trans-culturally. Different cultures might be different in terms of their practices and beliefs but, he maintained, the symbolic use of, for example, sun and water revealed an underlying unanimity of the unconscious. Thus, in this view of objectivity, we *know about* through, or because of, our experience, which gives rise to our being *acquainted with* universally available images and symbols, and we learn about these through our observation and dreaming (*know how*). Ontology (objective being) and epistemology are distinct, but linked through the activities of the psyche.

Philosophically speaking, questions about objectivity are not new. Famously, Immanuel Kant (after whom Carl Jung seems to have modelled some of his theoretical assumptions) posited the existence of a noumenal or objectively 'existing world', knowable only by divine intelligence. Immanuel Kant accordingly held that the human mind is not equipped to know such a world. What we perceive and know are phenomena that 'exist' within space and time which are not objective or absolutely 'out there'. Space and time are themselves sensible intuitions or forms that the human mind imposes on the noumenal world. What we experience 'within' these intuitions is structured by the categories of our human understanding. Knowledge, from a human perspective, is, then, a product of understanding and experience. In the Kantian view, we can never know things as they really are; our minds, through our sensibility, our understanding and the application of intellectual categories, always mediate what there really is, and what we can know about that 'reality'.

**xx** Introduction

Immanuel Kant's epistemological view has survived, I would argue, in some form or another to this day. While it might be the case that ontological 'objectivity' theorized as noumena or as independently existing 'objects' or relations remains contested, we have been seduced by Kant's commitment to the constructed nature of what we experience and know. Enquiries about the existence of any underlying 'reality' have been by-passed as we have begun to emphasize the affectivity of the social structuring of our experience. Theory which might appeal to 'natural' categories, that is to say, categories that clearly point to and/or reflect an allegedly natural world or a world as it is in itself, or objects, or relations that exist independently of the human mind behind or beyond social structuring, has been roundly criticized as untenable. We can never know objectively because we can never know things as they are; we can know only subjectively or relatively according to our situations in the world.

However, the case is not as clear as it might seem from what I have been outlining. Even if it is true that we can never know the world objectively in the sense I have just indicated, we might wonder if we are therefore 'trapped' by what might seem to be the limiting role of the social: the social is epistemologically formative. There is a sense in which the social acts causatively because the social in all of its dimensions moulds us not only as knowers but also what we know. On this account, the social plays a role as it 'triggers' our psyches, making us, in a robust sense, causal products or effects of our social environments and their influences. Note here, however, that I have invoked the notion of a psyche with which the social interacts. Interaction between psyche and the social might seem to ameliorate the strong effects the latter has on us as individuals and group members. After all, we are different, each and every one of us. Hence in recent theory, *social* categories such as class, 'race', skin colour, sex/gender, age, ability and sex/gender orientation have been introduced as modifiers of the notion of experience and knowledge within the social context. In social, philosophical, political and religious theory, for example, we have been introduced to the idea that our knowledge, attitudes, values and beliefs mirror our locatedness which reflects, to varying degrees, the social categories which are regarded as epistemologically formative. Difference counts.

The locus of that difference is in our bodies: psyche is embodied, the social acts on and in us as bodies. And all bodies, though anatomically and physiologically basically the same, are different. Weirdly enough, though, the social can 'pick up' and 'pick out' those differences resulting in a hierarchical ordering of human being from those with the 'best' qualities and relations on top, and those with the 'worst' on the bottom. The social itself is formed in and by preferences and desires that have an impact on each one of us, and the social groups to which we belong. Difference is thus expressed not only in bodies but also in the social itself. With difference operating at the level of embodiment and the social, we can see that what and how we know, and the perspectives we each and all have on and in the world, are going to vary greatly. We all have a view from somewhere, we are all positioned in the world. What we 'see' is heavily influenced by the interweaving of psyche, body and the social, by that positionality.

Introduction **xxi**

Anglophone feminist epistemologies and social ontologies have endeavoured to capture the importance of these factors. Standpoint theorists, for example, such as Helen Longino (1994: 393) and Sandra Harding (2009), began, and have continued to press for, acknowledgement of the relativity of knowledge and its objects in the humanities and sciences. Their view that objectivity in the Kantian sense (and in other 'scientific' senses) is not possible rests on the claim that we are all socially located and so our views about anything will always be influenced by who and what we are, and where we come from. Likewise, Iris Marion Young (1990b, 1990a), Kimberlé Crenshaw (Carbado *et al.* 2013) and Pamela Sue Anderson (1997), for example, have challenged objectivist understandings of politics, 'race', psychoanalysis and religion and pointed out the role institutions and their logics, and the intersection of 'race', class, sex/gender play in the power relations that dominate who and what we can know, understand and be, individually and as groups. Epistemic considerations around objectivity continue to exercise many anglophone feminist theorists up to this day including an interesting revisiting and review by Katharine Bartlett (2015) and a new collection of essays by Sandra Harding (2015).[1] Yet it is clear that these feminist theorists are not keen on a wholesale abandonment of objectivity precisely because of its value in theory and life practice. How do we bring together our own positionality and demands for truth and accuracy and recognition of the other?

Katharine Bartlett's review essay highlights the difficulties with developing a cogent notion of objectivity that is relevant across a range of disciplines. She figures objectivity as 'the quality of approaching decisions and truth claims without the influence of personal preference, self-interest, and emotion. The question of whether a decision or claim is objective can arise in law, morality, science, and any other area in which being "right" matters' (Bartlett 2015: 376). Yet, as I understand the issues involved, it is precisely the question of influence and value to which much of feminist scholarship has been devoted. How do we characterize truth? Can truth be absolute or is truth always partial and incomplete?

Hence problems with what we might think of as objective and subjective points of view are extraordinarily difficult to resolve and are not the sole concern of feminist and 'race' and class theorists. Given difference at the level of both the personal and the collective or social, how do we ever attain views that are outside our own particularities? How can we transcend our social, local situatedness, and indeed, is that at all possible? Furthermore, while we might begin with a notion of the objective, we seem to slide into notions of *objectivity*, or an attachment to a verbal and epistemological form of our original supposition (that there might be a world 'out there' beyond us). Can we make any sense of objectivity as an epistemic concept? In other words, is it possible to know objectively as distinct from subjectively, and if so, what would that mean? These questions continue to be salient and Bartlett's analysis, which ranges across legal theory, the sciences and humanities concludes with her view that we need a view of positionality that recognizes 'the limitations of our own objectivities, yet accepting the obligation to justify ourselves in terms intelligible from outside our limitations' (Bartlett 2015). Once we invoke

**xxii** Introduction

positionality we can see *position* as ground, as that in which and from which we grow, that gives us our own peculiar perspectives or views from which we cannot escape but which do not hold us into the ground. Rather, the very sociality of our being already ensures the possibility of movement beyond.

In *The View From Nowhere* Thomas Nagel posed a problem about these two standpoints or views: 'how to combine the perspective of a particular person inside the world with an objective view of that same world, the person and his viewpoint included'. For whom is this a problem? Nagel suggests that it 'is a problem that faces every creature with the impulse and the capacity to transcend its particular point of view and to conceive of the world as a whole' (Nagel 1986: 3). This theme is not unfamiliar to readers of Carl Jung. Thomas Nagel is invoking a specific idea of epistemic objectivity, one that involves a relationship with transcendence. As I see it, 'transcendence' is crucial to an understanding of subjectivity/objectivity debates. If we take the idea to invoke, minimally, the notion of going beyond, or exceeding one's own particularities, then we can work with an idea of a view from somewhere that is simultaneously objective and subjective. That is to say, we can invoke a notion of relativity that implies spatio-temporality. (Relative to who? To what?) This is not merely Bartlett's idea of accepting our limitations and then coming up with an intelligible justification 'from outside our limitations'. Rather, we can invoke the concept of psychic transformation in order to develop 'tran-scendence' as a whole being turn towards a world we embrace as potentially differ-ent from what we have previously understood and believed we have known.

There are two points to make here before I move on to discuss our contributors' views from somewhere. If we think of an individual as a biological, embodied, con-scious/unconscious intersection of a whole range of relational and social properties, then we can escape from a trap of conceiving of individuality as a private psycho-logical matter. We, as individuals, as selves, can be thought of as products of the interweaving of the factors about which I have been talking: we do not pre-exist ourselves as it were: we come into human being as biological creatures situated in language and social relations. The very fact that we use language and understand and can make ourselves understood suggests the transcendent nature of our being human. We are both in ourselves and beyond ourselves from the beginning, always in relation and tending towards transcendence. This is not something that happens to us once we are fully formed in our own selves: rather we can be fully formed only in the sociality of our nature, only in the beyondness in which we exist.

That we recognize our own positionality or situatedness, that we can situate ourselves as our selves in our living contexts and then come to have a view on those contexts, is a movement of transcendence, and a recognition of our immanence, of our being intimately aware of this being which we each are.

Secondly, truth, partial and fragile, will emerge from ground that will be con-tested. 'Feminist views from somewhere' as temporally modulated ground, will always display and express particularities, but those particularities can be, and often are, recognizable beyond the individual into whose world we are invited. That is the nature of writing, of language, of personal experience, of interpretation. Let us turn briefly, then, to the views of our contributors where we will find a polyphony of voices, of views, of expressive prose.

In her chapter, 'Explorations in the poetics of the feminine pronoun' Leslie Gardner raises some issues about uses of pronouns, depth psychology, and rhetorical considerations of grammar, arguing that grammar makes a difference. Taking her cue from Ursula Le Guin's idea of the novel as a container, Susan Rowland in 'Feminism, Jung and transdisciplinarity: a novel approach' proposes that the container metaphor can be extrapolated into Jungian and Depth Psychology's archetypal framework, already implicitly present in the work of Le Guin. Susan Rowland understands twenty-first-century feminism as a carrier bag for the constructive feminine voice. She suggests that the gendered voice, as a different voice, has the capacity to expose a respect for critical gender differences that can help to emancipate academic disciplines from their male strictures. Elizabeth Eowyn Nelson also explores the potential of the novel as a vehicle or container for a transgressive feminist voice in 'Fierce young women in popular fiction and an unpopular war'. She discusses the notion of the powerful woman that we can see in recent popular fiction for young adults. Elizabeth Eowyn Nelson contrasts fictional accounts of young women's power and aggression with accounts of what it is like to be a woman in the military in what she calls an 'unpopular war'. She works with what she sees as shifting archetypal patterns for women which she construes as a re-writing of 'true' femininity. Like Susan Rowland's, her work suggests that there are multiple ways in which women can be symbolized and that a wimpy, simpering or destructive anima-possessed characterization is necessarily limiting for women.

Susan Wyatt's 'Medial women: views from a feminist epistemologist' highlights Toni Wolff's pioneering work on figuring the feminine. She explores Toni Wolff's monograph, *Structural Forms of the Feminine Psyche*, and pays special attention to the notion of the medial woman, viz. the feminine psychic structure that acts, as she argues, as a bridge to the unconscious and effectively illuminates unconscious contents. Susan Wyatt explores this notion as she has been manifested in women's lives through history, for example, Hildegard of Bingen and the Virgin Martyrs.

In 'In search of the heroine' Coline Covington critically examines the idea of the heroine. She interrogates the hero as derivative of the maternal complex, and wonders if the anima is the hero's opposite. She argues that if we were to conclude that it is, then we are caught in a vicious cycle in which the hero is always, inescapably, indebted to the mother. Coline Covington uses the story, 'The Handless Maiden' to travers the territory of women's individuation from feelings of abandonment by the mother, to the restoration of the hands as symbols of psychic renewal and transformation outside the 'rescue me Prince Charming' paternalistic motifs of many fairy tales. She argues that hero as de-integration, and heroine as re-integration, from a dyadic relationship both of which are critical to the individuation process.

Cheryl L. Fuller's 'Emma Jung's pen: Jung, Feminism and the body' explores the notion of women's self-silencing. She discusses this in relation to what she sees as lack of focus on the body in depth psychology, in Jungian studies, and in the power

**xxiv** Introduction

of the male gaze. She directs us to think about bodies that are not thin, white and sculptured – the assumed body – but rather, full and fat. She uses the fat body as a type through which she explores cultural attitudes to atypical bodies, noting that transgender and 'wrong bodiedness' have become features of our current era.

Sue Austin's chapter, 'Working with a woman with binge eating disorder', engages with the concept of the emergent self. Using the insights of Carl Jung, Judith Butler and Jean Laplanche, Sue Austin argues that while externality in the form of coming together with others is crucial to our development, coming apart or coming undone initiated by others is existentially more salient in our experience of ourselves as selves. She examines the effect of others on the self, but significantly, engages with the concept of fantasizing about bringing others down or undone. Her chapter resonates with woman as 'container', a trope often associated with woman, symbolically, and in the mundane understanding of both 'woman' and the 'feminine'.

In Lyn Cowan's 'Women and land: reflections on physicality' we are invited into a poetic world of the body as an aging, declining presence in the world that needs to recover the notion of land. Rurality, dirt and earth feature as descriptive tropes to direct Lyn Cowan's attention to the reality of having to go underground, under the land, to retrieve a sense of our earthiness. Drawing on her biography, she appeals to the grounded-ness and fertility of the psyche as she realizes that bodily decline and dynamic, vital, psychic life can be co-present .

Amanda Dowd's chapter, 'Becoming human', explores the relationship between becoming human, the very meaning of that, and the perceptual frameworks we deploy in our meaning-making. She argues that psychotherapy is a potent way of exploring what it means to be human.

Our appendix, 'Voices', is a series of comments, arguments, wise observations and ideas that we have borrowed from the IAJS feminism archive from 2014.

We do hope that you will be challenged, alarmed and excited by this collection from eminent Jungian and post-Jungian scholars. We also hope that you will be delighted by the different points of view, the different feminist views from a multiple of somewheres. Read, question and enjoy.

## Note

1 Talk of objectivity has been less of a concern for French theorists who, it seems to me, have focused more on the phenomenological and hermeneutic dimensions of women's subjectivity.

## References

Anderson, Pamela Sue. 1997. *A Feminist Philosophy of Religion: The Rationality and Myths of Religious Belief*. Oxford, UK and Malden, MA: Blackwell.

Bartlett, Katharine T. 2015. 'Objectivity: a feminist revisit'. *Alabama Law Review* no. 66 (2): 375.

Carbado, Devon W., Kimberlé Williams Crenshaw, Vickie M. Mays and Barbara Tomlinson. 2013. 'INTERSECTIONALITY'. *Du Bois Review* no. 10 (2): 303–12. doi: http://dx.doi.org/10.1017/S1742058X13000349.

Harding, Sandra. 2009. 'Postcolonial and feminist philosophies of science and technology: convergences and dissonances'. *Postcolonial Studies* no. 12 (4): 401–21. doi: 10.1080/13688790903350658.

Harding, Sandra. 2015. *Objectivity and Diversity: Another Logic of Scientific Research*. Chicago, IL: University of Chicago Press.

Longino, Helen E. 1994. 'In search of feminist epistemology'. *The Monist* no. 77 (4): 472.

Nagel, Thomas. 1986. *The View From Nowhere*. Oxford: Oxford University Press.

Young, Iris Marion. 1990a. *Throwing Like a Girl and Other Essays in Feminist Philosophy and Social Theory*. Bloomington, IN: Indiana University Press.

Young, Iris Marion. 1990b. *Justice and the Politics of Difference*. Princeton, NJ: Princeton University Press.

**PART I**
# Theme: Viewing Earth

# 1

# WOMEN AND LAND

## Reflections on physicality

*Lyn Cowan*

In recent years I have become increasingly occupied with thoughts about physicality, about the place of the body in depth psychology, and particularly with my own body – that of me which is of the Earth, dirt, clay, sand, dead leaves, scrub brush, and still sprouting a seedling of something new now and then. It is this *humus* as much as the imagination that makes me one of the human species and connects me to all other living things on Earth. James Hillman wrote that "concrete flesh is a magnificent citadel of metaphors,"[1] which means to me that the body must have co-primacy of place in my imagination. This would not have been possible in the 1950s in America, when I came of age, because my female body then was considered useful or valuable only for the sexual pleasure it could provide men and for making babies. (And it had to look like Marilyn Monroe.)

My body doesn't work as well as it once did, and some parts hardly work at all, but my memory is sharp and my mind is intact, even retaining a certain suppleness and flexibility – in some ways, more so than in decades past. And so this latest concern with body is joined with another ongoing concern: language. How to speak the psyche's reality in its own language? If, as I think (following Jung), the psyche's mother tongue is the language of metaphor, then such speaking and writing must also be metaphorical language. Psychological writing is literary writing. Conceptual language, while often conveying deeply interesting and important ideas, has never touched me emotionally. Only the language of metaphor – poetry, literature, drama – can do this. And so I am casting this essay in the form of a reflection, a reminiscence, a metaphorical tour of that "citadel" and the land on which it lives.

Those things about which we ought to be most conscious and to which we ought to be most naturally and organically connected, are just those things from which cultural attitudes, prejudice, and history cut us off and keep us *unconscious*. I imagine as a psychological ideal an adaptation in which we have a sharper, instinctive sense of our own physical bodies, a sensitivity to wild animals and their habitats

**4** Lyn Cowan

as we are co-relatives and co-habitants, a responsiveness to climate, and an appreciation of the land itself.

Urban dwellers are perhaps most vulnerable to this kind of unconsciousness. Fitness programs, ski weekends, camping trips, and vacation tours to Mount Rushmore are fun but not radical attempts to see through to how subverted we've been and how deeply disconnected we are from the very ground on which we walk. It is no wonder that in our culture we do not usually and respectfully take off our shoes and call our ground "holy."

The fact and idea of "ground," its physicality, is worth examining as an experience from the perspective of the soul, and especially from a soul in exile from its ancestral land.

I used to think "land" was just "dirt." I used to think "land" was just "the ground," not hearing any metaphorical resonance in that, no deeper sense of ground, being grounded, standing one's ground. Ground was just something you were not supposed to be under, because if you were it meant you were a political threat or you were dead. "Ground" is not a very romantic word; it sometimes carries a suggestion of defeat, or exhaustion: being ground down, the daily grind, knocked flat on the ground, having the ground give way under you.

But "land" is nearly always a poetic, romantic word, a word that often appears with other pleasant, poetic words: the land of the free, a land of milk and honey, a green and verdant land, home land, promised land. We don't want to give ground, but we ask to be given land, lots of land.

Since I am only one part rural and three parts urban, my images of land have been somewhat romanticized in the absence of a solid, grounded relationship to land. I didn't even make mud pies when I was a kid. I was born in Brooklyn, New York, in 1942, and I knew only cement until I was six years old. I walked to school and back every day, but what I saw were cement and iron fences, cement and brownstone houses, cement and asphalt roads, cement sidewalks and cement subways.

Then, in 1951, we moved to a house my parents bought on Long Island. We were first-generation suburbanites, living just a few miles from famous Levittown in a large subdivision of houses still under construction when we moved in. There was dirt everywhere, of which my mother complained – we were not to track it in, the dust was impossible, there was gravel in the new wall-to-wall carpeting in the living room, when would they finish paving the roads already? My father set about immediately covering the exposed ground outside around the house, as if its nakedness were a silent criticism of his husbandry. The dirt of the plot was graded and topsoiled and graded again, and rocks were hand-picked out. We had a corner plot, and my father put little stakes all around it with little white rag strips hanging down. This was to keep human feet off the new grass that had been planted. Narrow cement walks were laid to the front and side doors.

None of us ever thought of this little corner plot as our *land*, our ground. We thought of it, and spoke of it, as "the house" and "the lawn." We lived in the house, and the lawn lived around us. For me growing up there and imagining my future, the "plot" came to mean a fearful conspiracy to trap me into the crushing conformity of suburban life.

Women and land: reflections on physicality **5**

But there was a rural part of me too. My grandfather owned about 200 acres in what was then a secluded, forested, mildly mountainous region of central New Jersey. I spent summers there for 16 years, although I only remember the years beginning at age six when I started riding horseback. When I was there, in the late 1940s and through the fifties, there were few paved roads, houses were miles apart and most of them were farmhouses. Within just half a mile of my grandfather's house you could be lost in the forest, and my cousin and I often were. But still, all that acreage in New Jersey, all that wilderness, that freedom of movement and sense of expansion – the exhilaration of unlimited possibilities because no one seemed to *own* all that land – with all this, there was no conception in my family of "the land," not even "our land." It was "property." Buildable, developable, taxable, rentable, appreciable property.

Brooklyn cement, Long Island plot, New Jersey property. These are not nourishing, romantic, poetic images. They are images of constrained living, with fixed social conventions and rarely questioned attitudes, life measured in square feet and acres, quality of life measured in the absence of weeds in the lawn.

My family was not psychologically able to put down roots that penetrated through the concrete; they were not able to develop and transmit to me a sense of rootedness and being grounded, even though they owned some land and the titles to it were legally secure. I do not think this was because they were just greedy materialists or because they were shallow and incapable of psychological depth. Not at all. I think it was rather that the collective prevailing attitude of *controlling* the land took as its sacrifice a sense of *working with* the land. And secondly I think it was because my family are all Jews, which historically has meant (among other things) a condition of exile and forced wandering. Our attitude toward land was conditioned more by our long Jewish history of migrancy than by the fact of actual ownership in modern America. After centuries of displacements, it is hard to settle down in just a generation or two.

One's ethnic history determines the basic formations of one's psyche, its geological configurations, if you will. But however modern and removed from the past we may think we are, psyche remembers the great mythic images of land: virginal and unspoiled, lush, like a woman's body: wild in dance, soft, curved, vulnerable to plows, receptive to seed, and capable of erupting with furious volcanic passion in fire that can melt rock and destroy what men have built. The somewhat romantic notion some of us have about "returning to nature" or "communing with nature" or "getting back to nature" is a recognition that we are separated from nature; we do not even know that we *are* nature. It is a double metaphor expressing the psychological reality that we have lost, or been robbed of, the sense of the natural world and the sensuality of our natural bodies. The separation of a woman from her "land" is an interior separation of a woman from her own body: both land and body have been appropriated to an unnatural degree primarily for male purposes, and both have become property, with all that implies: territorial rights, boundaries, No Trespassing signs, and control of production and reproduction. The evidence for this is everywhere visible in the world, under the guises of religion, politics, or commerce. And after all, a husband is both a keeper of the land and a husband with a wife.

**6** Lyn Cowan

I know in myself and in my body volcanic rage that accompanies enforced exile from the land. I know this in my blood as a Jew, having witnessed in my own life-time both Holocaust and re-creation of homeland in Israel. And I know the rage that is the proper and inevitable response of the dispossessed – of Native Americans, of Palestinians, of Syrian children, of African girls, too many instances to cite – and the fury that comes when my rage is dismissed as paranoia or personal psychopa-thology. It may be more than just a quirky personal association on my part to note that the gas chambers of the Nazi death camps were built of cement, and so are our so-called freeways and other reinforced concrete bunkers in our minds.

My own roots have to pierce through the concrete of Brooklyn pavement if I am to be grounded and rooted at all. I was born separated from the Earth by femaleness, by Jewishness, and by concrete, and at a time when my people were being returned by the millions to the Earth in ashes. And I believe that as women we share a collective psychic ground, which has also been covered over by concrete so that we often cannot see it, and sometimes we cannot even feel it.

The ancient image of women in relation to land is that women *are* land; but the reality of our lives is that this image has been both degraded and overly romanticized – and also concretized (made literal) so that we do not truly own our bodies anymore than we truly own any land. Most of the land now belongs to giant agri-businesses, or oil companies, or banks, or is owned by the State, to be controlled, managed, zoned, preserved or reserved, as if the living Earth – woman – doesn't know how or can't be trusted to take care of herself, and is incapable of *self*-possession.

We have to go *under* ground to find out who we are as women; self-knowledge requires that we be psychologically subversive. We are not just potentially fertile females waiting to be plowed and fulfilled – this is a male idea of woman-as-land. Under the ground, under this male image of land, there is another reality – other images of women's bodily and psychological reality. "Underground" is not just mysteriously dark and sexually damp, it is also brightly lit with hot fires at the Earth's core that keeps Earth alive with body heat; there are vast expanses of thick continental shelves, moving in shifts of slow, sure power to change the face of the world. Beneath the surface there are coral beds, artesian wells, oil deposits, icebergs, and fossils. All of which may have many meanings attached to them – coral beds of deceptive beauty and natural formations, wells of clean renewal, unlimited wealth of valuable deposits as yet unclaimed by women, icebergs of implacable purpose and hatred where necessary, and fossils – the memory of our foremothers, whose bodies bore us and whose images are still imprinted in our souls as rock, even though long sealed and buried under layers of soil and oppression. Remember Rosa Parks, carrying the fatigue of centuries, tired after a hard day's work, who sat like an immovable rock on an ordinary bus one day in Alabama, and whose "No" (the one word most commonly forbidden to women) helped ignite the volcanic erup-tion of a human rights movement. Remember Malala Yousafzai, young in years but ancient in wisdom, beautiful in compassion for her sisters, resisting with the power of spirit the guns of those who would destroy her.

# Women and land: reflections on physicality 7

A double reclamation of land by women has to take place. Literally, we must reclaim the land as Earth because she is our mother, and without her to nourish and provide foundation we all perish, and other species with us. The second reclamation is psychological: we need to reclaim the land and give it dignity in the form of our own bodies. We need to re-image land from a female imagination. This is a compelling necessity for women, whose bodies have been imaged in metaphors of Earth and ground and land and treated patriarchally and patronizingly the same way: owned, rented, harvested, exploited, exhausted, platted, plotted, parceled out, covered over, landscaped, plowed, stripped, furrowed, seeded, fenced, staked out, claimed, bought and sold. Even though every woman has an absolute, rightful claim to her own body, historically it too often has been physically hazardous, psychologically crippling, spiritually exhausting, and economically suicidal for her to exercise that claim, when it has been possible for her to do so at all. And in too many places of the world, at this moment, it is still so.

One of the ways this reclamation takes place is through memory. This is one of the ways historians and storytellers keep us alive. Think of Maya Angelou, who took the pain inflicted on her own body and helped work the redemption of her ancestors and sisters and mothers and daughters through the poetry of her story. I think of my own grandmother, my mother's mother, who conveyed to me the dignity and determination to survive that characterized our people's history through suffering, even though she struggled with a language that was not her own, and I received it more through the cellular memory of my body than through the understanding of my mind.

Another way of reclaiming our land, our bodies, is through poetry, a sensual body and language of images that speaks the way the land itself speaks: in pulsing rhythms, currents of rivers, falls of water, aspirations and hopes of mountain peaks, desolate beauty of deserts, and the horror and ugliness of landfills and toxic waste dumps. Women who are filmmakers, novelists, musicians, sculptors, intellectual theorists, gardeners, mothers, innovators in all areas of life – these women are at work reclaiming our creative ground: their generative work is regeneration for all of us, for we need their art, their produce, to live and to provide a future for our planet. Writers like Toni Morrison, filmmakers like Marleen Gorris, sculptors like Liza Todd, gardeners like my friend Bonnie Fisher, and farmers like my friend Anda Divine, all multiplied a million times over now and through past centuries, fertilize and feed us. Theirs is the fruit of the Earth.

Another way of reclaiming the land is the concrete working of it. This is very different from working concrete over it, which was the only way I knew as a child. Working it, tending it, turning it over, planting it, worrying about the weather and insects and diseases, dreaming it, sifting through it, feeding it, watering it, dancing on it, clearing it, leaving parts of it alone for a while – all of these are the labors of land workers, and they are also the labors of women caring for their physical and psychic bodies. One's psyche is a farm and must be worked the same way. One's physical body needs all this farming and one's soul needs all this cultivating.

**8** Lyn Cowan

Like the land, we are seasonal, we have psychological cycles and metabolic rhythms. And sometimes the process of reclamation, of restoring ourselves, requires a seventh day (or month, or year) of complete rest.

I don't know if death is the "last thing" or not, but I do know it is inevitable. I know this intellectually, of course, but I know it more surely in my body, which registers the smallest gradations of decline every day. But meanwhile, there is life to live and work to do. So I want to end here with part of a poem by Gertrud Kolmar, a German Jewish poet whose 48-year-old body was burned at Auschwitz sometime in 1943. She is one of our foremothers, whose ashes are now part of our Earth. The poem is called "Woman Undiscovered."

> I too am a continent.
> I have unexplored mountains, bushlands
>     impenetrable and lost,
> Bays, stream-deltas, salt-licking tongues
>     of coast,
> Caves where giant crawling beasts gleam
>     dusky green,
> And inland seas were lemon-yellow
>     jellyfish are seen.
>
> No rains have washed my budded breasts,
> No springs burst forth from them: these
>     gardens are remote from all the rest.
> And no adventurer has claimed my desert
>     valley's golden sands,
> Or crossed the virgin snows atop my
>     highest barren lands.. . .
>
> Above me, often skies are black with stars
>     or bright with thunderstorms;
> Inside me flicker lobed and jagged craters
>     filled with violent glowing forms;
> But an ice-pure fountain I have as well,
>     and the flower that drinks there quietly:
> I am a continent that one day soon will
>     sink without a sound into the sea.[2]

## Notes

1  James Hillman, *Re-Visioning Psychology*. New York: Harper & Row, 1975, p. 174.
2  Gertrud Kolmar, *Dark Soliloquy: The Selected Poems of Gertrud Kolmar* (translated from the German by Henry A. Smith). New York: The Seabury Press, Inc., 1975, pp. 59, 61.

# 2

# BECOMING HUMAN

*Amanda Dowd*

## Introduction

> *Art does not reproduce what we see. It makes us see.*
> *When looking at any work of art remember that a more significant one has probably had to be sacrificed.*
>
> —Paul Klee

In 1921 Paul Klee painted *Revolving House*. It captured a significant 'moment' of change in our capacity to perceive – from the position of a single 'view' and 'viewer' he anticipated the postmodern shift to the recognition of the simultaneous presence of a number of vertices of possible perception of the same object – if we could but 'see'. The painting helps to give visual form to something that speaks to the heart of what I am trying to convey in this chapter: the necessity of holding in mind multiple simultaneous perspectives on psychic pain, healing, relational trauma, the nature of the self, unconsciousness and the psychotherapy project itself. How we imagine the human project depends on one's point of view – and in turn our perception from that point of view will influence how we think and theorise the human condition, make meanings and even 'decide' what is meaningful. This, in turn, will affect our ongoing capacities to perceive.

Finding and creating ways to make meaning out of our experiences and hence give meaning to our existence on this planet is what we humans do: we need to find our place in the 'scheme of things'. It was with the discovery of unconscious mental life – did we find it or did we create it? – that our *perceptions* of what it means to be human and to make meanings took an evolutionary and revolutionary turn and during the past 100 or so years psychoanalysis has added its perspective to the range of points of view from which we perceive the human project.

**10** Amanda Dowd

I think we are now in a similar turn of the century 'moment' of perceptual evolution regarding the psychotherapy discipline itself and therefore how we make meanings about being 'human': we are challenged to question and critique foundations without destroying them, to hold onto 'essentials' while incorporating new perspectives, in other words to develop an attitude of disciplined pluralism with regard to our ways of thinking and theorising psychic structures, psychic distress and the alleviation of psychic suffering. I think of this as an attempt to find coherence within multiplicity and difference; something we are all challenged with as we seek to learn how to live beside one another; how to 'be' together so that 'we' or 'us' makes sense.

This paper is about the humanising potential of psychotherapy; it is about beginnings, 'coming into being' or psychological birth and evolutionary change; it therefore is about embodiment because to become *fully* human the human spirit and soul must incarnate in a feeling body.

> *The thickness of the body, far from rivalling that of the world, is on the contrary the sole means I have to go into the heart of things, by making myself a world and by making them flesh.* (Merleau-Ponty, 1968, p. 135)

But we can't think about 'becoming human' without at the same time recognising something of the ways in which we are thinking about 'becoming human' – that is our perceptual frameworks for making meaning.

## 'Doors of perception ...'

Change takes place through time, in places and through human embodied experience. Our shared 'human project', I believe, is not about transcendence but about immanence and the freedom to become more fully human and so more and more able to experience and participate feelingfully in the 'aliveness of the world'; a world that calls us forth into relationship with it if we are open to perceiving and receiving it. A world always already here.

I do not believe we can separate our humanness from the profound relational matrix – physical (animate and inanimate), cultural, ecological and spiritual – out of which all life, as we know it, evolves. We also of course can't separate our ways of thinking – our cultures of understanding – from the truth of these relational matrices either. My own work has consistently explored the theme of 'place' as 'background of meaningful containment' (Dowd, 2011), which I envisage as a continuum of internal/external experience through bodies, skins, minds, places and time. I see this as constituting a profoundly feminine and ecological approach to the question/problem of 'becoming human'.

I was listening to a poignant interview with the Australian author/poet Clive James as I was thinking about this paper and he spoke of a 'good' poem as a manifestation of 'abundance in a small space'. It captured something for me about what Daniel Stern (2004) calls 'moments of meeting': an experience in the space between two that can shape and direct or re-direct a life path. A moment during a breast feed; a moment in union with nature; a moment making love; a smile at just the right moment; a moment of recognition between two minds; a moment of linking in the therapy room. Such moments open up an opportunity for 'becoming ...' as the continuum of time/space shifts and *Topos* gives way to *Khóros* – in other words a space opens up for something to emerge – a 'happening' – which potentially could be realised and emotionally experienced – 'taken in' and made flesh.

*Khóros* was conceived by the Greeks as a middle term between *Topos* on the one hand and *Cosmos* on the other: *Topos*, as place, evokes something of the particular and hence also a particular time or quality of time – it is linked with historical and developmental time; *Cosmos* evokes the universal; it has its own distinct quality of expanded or expansive time – of ages or aeons. The middle term, *Khóros*, denotes region, space, interval, site and receptacle; it is paradoxically both container and space. According to Casey (1993, p. 19) it is a region or space with 'sensible qualities' and its own 'determinacy'; he also notes that Plato used the word *Khóra* to characterise the initial state of the universe in his account of creation in the *Timaeus*. *Khóra*, then, is also akin to *chaos*, as in a necessary state prior to creation or 'something coming into form'. *Khóra/Khóros* has also been called the nursery of, or basket of, creation. Embedded in the notion of *Khóra* then is another dimension of time – of 'time going on ...', endless eternal time rather than timelessness.

Heidegger refers to *Khóra* as a 'clearing in which being happens or takes place' and Derrida (1993) uses *Khóra* to name a radical otherness that 'gives place' for being and which 'defies attempts at naming'. Kristeva (1984, p. 26) designates *Khóra* as a 'presignifying state which can be designated and regulated' but which can 'never be definitively posited'. Caputo (1997, pp. 35–6) on the other hand describes *Khóra* as 'neither present nor absent, active nor passive, good nor evil, living nor non-living – but rather atheological and non-human ... she/it receives all without becoming anything ...'. Returning to Plato, I will use the term to designate a space/interval/site/receptacle between the sensible or felt and intelligible or thought through which everything passes but in which nothing is retained; a contained space which at the same time provides access to or linkage with what I call a background of meaningful containment (Dowd, 2011, 2012).

Clinically, Donald Winnicott (1971/1985) comes closest to this in his perception of what he called a 'potential space'. We neither find nor create it ourselves; it is, as Winnicott understood, always only a potential and significantly the possibility for its emergence arises 'between two subjectivities'. Winnicott perceived this 'space' in his close observational work of mothers and babies and postulated that, in health, this potential space emerges between mother and baby as a function of mother's capacity to perceive her infant as a whole and separate person from the beginning; this in turn facilitates the emergence of an internal symbolic space in baby's mind and both contribute into the establishment of the ongoing potential for the emergence of potential spaces between persons and between person and world during the maturational process. The potential space becomes an 'area of faith', it *is* the space or region, the *Khóra*, through which we continue to find/create the

**12** Amanda Dowd

possibility of becoming more and more human. It is the necessary prerequisite for the experience of a sense of continuity of self over time – for the possibility of continu*ing* to come into form or become; for the incarnation of the human spirit and soul and the freedom to be.

Eric Rhode approaches this notion of *Khôra* – the 'clearing in which being happens or takes place' or that which 'gives place for being' – from a different vertex. He describes this space/region/interval as an intersection and he locates the site of psychoanalysis in this region. 'From its beginning' he writes 'psychoanalysis knew that its site was the intersection between history and myth, and not history alone' (Rhode, 1994, p. 290). What he means by this is that the 'site' at which and in which psychoanalysis 'happens' is the intersection between the unknown and unknowable (variously termed mythic, archetypal, unconscious, undimensioned life, unformulated experience, un-contained or un-embodied life, the subsymbolic, depending on one's perspective) and the known and knowable (historical/temporal, conscious, dimensioned, ordered, limited, embodied life). Rhode's intersection is a way of describing a prerequisite for psychic birth – he is bringing our attention to *Khôra* imagined as an intersection between two perspectives on *time* – time before birth or coming into being (eternal or limitless time) and time after birth (historical or developmental time).

And he continues, 'if history and myth are isolated from each other, thought finds itself unable to be mobilised' (Rhode, 1994, p. 291). That is, if the intersection isn't there then something can't 'happen': in Rhode's vision, 'thought' cannot be mobilised. Rhode is not speaking to an intellectual 'idea' but to the realisation and so embodied experience of an emotional impact or 'happening'. In order for an emotional event to be 'humanised' or made flesh, it must be 'been' (after W. Bion), that is psychosomatically metabolised and incorporated into the experience of being itself; embodied.

If the link between myth and history is present enough, that is if *Khôra* is open enough in an individual psyche it means that humanised emotional experiences of 'being itself' (being a feeling body) are able to keep contributing to an ongoing process of what we might call 'mineralisation' of our human psychic structural bones. It is a vitalisation process out of which emotional 'happenings' and 'ideas' or 'knowings' about being 'a' particular human self arise which can then be incorporated into developing 'knowings about me' and therefore 'knowings about you' and 'us' as humans. If the link is lost and these two domains are isolated or dissociated from each other then psychic events may 'happen' but they cannot be 'been' or experienced – that is they remain dissociated from a 'me'; they become 'not' me and are destined to remain outside of historical time and embodied dimension, unavailable therefore for developmental incorporation into biography and identity. Experience, then, cannot build and be built upon.

Unprocessed 'happenings' are sometimes referred to as unformulated experience – in other words 'content' without 'form'. Philip Bromberg (2011) calls these unprocessed happenings 'dissociated not-me self states'; the Buddhists might call them 'hungry ghosts'. Such 'happenings' are not lost from or excluded from

Becoming human **13**

consciousness because they have never been conscious; they cannot therefore be called unconscious in our historical understandings of this term, that is either the repression or pulling down of ego-alien content into a substantive unconscious from the Freudian perspective or, from a Jungian perspective, the splitting off or dissociation of disavowed ego-alien content into complexes. They are a part of what we now call the dissociated unconscious.

For all of its 100 or so years, the 'site' of psychoanalysis (and I use this term to denote all depth psychoanalytical psychotherapies) has been conceived as facilitating the 'unconscious becoming conscious' – and this is one way of conceiving Rhode's somewhat enigmatic statement. Facilitating this psychic movement is what distinguishes our profession from all other psychological approaches to healing. The image that holds this rather abstract notion in place for us is often one of stratified or archaeological layers or levels and a movement up or down – things coming up, things sinking down, travelling up and down. This vertical perspective and axis has been privileged as the psychoanalytic Delphic mantra of 'know thyself' was imagined as a deeply personal descent into the dark unknown depths of the self, a stripping bare, a recovery of something buried or lost, its reintegration and eventual ascent into the light of renewal (Dante's *Divine Comedy*, Innana's descent, St John of the Cross, etc. come to mind). These mythic patterns have great psychological and spiritual significance and validity and at certain points in a life path offer a guiding way to proceed, a necessary perspective. The vertical offers a point of view.

But our notions of what actually constitutes an 'unconscious' or indeed whether we can now speak of a substantive unconscious (personal or collective) at all are changing. As eminent post-Jungian theorist Jean Knox (2014) puts it:

> there is enough empirical evidence from other disciplines to enable us to show that some of the core psychoanalytic theories about the nature of the human unconscious mind are based on inaccurate and outdated assumptions about neurobiology, genetic inheritance and developmental processes. For example, both Freud's and Jung's discoveries were rooted in a 19th century modernist paradigm in which there are absolute and universal truths that structure our existence. Freud's libido theory and death instinct define a universal human nature, as aspects of biological, instinctual drives. Jung's attempt to define a different kind of universal human nature led to his idea of a collective unconscious and archetypes, psychic structures that are 'an inherited organization of psychic energy (CW 6, p. 447)'.

However, as Knox and others also acknowledge, there are other aspects of Jung's theories that anticipated the postmodern zeitgeist, his theories of transference, for example, which point to emergent patterns of unconscious relational communication between people and which recognise the fluidity rather than fixity of mental processes, his concept of the psychoid unconscious and placing imagination and dissociation as central to his theory are others. In fact both Freud and Jung anticipated something of the implicit relational nature of psychic processes inherent in

**14** Amanda Dowd

their revolutionary discoveries of unconscious mental life. But note Knox's recognition of the attempt to 'define' a universal human nature.

George Hogenson (1994) offers an enlightening perspective on the struggle between these two men and suggests that their *relationship* and hence the creative/ destructive tension between them not only influenced each profoundly but set the scene for a 'struggle' or battle for 'authority' within the field of psychoanalysis and therefore and especially the authority to write the dominant 'myth' or universalised pattern of the genesis of human development and meaning making. As Hogenson notes: 'a serious problem confronted the founders of modern depth psychology in that they must give an account of how and why there is an unconscious in the first place. But the account given … is itself mythical' says Hogenson. 'It has all the qualities of a creation myth … a cosmogony, a story about the origins of the world'.

He continues:

> as creators of mythic systems, both Jung and Freud can be understood as cosmogonists. The struggle over the redefinition of biographical understanding [of what it means to be human, of the relationship between time and space and therefore of what kinds of 'data' have validity] is nothing less than a primordial struggle of world constitution. (p. 5)

Hogenson again: 'Freud and Jung [both] derive their respective myths from a combination of deep personal experience with the unconscious [their respective self-analyses] and highly idiosyncratic investigations of the religious traditions of the world' (p. 6) and, he also notes, these are formulated out of highly idiosyncratic patterns of disclosure and foreclosure; the personal equation we might say – what each allowed into interpersonal/public discourse; what remained hidden from themselves and others. When method and insight link the individual with the universal, individual biography becomes mythologised into 'metabiography' and hence 'metapsychology' which can then become normative or lead to reification and monotheism. The problem, according to Hogenson (1994, pp. 2–3), 'lies not in self-analysis per se, but rather in the problematic of generalisation from the individual to the universal' and he asks the question, 'what is at stake when the life narrative of one individual … becomes normative for the interpretation of other lives?' (p. 3).

Very briefly, on the one hand we might say that Freud's system of interpreting human experience occupied a primarily retrospective point of view privileging repression/prohibition as the primordial world constituting (and hence culture/ civilisation constituting) act (after Hogenson) and privileging language over image. Its perspective represents something of the 'law of the fathers' enabling thinking and imagining about structures, 'objects', boundaries and it gave rise to object relations theory. On the other hand, Jung's system of interpretation takes a primarily prospective point of view privileging projection (as the world or culture constituting act) and dissociation; it linked psychic energy to image rather than object and has come to represent something of the 'law of the mothers' or maternal order enabling thinking about creativity, image, imagination, alignment with 'inner authority' and reorientation towards the world. I think we could say that the Freudian tradition has privileged differentiation and the Jungian inter-connection; perhaps, somewhat crudely, left brain/right brain preferences.

As a Jungian psychoanalyst I need both 'cultures' and perspectives because I need to keep 'looking both ways'; retrospectively towards historical (biographical) and mythic (ontogenetic and phylogenetic) time, towards what has become structuralised, life preserving, rigidified, towards what has gone before and what *goes before*; and prospectively towards loosening structures, facilitating dynamic process, finding/creating meaning and opening possibilities for life and relationships continuing in new ways.

Myths are universalised patterns of meaning – they are forms with which human beings comprehend and make sense of themselves and the world – past, present and future. If we conceive of our theories or cultures of understanding as supporting mythologies we can see that our psychoanalytical foundation myths are both creation myths concerned with genesis – world (person/culture) constitution – and healing myths concerned with the loss (pain and suffering) and recovery (healing) of that world.

It has been our efforts to better understand the origin and nature of trauma (individual and cultural), structural dissociation, depersonalisation, despair, suicide, 'problems of being' (disorders of the self) and 'problems of being with' (disorders of relationship) along with our attempts to formulate theories that better match our actual clinical experience that has changed our perceptions and so changed our thinking. Together with recent research into infant development, attachment theory, neuroscience (left and right brain systems and fore and hind brain systems), memory and the emerging field of neuropsychoanalysis, we have learned more about the ways in which mind and self form and about what the brain has to do with it. This has generated a shift in perspective which brings the lateral, positional, horizontal and therefore relational axis into the foreground in a new way because this is where we all start from on our journey to become human. This means that our discipline is shifting its emphasis more towards an ontological, developmental psychobiological and complex dyadic systems theory approach.

I think that a new mythology is emerging as both founding perspectives are being re-oriented towards and by new research in infant development, attachment theory and neuroscience; all areas of investigation which privilege *relationship between two* or the horizontal axis or perspective – mother/infant, left/right brain – and therefore the affective/developmental/corporeal domains. Metabiography and its correlate metapsychology no longer have primacy and changes in our capacity to perceive mean that we are getting better at 'seeing' what's there.

The new myth brings a new form of comprehension, a story of origins or genesis that comes not from the experience of one mind but out of the shared and co-created experience of two and out of a primal pattern of origin that we all share: birth, the relationship between infant and mother and the development of mind and self. The paradigm shift in our turn of the century moment is to privilege the *relational* because it is ontology, the nature of being and being with, rather than the interpretation of

**16** Amanda Dowd

symbolic content that psychoanalysis now finds itself preoccupied with more of the time as analysts recognise that they sit with patients whose ontological foundations are 'in doubt'; souls who have suffered 'mismanaged' psychological births and who consequently lack what ought to be implicit – a sense of 'how to be' or 'feel like' a person or 'do' relational life in sustainable ways. (Actually it was ever thus – it's just that now we see it differently.) For such patients something that ought to be there is not.

This brings more attention to bear on the conditions which both facilitate and hinder the process of humanisation and embodiment of life's 'happenings' – both intrapsychically and interpsychically; in infancy, adult life and in therapy. The analyst–patient relationship shares with the parent–infant relationship the common focus of facilitating psychological birth and consequent developmental growth and change especially, as we are now understanding this, new possibilities for navigating and negotiating intersubjective experiences; 'the analyst, though, has the much more demanding charge of facilitating the [extremely slow] deconstruction of established but unsatisfying was of "being with" [the trauma complexes] while simultaneously moving towards the new' (Lyons-Ruth, 1999, p. 582). In practice this means facilitating emergence from those defensive protective psychic retreats and re-locating the soul or true self on/in more sustainable and fertile ground within a new psychic skin.

And this returns us to Rhode's crucial insight regarding the 'site' of psychoanalysis as the 'intersection between myth and history'; world-constituting acts then become humanisations (or bringing to birth) through *Khôra* of previously unhumanised affects and unremembered 'memories' as well as unrealised potentials leading to embodiment and 'bodying forth'; the 'loss and recovery of the world' becomes the recognition of dissociative gaps as 'sites' where *Khôra as site of becoming was foreclosed* and their recovery or re-opening between two. Clinical authority then resides not within whichever mythical system one has subscribed to but out of the felt immediacy over time and in place of the experience of sitting at that intersection with many people engaged in what Neville Symington has called 'mutual myth-making'. To my mind we now have the possibility of a more democratic and holistic approach to suffering and healing the problem of becoming and continuing to become human. This is an implicitly relational, emotional, psychological, philosophical, ecological and spiritual matter. It also describes a particularly feminine perspective.

## The two-person relational unconscious and relational trauma

The term two-person relational unconscious makes explicit what has always been implicit: that we come into being through being 'been' by the being of another, we come to know our own minds through being known by another mind, we arrive at a sense of self through being recognised as a self by another, we dream/imagine because we have been dreamt/imagined by another. We come into being though that intersection Rhode described – through *Khôra* – which in the first instance, our actual biological birth, is instantiated by another. Our ways of being with another precede our ways of being with our self. We are both one-person psychologies in our separateness from others but also always at the same time two-person relational and cultural psychologies. This is why Hogenson's argument about metabiography and metapsychology – the patterns laid down by Freud/Jung – is so apposite to where we are now.

We now have irrefutable evidence for the recognition of the biological/corporeal basis of mind and self and the relational or dyadic structure of unconscious process. The term relational unconscious refers to the way in which the psychobiological substrate of the infant which maps patterns of 'being' and 'being with' (the neuronal systems, implicit procedural memory, basic image schemas and later internal working models) is scaffolded by and in relation to primary caregivers. This is mediated primarily by the implicit, emotional, corporeal right-brain self-system of the mother boot-strapping we might say the implicit emotional corporeal self-system of the infant through a process whereby one unconscious mind communicates with another unconscious mind (Schore, 2011). Both Freud and Jung recognised this unconscious communication of course, but 100 years ago it was not perceived as being a part of universal emotional developmental process. Infant researchers have provided us with substantial evidence that 'the intersubjective field is a continuous reciprocal system in which each partner is contextualised by the other … [and infant] development proceeds as self and other are involved in interactions which are mutually regulating' (Feldman, 2014, pp. 188–9). This is a good description actually of an ecosystem.

For the infant this is primarily about affect regulation; a psychobiologically and emotionally attuned mother will intuitively and implicitly both recognise and respond emotionally to her infant's distress, making sense of it, modifying it thereby providing the emotional buffer necessary between infant and her or his experience until the infant has developed the psychic structure to gradually take over some of these buffering processes. Relational trauma then refers to a pattern of consistent failure in this dyadic process. The failure to recognise infant experience and respond to it appropriately is experienced by the infant as a lost emotional link to mother and therefore a loss of a link to safety. If the lost link is not repaired quickly enough it leaves the infant's immature psyche alone with un-humanised and disorganising (because unmodified by mother) affect. This rupture then becomes represented in the developing infant's psyche as an absence or void and the infant will begin to self-modify in order to protect herself or himself from unbearable states of anguish and dread. Relational or developmental trauma therefore also refers to a pattern of consistent failure of emotional right-brain to right-brain (body to body) communication necessitating detachment from the unbearable and unsafe situation; attention is directed away from painful internal states in order to begin to feel safe. This then becomes habitual.

Bromberg (2011, dustjacket) describes it this way:

> During early development, every human being is exposed to the relative impact of relational trauma – disconfirmation of aspects of oneself as having

**18** Amanda Dowd

legitimate existence in the world of others – in shaping both the capacity for spontaneous human relatedness and the relative vulnerability to 'adult-onset trauma'. To one degree or another a wave of dysregulated affect – a dissociated tsunami – hits the immature mind, and if left relationally unprocessed leaves a fearful shadow that weakens future ability to regulate affect in an interpersonal context and reduces the capacity to trust, sometimes even experience, authentic human discourse.

Dissociation:

> involves more than an alteration of mental processes … it ruptures the integration of psychic and somatic experience … [this] right-brain strategy … represents the ultimate defence for blocking emotional bodily-based pain. The endpoint of chronically experienced catastrophic states of emotional trauma … is therefore a progressive impairment of the ability to adjust, take defensive action, act on one's own behalf and a blocking of the ability to register affect and pain, all critical to survival. (Schore in Bromberg, 2011, pp. xxiii–xxiv)

Importantly here the mother or care-giver need not be perfect, ruptures happen and indeed mother-infant attachment studies have shown how crucial this actually is because it is the process of repair that goes on to establish faith in the process of 'being with' and therefore later 'being'; to have faith that it is safe to become 'human' (embodied) we have to implicitly know that relational failure is okay because relational repair is possible. This is the mechanism through which intergenerational relational trauma happens. In other words, if a child grows up without this implicit knowing then she/he will be unable to represent such patterns of rupture and repair to her/his own growing infant; relational failure repeats because relational repair seems impossible; impossible because disorganising states of infant distress are simply not processable by a mother who lacks the representations of re-organising repair.

Karlen Lyons-Ruth (1999, p. 577) states:

> Psychoanalysis has always been concerned with understanding the organisation of meaning with affects viewed as the central guides and directors of meaning. The paradigm shift is to expand accounts of how meaning systems are organised to include implicit or procedural forms of knowing – the 'how' to do something and how to behave adaptively rather than knowing information or images that can be consciously recalled and recounted. The organisation (and so re-organisation) of memory and meaning in the implicit or enactive domain only becomes manifest in the doing.

That is within a facilitative relationship. In other words, the psychobiological substrate or implicit procedural memory of 'being with' can only come into being and become part of psychic structure via the processing of the 'happening' of being with another into the *experience of being with* another.

This perspectival shift towards the affective/corporeal/developmental also changes the ways in which we have imagined transference and countertransference dynamics. There is less emphasis on projection and projective identification (on what who is doing what to whom) and more emphasis on 'moments of meeting' and working through relational impasses and misunderstandings where what is happening to the relational link between therapist and patient is the 'object' we might say of the investigation more often (in practice this means mapping patterns of dissociation). What are termed 'enactments' or misunderstandings are imagined not as 'failures' of therapist/patient/therapy but as communications regarding dissociated material and so a necessary part of the essential developmental processes of 'rupture and negotiated repair'. This has led to more fluid perceptions of the psychoanalytic dialogue, the 'talk' (what can be symbolised into language and made explicit) and its relation to what is happening implicitly – what cannot be known but can be experienced.

And so when we now think of what the 'unconscious becoming conscious' means we need to add other perspectives – a dissociated unconscious and relational unconscious which give more attention to emergent experiences of 'coming into being' and embodiment via 'moments of meeting or emergence' – possibilities for 'abundance in a small space' – than to the interpretation of symbolic content. Indeed, 'at the more severe levels of psychopathology, it is not a question of making the unconscious conscious; rather it is a question of restructuring the unconscious itself' (Schore, 2011, p. 94).

## Variations on a theme – Khôra, psychic skin, a place to stand

> *Give me a place to stand, and I will move the world* (Archimedes in Casey, 1993, p. ix)

The final part of my chapter addresses itself to *Khôra* – the space that 'gives place for being' which is at the same time a receptacle through which everything passes and in which nothing is retained and yet, potentially links 'being' as if by an unbroken thread in continuity before, now and after ...

Finding words for what is fundamentally irrepresentable because unknowable is the challenge of all psychoanalysts – often we can only know something of the nature of these phenomena by the traces left behind by their absence. The Italian poetess Alda Merini said: 'Psychoanalysis always looks for the egg in a basket that has been lost'. Merini's observation and image speaks to something that is difficult to put into words any other way. She brings our attention to something that can keep getting 'missed' in the therapy situation in the same way that it was 'missed' in development; we can fail our patients if our attention is directed in the wrong place too often – searching for the egg (the self, 'content') whilst not seeing that it is the basket itself which is lost, missing or damaged.

**20** Amanda Dowd

Relational trauma is *trauma* because there has been a catastrophic rupture – a tearing away from and sudden catastrophic loss of the link with a sense of sheltering containment that organises the emotional self, enabling meaning to be made out of experience. In the first instance, infancy, the location of this sheltering containment is literally mother's mind/body (Merini's basket). Bion best approaches this with his notion of the relation container/contained; Winnicott approaches this with his formulation of the environmental mother. But Bion also approaches an enigmatic unknowable aspect of *Khôra* via his formulation of O – *ultimate unknowable reality*.

The poet Rilke (1987) approaches this from another direction:

> Oh this is the animal that never was.
> They hadn't seen one; but just the same, they loved
> Its graceful movements, and the way it stood
> Looking at them calmly, with clear eyes.
>
> It had not been. But for them, it appeared
> In all its purity. They left space enough.
> And in the space hollowed out by their love
> It stood up all at once and didn't need
>
> Existence. They nourished it, not with grain,
> But with the mere possibility of being.
> And finally this gave it so much power
>
> That from its forehead grew. One horn.
> It drew near to a virgin, white, gleaming—
> And was, inside the mirror and in her.[1]

Rilke's perception of a 'space hollowed out by ... love' implies a 'making way for'; through love a space is 'given' for 'being' – for the arrival into or through that space of something that has 'not yet been'. Its arrival is made possible by the 'nourishment' provided by the validation of its 'mere possibility'. Here is an exquisite expression of the nature of *Khôra*.

To conceive is an act of imagination and the representation of the nascent infant self in mother's mind as 'mere possibility' or 'idea' is an act of creation – thought is being mobilised in the service of the actual baby coming into being. In this very first instance, what mother 'gives' to baby by making space in her mind is an implicit recognition and confirmation of the fact 'baby as whole person'. Such an act of love implicitly confers and confirms baby's right to exist as one human being among other human beings; the 'right' to leave an impression on the earth – or her/his 'stamp upon the ground' as one of my very ill patients has said.

I call this experience a primal recognition (Dowd, 2012); Grotstein (2007, p. 313) refers to the blessing of an 'initialising experience of containment'. This *blessing of recognition* (or validation or confirmation) implicitly confers a sense of legitimacy:

acceptance and belonging to the human category of relations. A mother who can recognise her infant and feel recognised in turn is engaged in a creative act of linking both personal and cultural past (including pre-birth), present and potential future for her newborn thus establishing an experience of continuity which can be taken-for-granted.

If such an initialising recognition is followed by a consistent and reliable process of ongoing implicit recognitions by mother of the meaningfulness of all or most of baby's communications – bodily/emotionally/spiritually – it affords the infant with shelter from her or his affective storms. By her ongoing reveries mother provides an essential but illusory post-natal womb which relieves her infant of sensory overload and buffers the infant's nascent sensory apparatus from the annihilatory threat of disorganisation. When bodily-cum-emotional/psychological states are contained well enough, baby feels 'rooted' in safety, a sense of basic faith or primal trust is established and there is a growing sense of taken-for-granted boundedness within which sensations ('happenings') can be tolerated.

A magical thing happens: maternal sheltering begins to be internalised, forming what I call a background of meaningful containment (Merini's basket); Grotstein (1981) approaches this with his formulation of the 'mythic carpet on the floor of thought'. By this process, 'being' and meaningfulness of being begins to take shape or form, that is psychological birth within a psychic skin is achieved, body becomes a safe place to be and continuity of being becomes implicitly taken-for-granted.

When this happens consistently enough infant development progresses into relationally based and interconnected personhood; there is a felt place to stand, a sense of comfort in one's own skin, a taken-for granted acceptance of the reality inside and outside of one's own mind, a capacity to be one amongst others. The formation of a good enough psychic skin is one of those everyday miracles – the poesis of love in action – that is rarely thought about but essential for psychic survival and ongoing development.

Psyche needs containment to give it form or shape otherwise infants experience what are termed existential or formless dreads – falling/spilling out, falling to pieces. At its worst, instead of a primal recognition there can be what I have called a primal negation (Dowd, 2012) which results from a foreclosure of the 'place of becoming' – a foreclosure of *Khôra*. Instead of 'being' being represented in mother's mind (i.e. emotional being) there is a non-representation or void. Not finding oneself represented in mother's mind threatens the infant with non-existence; human beingness itself is disconfirmed. What ensues is overwhelming anxiety as self-states remain not only not represented but also dreaded as not-representable because unformulated. This leads to existential ontological doubt bringing with it disorganising primitive shame to hide/camouflage this primary lack. Shame and self-disgust intensify when there has been a rupture of self-continuity and an implosion of the implicit self. The infant can feel left as it were 'placeless' – a state of intolerable existential homelessness. To feel 'outside' of mother's mind is to feel estranged/alienated – dispossessed of validity and deprived of a legitimate place in the scheme of things within the realm of history and time.

## 22 Amanda Dowd

This experience and indeed all infant self-experiences not recognised and made meaningful by mother at this stage remain as unformulated experience or dissociatively 'unconscious'. If this happens too much we can then speak of a mismanaged birth or a partially unbirthed self, an unformed or only partially formed psychic skin. It is this which leads to the missing 'feeling of being a person' and primitive ontological doubts about being viable and legitimate as a human person mentioned earlier.

When *Khôra* is foreclosed, psychic skin formation is severely impaired necessitating the formation of what are called secondary skin defences which provide the 'missing' felt sense of boundedness and containment and hence safety and security. It makes sense to speak of a false body or false sense of embodiment in such cases. But this 'body' is in a form which prevents growth – instead of a humanised, flexible, organic system governed by the rules of biology and ecology, a super-human (in-human), life-preserving but stultifying and distorting, inflexible, tyrannical system shapes, structures and organises psyche and life. Secondary skin defences develop into psychic retreats or trauma complex systems – the obsessive, autistic, psychotic, schizoid, narcissistic and borderline defence systems we discover when people come into therapy to seek help.

Implicit in secondary skin defences is a soul in hiding – sequestered off in desperate protection against the feared threat of annihilation by a tsunami of unmediated affect – terror, grief and rage at the loss of the link to sheltering and meaning making. Soul (the true self) alienated from the rest of the personality leads to intolerable loneliness, unbearable doubt and shame and loss of hope because the hope that soul protects is unavailable – a seemingly 'lost' resource.

Coming into being or becoming human, then, is instantiated through a continuum of *Khôric* space – the 'space' or place in mother's womb/mind becomes the space or place in mother's mind/womb becomes the sheltering space between mother and infant becomes the symbolic space or place in baby's mind becomes the space or place between developing baby/child and world, becomes a felt place to stand on this earth embodied within a psychic skin implicitly linked within the ecosystem of human, world and spiritual relations. With luck, a feeling for and knowing oneself to be a part of a reciprocal, continuous system develops as *Khôra* as intersection between myth and history, between the unknowable and knowable between times past and time present, between the ineffable and mortal realms establishes itself as site of continual emergence of that unbroken thread that can potentially sustain one through life unto death.

In order to be able to think about the experience of relational trauma and what that means for psychotherapy and possible psychic change we need to be able to get a hold of the simultaneous way in which *Khôra*, potential space, Rhode's intersection, the background of meaningful containment and psychic skin are all implicitly inter-related; they are ways of representing and thinking about different perspectives on, not quite the same phenomena, but phenomena that are so inter-related as to be almost indistinguishable because each implies and contextualises the other. This is the main point because it is the rupture of

Becoming human **23**

the link to this that constitutes relational trauma – the impediment to becoming fully human.

It is the re-establishment of that link that facilitates potential psychic change as previously dissociated and unrepresentable self-experience has the opportunity to be represented in the shared minds of both patient and therapist until it can be fully accepted and returned home to the mind and self and body of the patient.

Recognition of a dynamic two-person relational and dissociated unconscious in this new way as an additional perspective brings us a new understanding of what the 'loss and recovery of the world' might mean; an expansion of the way in which we imagine the 'site of psychoanalysis'. I think it distils our awareness of our shared 'human' condition and enables deeper appreciation of the suffering of the struggle to *be* who we were always meant to be – a human being amongst 'other' human beings and to be able to feel as if we belong, or, as the poet Raymond Carver said in his poem *Late Fragment*, 'beloved of this earth'.

## Epilogue

Accepting the validity of multiple cosmogonies and shifting perspectives from the primarily vertical and generational point of view to the horizontal and lateral and so relational dimension is, I think, a profoundly ecological and feminine approach. Returning to feeling bodies returns us to our rightful place in the scheme of things, to the human and so cultural dimension where we can speak of love as a meaningful emotional and spiritual link which connects self with other with place.

## Note

1 Translation © 1987 by Stephen Mitchell. Used by permission.

## References

Bromberg, P.M. (2011), *The Shadow of the Tsunami and the Growth of the Relational Mind*, Routledge, New York and Abingdon

Caputo, J.D. (2004), 'Love Among the Deconstructibles: A Response to Gregg Lambert', *Journal for Cultural and Religious Theory*, 5, 2, pp. 37–57

Casey, E. (1993), *Getting Back into Place: Towards a Renewed Understanding of the Place-World*, Indiana University Press, Bloomington and Indianapolis

Derrida, J. (1993), '*Khora*', in T. Dutoit, 1995, *On the Name*, Stanford University Press, Stanford

Dowd, A. (2011), 'Finding the Fish: Memory, Displacement Anxiety, Legitimacy and Identity', in *Placing Psyche: Exploring Cultural Complexes in Australia*, eds Craig San Roque, Amanda Dowd and David Tacey, Spring Journal Books, New Orleans

Dowd, A. (2012), 'Primal Negation as a Primitive Agony: Reflections on the Absence of a Place-for-Becoming', *Journal of Analytical Psychology*, 57, 1, pp. 3–20

Feldman, B. (2014), 'Creating a Skin for Imagination, Reflection and Desire', in *Transformation: Jung's Legacy and Clinical Work Today*, Karnac, London

## 24 Amanda Dowd

Grotstein, J.S. (1981), 'Who Is the Dreamer Who Dreams the Dream and Who Is the Dreamer Who Understands It', in *Do I Dare Disturb the Universe? A Memorial to Wilfred R. Bion*, ed. J. Grotstein, Caesura Press, Beverly Hills

Grotstein, J.S. (2007), *A Beam of Intense Darkness, Wilfred Bion's Legacy to Psychoanalysis*, Karnac Books, London

Heidegger, M., https://en.wikipedia.org/wiki/*Khôra*

Hogenson, G.B. (1993/1994), *Jung's Struggle with Freud*, Revsd edn, Chiron Publications, Wilmette, Illinois

Klee, P. http://www.goodreads.com/author/quotes/122182.Paul_Klee (accessed 5 August 2016)

Knox, J. (2014), 'Imagining the Past, Remembering the Future', public lecture given in Sydney, Australia as part of the professional development programme offered by ANZSJA (with permission from the author)

Kristeva, J. (1984), *Revolution in Poetic Language,* Columbia University Press, New York

Lyons-Ruth, K. (1999), 'The Two-Person Unconscious: Intersubjective Dialogue, Enactive Relational Representation and the Emergence of New Forms of Relational Organisation', *Psychoanalytic Enquiry*, 19, pp. 576–617

Merleau-Ponty, M. (1968), *The Visible and the Invisible*, Northwestern University Press, Evanston, Illinois

Rhode, E. (1994), *Psychotic Metaphysics*, Karnac Books, London

Rilke, R.M. (1987), 'The Sonnets to Orpheus, II, 4', in *The Selected Poetry of Rainer Maria Rilke*, trans. Stephen Mitchell, Picador, London

Schore, A.N. (2011), 'The Right-Brain Implicit Self Lies at the Core of Psychoanalysis', *Psychoanalytic Dialogues*, 21, pp. 75–100

Stern, D. (2004), *The Present Moment in Psychotherapy and Everyday Life*, W.W. Norton & Co., New York and London

Symington, N. (pers. comm.)

Winnicott, D.W. (1971/1985), *Playing and Reality*, Penguin Books, Harmondsworth

# 3

# MEDIAL WOMEN

## Views of a feminist epistemologist

*Susan Wyatt*

The first theory of the feminine developed by a woman in Carl Jung's circle was presented by Toni Wolff to the Analytical Psychology Club in Zürich in 1934. Toni Wolff was involved with Jung throughout most of her life in a complex relationship which included student and analysand as well as "assistant, collaborator, the Other Woman, a *femme inspiratrice, soror mystica*, and *anima*" (Corson, 1998, p. 18). She described her theory in a monograph entitled "Structural Forms of the Feminine Psyche." After its first reading in 1934, the monograph was presented in a more detailed version in 1948 at the C. G. Jung Institut in Zürich. It was published in 1951 and was then printed only privately for more than forty years. It is still an important source for a Jungian theory of the feminine because it was woven from her own subjective experience and her clinical work as a highly regarded analyst as well as her grounding in Jung's ideas about archetypes and individuation.

In the monograph, Toni Wolff identified four patterns that structure the feminine psyche in women, as well as in the male anima, that she named the mother, the hetaira, the amazon, and the medial woman (she was aware of the problems with this terminology). The first two of these structures, the mother and the hetaira, are primarily expressed through personal relationships. The mother relates to what is unfinished and nurtures all that is growing and becoming. Toni Wolff pointed out that she can find fulfillment in any profession or human relationship that has scope for maternal activity, specifically mentioning Florence Nightingale. The hetaira or companion relates to individual relationships in all their dimensions and awakens the psychic process. She is sometimes seen as a muse or a *femme inspiratrice* represented mythically by Calypso. The amazon and the medial woman, on the other hand, are influenced by impersonal relationships. For the amazon, this means living in relationship to objective cultural values and achievements. Her fulfillment comes through the accomplishment of objective achievements. The perception of the medial woman relates to the impersonal unconscious out of which these objective cultural values grow.

In any particular woman one, or at most two, of these structures are dominant. One of the basic psychological problems for women is that the culture she lives in may not allow possibilities of expressing her dominant structural form: "… more often than not the structural form of the psyche will fit into the outer form of life only with difficulty, resulting in insecurity and conflicts" (Wolff, 1951/1995, p. 3). (It is interesting that even in the earlier part of the twentieth century Toni Wolff thought that the cultural values offered the greatest scope to the amazon structure.) The primary developmental tasks of a woman are, therefore, twofold. The first is achieving consciousness of the structural form that is most consistent with her nature. The other is the integration of all four structural forms, at least on a symbolic level. Coming to terms with all four functions is the basic path of individuation for women.

Toni Wolff's project was to describe structural forms that characterize the feminine psyche regardless of the outer form of life that is often imposed upon women by historical, environmental, or social factors. One of the concerns of the monograph and early commentators was the relationship of each of the structural forms with men. The medial woman, for example, could personify the impersonal side of the anima. However, the forms can be seen through a number of lenses. One perspective, for example, is to focus on women's ways of discovering and creating knowledge that can include methods such as nurturing, inspiring, doing, narrating, and imagining. Toni Wolff implied that these ways of knowing are just as valid as epistemically privileged ways of knowing such as rational analysis.

It is worth noting that Toni Wolff's basic two-dimensional model has no intrinsic gender characteristics. One axis differentiates between being personally related and being related to the impersonal or collective. The other axis distinguishes between relating primarily to the conscious or the unconscious. The four quadrants of the model might just as accurately be called structural forms of the relational psyche. Thus, as early as 1934, Toni Wolff was arguing that women grow in connection.

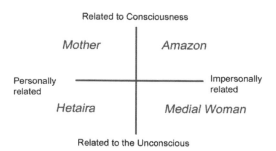

The focus of this chapter is on the least well known of the forms, the medial woman. Toni Wolff described this structural form as a bridge to the contents of the

Medial women: views of a feminist epistemologist **27**

collective unconscious. The medial woman engages with the collective unconscious, constellates it, and finds and expresses its meaning.

> The medial woman is immersed in the psychic atmosphere of her environment and the spirit of her period, but above all in the collective (impersonal) unconscious. The unconscious, once it is constellated and can become conscious, exerts an effect. The medial woman is overcome by this effect, she is absorbed and moulded by it and sometimes she represents it herself. She must for instance express or act what "is in the air," what the environment cannot or will not admit, but what is nevertheless a part of it. (Wolff, 1951/1995, p. 6)

Toni Wolff was sparing in her use of examples. She did point to the early Christian martyrs and the female mystics of the Middle Ages as medial women who exerted a positive cultural influence. Her examples also included creative medial women such as Italian actress Eleonora Duse and German historian Ricarda Huch. Medial women may come to personify the impersonal shadow as, for example, a witch or a heretic, and another of the monograph's examples was a nineteenth-century case of demonic possession. Some of these examples are not so familiar to contemporary readers and may not provide the illumination that the monograph intended. The purpose of this chapter is to explore the lives of some of these cases to gain a better theoretical understanding of the medial woman. The specific objective guiding the inquiry is to gain insight into how the medial woman knows what she knows. According to Toni Wolff, this is a process of immersion and constellation. But what is a medial woman's subjective experience of knowing?

## Virgin martyrs

There are many narratives from the early years of Christianity in the third and fourth centuries of a young woman who "consecrates herself to the service of a new, maybe yet concealed, spirit of her age" (Wolff, 1951/1995, p. 6) and ended up as a martyr for her faith. Stories such as those of the saints Margaret, Catherine, and Barbara have similar patterns with various legendary elements.

Saint Margaret, the daughter of a pagan priest of Antioch, converted to Christianity and dedicated herself to virginity. When she refused to marry the Roman prefect, he tried to execute her in various ways. One of these involved throwing her in a river where she was swallowed by the devil in the form of a dragon. The dragon was forced to disgorge her because the cross that she was carrying irritated its throat. Attempts at execution by methods such as fire and water failed because the wounds were miraculously healed. It was only by cutting off her head that the prefect succeeded in ending her life.

Saint Catherine was a princess of Alexandria who decided to convert to Christianity as a teenager. She became a scholar and visited Rome in an attempt to convert the emperor. He set up a debate between her and the leading pagan philosophers

**28** Susan Wyatt

that resulted in her adversaries converting to Christianity. The emperor then had her tortured and attempted to execute her by various methods that included being broken on a wheel. Although this is the image most often associated with Catherine, it was not the way she actually died because her wounds were miraculously healed. Eventually, the emperor had her beheaded.

The final example of these early Christian martyrs is Barbara, the patron saint of a city near an important center of archetypal scholarship. Saint Barbara was born in the Roman province of Asia Minor. Because she was so beautiful, her father Dioscorus imprisoned her in a tower to make sure that she would not marry someone of whom he did not approve. There she was provided with every luxury and spent her days in the study of philosophy and poetry. From her tower she heard about the teachings of Christianity and became a convert. She corresponded with the early Christian philosophers and modified the architecture of her tower to include three windows to represent the Holy Trinity. In the meantime, her father had her betrothed to be married but, when he discovered that she had become a Christian, he turned her over to the local prosecutorial authorities. She escaped, but Dioscorus hunted her down and turned her over to be tortured in various gruesome ways. When she persisted in her faith, her own father cut off her head. He was immediately struck by lightning.

While all of these stories are semi-mythical legends, they also represent the dynamics of a transitional age in the culture in which these women lived. Paternal control, the father over his family and the emperor over his subjects, was a defining dynamic of the Roman Empire and control of men over women one of the essential elements of its legal system. The ultimate crime was defiance of the paternal authority of father, husband, emperor, or the Roman gods. The coming of Christianity to the Roman Empire created a collision of traditional values with those of the new Christian ethos. In resisting paternal authority, the martyrs brought into consciousness the life of faith and embracing of suffering that were to become essential features of Western culture in the following centuries. Both Catherine and Barbara expressed this new consciousness through words, Catherine in debate and Barbara through correspondence. Barbara also expressed her knowledge through architecture in redesigning her tower.

Since these stories are legends and rich in imagery such as the wheel, the dragon, and the tower, they lend themselves to a medial approach in exploring these women's way of knowing. The common image of losing one's head provides an essential clue. I imagine that each of these women had an experience of divine love that took her completely out of her head and, in fact, made her headless, because such an experience cannot be understood in any intellectual way. As a symbol, the head often represents consciousness and one way to interpret the loss of one's head is the loss of duality implicit in the experience of consciousness. In my imagining of this experience, this feeling of headlessness was quite exhilarating. Body was no longer separated from mind, Logos from Eros, or, for that matter, knowing from not-knowing. The paradox is that it is only by losing their head could these women lose the separation from their head.

## Hildegard of Bingen

Unlike the early Christian martyrs who left no first-hand accounts, several of the female mystics of the Middle Ages left records of their experience. One of the most influential of these mystics was Hildegard of Bingen (1098–1179) and we have insight into her experience of knowing from her own account. From the age of three, Hildegard experienced visions of an inner light. She made it clear that these visions were part of her waking experience and not the result of trance states. While her primary experience of the impersonal unconscious arose from her compelling internal visual images, she also perceived "the sacred sound through which all creation resounds" (Hildegard, 2001, p. 5). However, she did not share these visions publicly until her early forties after she had been elected abbess by the members of her monastery. Her life shows a progression of confidence in the significance of her visions for the collective. In an early letter to Bernard of Clairvaux (Hildegard, 2001), she questioned whether she should even reveal these images. The more that she wrote about and interpreted her visions, the more confidence she seemed to acquire that they had a meaning that transcended her personal spiritual development.

Toni Wolff wrote that the concern of the medial woman is not herself alone. Her mediation of the collective unconscious can be a service to her community.

> But if she possesses the faculty of discrimination, the feeling or the understanding for the specific values and the limits of the conscious and the unconscious, of the personal and the impersonal, of what belongs to the ego and what to the environment, then her faculty to let herself be moulded by the objective psychic contents will enable her to exert a positive cultural influence …. (Wolff, 1951/1995, p. 86)

One way of performing this service is by embodying and living her perceptions of the unconscious. Hildegard, one of the most extraordinary women of all ages, lived a life guided by her inner vision. She also strove to communicate this vision in as many forms as possible. She not only wrote of her inner experience, but also created images and composed music. She authored a morality play as well as books on science and medicine. She corresponded with emperors, popes, and other mystics as well as ordinary people seeking guidance. At the age of sixty, she embarked on a series of preaching tours.

In these texts, Hildegard revealed a woman who, almost 900 years ago, struggled to develop a methodology for interpreting her inner experience. She created an approach that involved body, mind, and spirit as well as memory, will, and attention (Atherton, 2001). In interpreting the meaning of these sounds and images, she placed them in the context of a broad range of sources including Christian theology, the Old and New Testaments, Plato and the neo-Platonists, and St. Augustine, as well as numerous ancient and contemporary references in a process very reminiscent of amplification. She recognized that her images might have layers of meaning and often provided multiple interpretations.

**30** Susan Wyatt

Hildegard lived at a time when the church in Europe was expressing itself in building great stone cathedrals. While beautiful, these structures also symbolized a rigidity that was becoming entrenched in religious life. As the clergy pursued political power, both authority and dogma were being consolidated and canon law solidified. While many of the cathedrals were dedicated to Mary as a transcendent woman, real women were being increasingly marginalized from significance in public life. In counterpoint to these rigid stone structures, Hildegard saw the universe as imbued with God's creative power. One of her central concepts was *viriditas* – the greening power of all life. The images that she created to represent her inner experience took the form of very striking mandalas, to Jung symbols of wholeness, the union of all opposites (Jung, 1959). In her words, images, and music, Hildegard conveyed a vision of the wholeness and interconnectedness of all life. "Hildegard's worldview was basically therapeutic: humanity-in-creation has the purpose and mission of being healed and saved and, in turn, of healing and saving" (Clendenen, 2012, p. 90).

In Hildegard's visions, divinity was often depicted symbolically as well as by figures of both genders. Her *Scivias* (Hildegard, 1151/1986), which described and interpreted her visions, was divided into three sections, which she correlated with the Christian Trinity. In the third section, which consisted of thirteen visions, her interpretation focused on the Holy Ghost. The number thirteen has often been associated with the Goddess and, although she was careful to keep her interpretations within the bounds of orthodox twelfth-century theology, the images that she described in this section could also be seen as representations of the divine feminine.

Although the capacity to perceive patterns of the impersonal unconscious is the gift of the medial woman, the ability to understand and communicate their meaning requires art and craft. Hildegard had the talent to interpret her visions in music and art as well as words. For any medial woman, making meaning of archetypal images and learning how to express those meanings are hard work requiring skills that must be acquired and practiced. Hildegard was able to transcend the cultural context of her time to produce works that still seem fresh, relevant, and profound.

## Eleonora Duse

Toni Wolff (1951/1995) wrote that the challenge of the medial woman is to find an adequate language to express the contents of the collective unconscious. For Eleonora Duse, that language was acting. "Beneath our surface differences, Duse believed, we share a common human core, and she communicated that truth through the medium of the theater and the women she portrayed" (Sheehy, 2003, p. 116). Her technical skills were so great that they appeared effortless to her audiences. However, Duse worked unrelentingly from the time when she first became aware of herself as an actress to achieve this virtuosity.

> She welcomed the applause and cheers of the crowd because they were a proof of her work well done, but they were forgotten as soon as they were

Medial women: views of a feminist epistemologist **31**

over, and what remained was the challenge, the constant aspiration to perfect herself as an even finer, more sensitive, more revealing instrument with which to serve. (Le Gallienne, 1965, p. 37)

Eleonora Duse grew up in a family troupe of itinerant actors in mid-nineteenth-century northern Italy. She made her acting debut at the age of four in the role of Cosette. She wrote a brief memoir in which we can see that her experience of knowing involved interaction with the voices of her characters. When she was fourteen she played Juliet in Verona. She wrote of her performance, "(E)very word seemed to go through the heat of my blood. There was not a fiber in me that did not contribute to the harmony" (quoted in Sheehy, 2003, p. 4). She felt that she was guided by a secret voice aimed at transformation. Juliet, Marguerite, Nora, Hedda, and her other characters not only guided her performances but provided consolation through her troubles. The dominant style of acting at the time involved striking poses and declaiming speeches. Duse, however, insisted on a naturalistic style that was an inspiration to a modern generation of actors such as Constantin Stanislavski. Since her roles were conjured from her experience with her characters and their varying moods, each performance was unique. This was in sharp contrast to her rival Sarah Bernhardt, who was famous for playing a role exactly the same in every performance.

When she played in North and South America as well as all the major countries of Europe, Eleonora Duse (often referred to as *La Duse*) was acclaimed as the greatest living actress; yet she never performed in any language other than Italian. As an actress and director, she may have had an advantage in portraying the archetypal dimensions of her characters because she relied on the words of others. Her language consisted of the images that she created with her body, spirit, and emotions. She felt her greatest performances had been given not by, but to her. Perfecting herself as an instrument was essential to her ability to communicate meaning to an audience. "She worked to enrich the resources of her mind and spirit; to deepen her perception; sharpen her imagination; widen her understanding; develop a power of concentration so intense that it could translate a mental image into reality" (Le Gallienne, 1965, p. 125).

The most striking quality of Duse seems to have been, paradoxically, her transparency. "She is no longer herself when she plays a character; she becomes the character she plays to such an extent that she herself disappears entirely" (Le Gallienne, 1965, p. 127). Although Duse must have had an immense talent for acting, this transparency was not achieved without effort. The elimination of ego from her playing took years of hard work and practice. "[H]er aim throughout her live was the elimination of self—the 'self-naughting' of the mystic—in order that she should become merely the instrument by which the Universal Self could be expressed" (Le Gallienne, 1965, p. 19).

Eleonora Duse was also a successful producer and manager of her own acting company but her work and the extremes of her emotional life often left her exhausted. She had one daughter but she was not an attentive mother, leaving the

**32** Susan Wyatt

girl to be raised by a wet nurse until she was old enough to be sent to boarding school. Unlike the virgin martyrs and mystics, she had a life filled with liaisons with men. At the beginning of the most fervent of these, with the poet Gabriele D'Annunzio, she took on the role of muse with as much intensity as any of her stage performances. Her first loyalty, however, was always to Dionysus and to the transforming power of the ritual of theater. After a brief retirement, she was on the stage up to the time when died in 1924 and it is tantalizing to wonder if Toni Wolff ever saw her in performance.

## Ricarda Huch

Of all Toni Wolff's examples, the most intriguing from a scholarly point of view is Ricarda Huch because she was a distinguished scholar and historical researcher herself. There was nothing out of the ordinary in her early education in northern Germany, where she was born in 1864. However, when she was thwarted in her desire for a college education because German universities did not award degrees to women, she set forth to Zürich to study history, philosophy, and philology. In 1891 she became one of the first women in the world to earn a Ph.D. and went to work as a librarian. Five years later, she returned to Germany to teach history, but soon liberated herself from these duties to become what she termed a "free authoress" (*Biographie*, n.d.). Her major historical works focused on such diverse topics as Garibaldi, the Thirty Years' War, the Revolutions of 1848, and Michael Bakunin. However, much of her research concentrated on the influence of romanticism in literature with the avowed purpose of contributing to the renewal of her era in the spirit of romance. Her work was very highly regarded and she was the first woman invited to join the Prussian Academy of Arts. Thomas Mann referred to her as "the first lady of German letters" (Schaffrodt, 1999).

Ricarda Huch's historical works have been challenging for both her contemporaries and present day historians. Although her research was admired for its meticulousness and the breadth of its vision, her works are now usually classified as fiction (Smith, 1998), for she believed that poetic imagination is just as important for capturing history as the collection of facts that dominated historical research among her contemporaries. The preface she wrote to a collection of early Christian mosaics (1946) seems to shed light on how she conducted her research. A traditional hermeneut would have surrounded the mosaics with texts to interpret their meaning. Instead she used the images themselves–their placement, contents, symbolism, shapes, symmetries, colors, and the moods they evoked–to imagine the worldview of the human subjects of the late Roman empire. Toni Wolff identified Ricarda Huch as a medial woman for her ability to "evoke historical situations and persons" (1951/1995, p. 5) and this evocative element was crucial to her research.

> Ricarda Huch proposed that it was the imagistic quality of a historical fact that mattered, the resonance that would strike readers enough to grab their intellect and emotions. With the factual being used as domination, the

Medial women: views of a feminist epistemologist **33**

fantastic in history was an important means of keeping this source of oppression under control. (Smith, 1998, p. 233)

Ricarda Huch wove her histories from the stories of individuals and from the ordinary events of everyday life. "Historiography is for her both an intensely personal experience and a public event" (Anderson, 1998, p. 471). This was quite baffling for her contemporary readers who were accustomed to thinking of history as big events, military campaigns, and great men. In order to evoke a response from her readers, she presented not only the facts and recorded words of the individuals who comprised her histories; she revealed their thoughts and feelings, their quarrels and intrigues, their reactions to both failures and triumphs. Her characters included not only the great, but the small—"any number of anonymous monks, society ladies, and children" (Smith, 1998, p. 168) who contributed their own thoughts and feelings.

In Ricarda Huch's work, the basic dynamic of history was the movement of human consciousness towards something that is at the same time deeper and higher. She attempted to show "how each individual is capable of disintegrating his moral structure and reassembling it in a new and higher arrangement, under the katalysis of a powerful emotional experience or conviction" (Drake, 1931, p. vi). Her approach to historical research was grounded in her teleological viewpoint that the purpose of human life is to achieve personal harmony. "Man is a representation of the universe consisting of nature, spirit and soul. The meaning of human life is in a harmonious balance of character within the environment which creates a readiness to do good" (Smolenski, 1989, p. 1). Ultimately this inner harmony will lead to a balance between the self and the other that provides the foundation for a harmonious, just, and community-oriented collective. One particular facet of this harmony is the balance between the rational and irrational. Ricarda Huch suggested that, in Germany at the beginning of the Weimar years, the rational had gained the upper hand, resulting in depersonification (Skidmore, 1993). She saw her evocative and poetic approach to historical research as one way of restoring the balance.

In addition to her historical works, Ricarda Huch was admired for her poetry and fiction. The best insight into her experience of knowing can be found in a story that she wrote in 1899 that resonates with themes familiar from traditional fairy tales such as the search for enlightenment and the relationship between knowing and loving. In synopsis, the story reads:

> Once upon a time there was a youth who wanted to find a shortcut to hard work and study in his quest for knowledge. He read in a book how mermaids could sing so sweetly that whatever heard their song revealed itself without resistance and he decided that this was the way to induce the universe to open up its secrets to him. Once he succumbed to this desire, it was not long before he came upon a mermaid. She, however, had designs of her own. For a mermaid, though she can live a long time, is not immortal unless she can induce a human to willingly give her his heart. The mermaid agreed to teach the

youth her song in exchange for his heart. She even gave him a beautiful crystal blade with which to cut it out quite painlessly.

It seemed dubious to the youth that he would continue to thrive without a heart. Nonetheless, he was not willing to do without the siren song, so he procured the heart of a calf that he offered to the mermaid, reminding her of her promise to teach him the secret of her magical singing. There was no need to teach him, she explained, because the song of the mermaids is magical precisely because they have no heart and he acquired the talent the moment he cut his out.

The title of the tale is "The Pack of Lies" (Huch, 2001) and Ricarda Huch left it to the reader to sort out just which are truths and which lies.

Towards the end of her life, Ricarda Huch herself was confronted with the pack of lies. She despised National Socialism and wrote an intentionally provocative chapter on the persecution of the Jews in her study of the Holy Roman Empire. Even though she was an outspoken opponent, the Nazis did not suppress her work, but rather used her conservative nationalist and romantic themes for their own ends (Condray, 1980). In 1936, however, German writers were required to take a loyalty oath to the National Socialist Party. Ricarda Huch's response was to resign from the Prussian Academy. After this her work was suppressed and a review of it in *The National Socialist Monthly* closed with the words: "Adolf Hitler's Germany has no place for sorceresses of this ilk" (Schaffrodt, 1999). She fled to Jena to live out the war years in obscurity and poverty. After the war, when it became clear that Jena would be swallowed in the Soviet zone of occupation, she once again took flight, this time to West Germany where she started work on a book about the German resistance. No longer young and, weakened by the arduous journey and the privations she suffered during the war, she died in 1947.

In the more than half century since her death, Ricarda Huch has not been an influential figure in historical research. Her romantic sensibilities and worldview seem quite nineteenth century and her work has been criticized for not touching the reality of human lives. However, her resistance to those who would exercise tyranny over or through scholarly research is as relevant as ever. In Toni Wolff's model, the medial woman performs a life-promoting function by compensating for what has become overly dominant in the collective conscious. Ricarda Huch's conviction that knowing is a matter of the heart and that the purpose of research is to tap into the wellsprings of human values and "assist people in developing new life forms" (Skidmore, 2001, p. 102) undermined the notion of a scholar's responsibility to contribute to some ever-increasing body of objective knowledge. Her view that facts are a source of oppression confronted assumptions about research that even now many do not question. Her digressive style of writing as well as her emphasis on art and culture and on everyday life and people violated ideological theories of research. Her argument that the violence of cutting one's heart, spirit, or imagination out of one's research methodology produces an

Medial women: views of a feminist epistemologist **35**

imbalance in the individual that is at the root of injustice and violence in the collective challenged many of the still dominant contemporary models of inquiry.

## Conclusion

What Ricarda Huch, Eleonora Duse, Hildegard of Bingen, and the Christian martyrs had in common is a way of knowing that is a matter of the heart and imagination. Their actual experience included inner visual images as well as sounds and voices. Their knowing involved creating of themselves vessels that were structured enough for constellating the energy of the archetypes and yet permeable enough to be receptacles for the collective unconscious:

> to deal with the collective unconscious demands a solid ego consciousness and an adequate adaptation to reality. As a rule the medial woman disposes of neither and consequently she will create confusion in the same measure as she herself is confused ... But if she possesses the faculty of discrimination, the feeling or the understanding for the specific values and the limits of the conscious and the unconscious, of the personal and the impersonal, of what belongs to the ego and what to the environment, then her faculty to let herself be moulded by the objective psychic contents will enable her to exert a positive cultural influence.... (Wolff, 1951/1995, p. 7)

The work of these medial women went beyond their individual development or even the developmental relationships they had with other individuals. Their engagement with archetypes contributed to the integration of their culture and the development of the consciousness of their collective.

Although she titled her four categories "structural forms," Toni Wolff observed that they "probably are of an archetypal nature" (1951/1995, p. 80) and the structure of mediality can be seen as having origins in mythology. The Pythia of the Delphic Oracle was a medial woman whose role involved mythic dimensions. Laurie Layton Schapira (1988) has identified the Trojan prophetess Cassandra as a medial woman whose feminine values have been repressed. Toni Wolff observed that medial women have always had a social function as seers, sibyls, medicine women, and shamans. Sometimes I imagine what it would be like if our social organization included a Department of Consciousness. Lacking such a place of employment, many medial women can only serve their collective through their spiritual practice. Many artists, such as poet Adrienne Rich and singer Nóirín Ní Riain, express the meaning of the collective unconscious in their work. Women in the visual arts such as fashion designer Vivienne Westwood and costume designer Emi Wada also mediate such meaning in their images. A particularly inspiring contemporary example of a medial woman is Sister Wendy Beckett, who can be seen as a mediatrix of the spiritual in art.

A number of scholars have begun to incorporate mediality into their research methodology, although including imagination and intuition in their approach can

**36** Susan Wyatt

still provoke controversy. However, since the role of medial women includes representing contents that have been submerged in the collective unconscious, it is not surprising that almost all the examples in this chapter struggled with defining themselves on their own terms, often in defiance of the norms of their collective. While one or two forms are usually predominant in a particular woman, Toni Wolff noted that it is possible, with difficulty, to develop and integrate the third and fourth form as an approach to individuation. Any of us can experiment with weaving the medial structure into our work and our research as well as our creative and spiritual lives.

## References

Anderson, S. C. (1998). The insider as outsider: Ricarda Huch's autobiographical texts. *German Life and Letters*, 51: 4, 470–83.

Atherton, M. (2001). *Introduction to Hildegard of Bingen, selected writings*. London: Penguin.

*Biographie Ricarda Huch, 1864–1947*. (n.d.) Retrieved March 20, 2015 from the German Historical Museum website. http://www.dhm.de/lemo/html/biografien/HuchRicarda/

Clendenen, A. (2012). *Experiencing Hildegard: Jungian perspectives*. Wilmette, IL: Chiron Publications.

Condray, K. (1980). *Women writers of the journal* Jugen *from 1914–1940*. Lewiston, NY: Edwin Mellon Press.

Corson, R. B. (1998). *Wounds of the medial woman in contemporary Western culture*. Unpublished Ph.D. Dissertation, Pacifica Graduate Institute, Carpenteria, CA.

Drake, W. A. (1931). Introduction. In R. Huch, *Eros invincible* (pp. v–xi). New York: MacCaulay.

Hildegard of Bingen. (1986). *Mystical visions (Scivias)* (B. Hozeski, Trans.). Santa Fe, NM: Bear.

Hildegard of Bingen. (2001). *Selected writings* (M. Atherton, Trans.). London: Penguin.

Huch, R. (1946). Preface. In *Early Christian mosaics from the fourth to the seventh centuries* (pp. 5–7). New York: Iris Books.

Huch, R. (2001). The pack of lies. In S. C. Jarvis and J. Blackwell (Eds. and Trans.), *The queen's mirror: Fairy tales by German women, 1780–1900* (pp. 353–58). Lincoln, NE: University of Nebraska Press.

Jung, C. G. (1959). Concerning mandala symbolism (R. F. C. Hull, Trans.). In *The collected works of C. G. Jung* (Vol 9i). Princeton, NJ: Princeton University Press.

Le Gallienne, E. (Ed.). (1965). *The mystic in the theatre: Eleonora Duse*. Carbondale, Il: Southern Illinois University.

*Ricarda Huch*. (n.d.) Retrieved July 29, 2015 from the Ricarda Huch School website. http://www.ricarda-huch-schule-giessen.de/

Schaffrodt, P. (1999). *Ricarda Huch manuscript discovered in Heidelberg University Library*. Retrieved March 20, 2006, from the University of Heidelberg website. http://www.uni-heidelberg.de/press/news/press56_huch_e.html

Schapira, L. L. (1988). *The Cassandra complex: Living with disbelief*. Toronto: Inner City.

Sheehy, H. (2003). *Eleonora Duse*. New York: Albert A. Knopf.

Skidmore, J. M. (1993). *History with a mission: Ricarda Huch's historiography during the Weimar Republic*. Unpublished Ph.D. Dissertation, Princeton University, NJ.

Skidmore, J. M. (2001). "Nestorin der deutschen Lieratur" or "Parasit Hitlers"? The early East German debate about Ricarda Huch. *The Germanic Review*, 76: 1, 3–14.

Smith, B. G. (1998). *The gender of history: Men, women, and historical practice.* Cambridge, MA: Harvard University.

Smolenski, E. (1989). *The problem of fate and human embodiment in the works of Ricarda Huch.* Unpublished Ph.D. Dissertation, University of Pretoria.

Wolff, T. (1951). *Structural forms of the feminine psyche* (P. Watzlawik, Trans.). Zürich: privately printed for the Students Association, C. G. Jung Institut.

Wolff, A. (1995). Structural forms of the feminine psyche. (G. Jacobson, Trans.). *Psychological Perspectives*, 31: 1, 77–90.

**PART II**
# Theme: Clinical Perspectives

# 4

# WORKING WITH A WOMAN WITH BINGE EATING DISORDER

*Sue Austin*

## Introduction

In this chapter I will extend the Jungian/post-Jungian view of the self as an emergent phenomenon through Judith Butler's idea that the self is ec-static. By this Butler means that our sense of self is located 'outside' ourselves (2004a, p. 24) and that our experience of interiority is made up of an assemblage of alien pockets of inner otherness.

On this basis I suggest that what matters most in our experience of selfhood is not how we come together, and/or what we come together around, but what it is like when we come apart or come undone, what shapes and informs how and when we do so, and the ways we long to be (and fear being) brought undone by others. Of course, these longings and fantasies are interwoven with our terrors and longings about bringing others undone.

As well as providing a theoretical perspective, this view of interiority offers clinicians ways of thinking about and working with clients and their 'symptoms' which can lead to powerful insights. Given the cultural pressures on women to perform a (default) social function as 'containers' for others, insights into our longings to come undone and bring others undone can be especially valuable for girls and women and, in particular, those with eating disorders. To illustrate this I will describe my work with a young woman who suffered from a binge eating disorder.

## Centripetal and centrifugal dynamics in Jung's work

While Jung was explicitly committed to an *a priori* view of the self, there are currents in his work which support a more emergent view of self experience and Susan Rowland's identification of centripetal and centrifugal dynamics in Jung's texts helps to clear a space in which to draw out this emergent aspect of his thinking.

**42** Sue Austin

Rowland's distinction is based on the ideas of literary theorist Mikhail Bakhtin who suggests that:

> language and social representation ... [are] a constant battle between centralizing energies that aim to standardize meaning and linguistic form, versus centrifugal forces of dispersion and difference as language is embodied in actual social situations (Rowland 2005, pp. 101–2).

### Centripetal dynamics in Jung's view of the self

The centripetal, centralizing energies which dominate much of Jung's work on the self are visible in his many discussions on the subject which are arranged around themes of wholeness and unity and which grant the self an *a priori*, universal, ahistorical status. This privileging of centripetal dynamics in the concept of the self was cemented into place by a number of Jung's followers whose writings on it placed strong emphasis on structure, order, wholeness, completeness and processes of 'coming together' (e.g., Jacobi 1974).

This focus needs, however, to be seen in context. For example, Marilyn Nagy writes that:

> Jung's psychology of individuation must be seen *not only* in terms of its practical merits as a theory of psychic process, but *also* in its historical context as one kind of attempt at resolution of the dilemma between science and religion which formed the major issue for turn-of-the-century intellectuals. (1991, p. 236; original italics)

Zinkin contextualizes the power of the centripetal dynamics in Jung's work in a different way, suggesting that Jung's thinking bears the marks of having developed out of his own need to manage the deranging centrifugal dynamics he found within himself:

> [w]hatever the value may be of seeing experience as archetypal, it seems likely from Jung's autobiographical material that for him personally it had the value of helping him feel sane through recognizing that his strange fantasies were not his alone but belonged to the whole of humankind. (2008, p. 398)

### Centrifugal dynamics in Jung's view of the self – the normally dissociable psyche

In contrast to this focus on wholeness and coming together, the centrifugal, unravelling energies in Jung's thinking are most visible in his earlier work on the dissociability of the psyche and in his doctoral thesis on the supposed mediumistic talents of his 15½-year-old-cousin, Hélène.

Working with a woman with binge eating disorder **43**

Here Jung was engaged with the irreducibly unresolvable, fragmented and fragmenting nature of subjectivity. This is also where I believe his most powerful clinical insights and techniques are to be found and it is important to understand why these insights were and are more easily available to Jung and the post-Jungians than they are to other psychoanalytic traditions.

Freud was aware of the dissociative split in libido (in other words, its tendency to fragment into seemingly disconnected parts), but saw it as pathological and pathogenic, while Jung saw it as normal and a natural prerequisite for the movement of psychic energy (Hartman 1994). As John Haule (1992, p. 247) points out, Freud chose to stay away from the ideas of the dissociationist movement of the late nineteenth century (with its links to spiritualism) because he wanted psychoanalysis to be regarded as a science, with its own independent credibility.

Jung, on the other hand, was strongly influenced by the dissociationists who:

> held that every aggregation of ideas and images possessed, in some measure or other, its *own personality*. The guiding image for this was the phenomenon of multiple personality, for which there was already a hundred-year-old therapeutic tradition, going back to Mesmer, Puységur, Despine, Azaam [and others] (Haule 1992, pp. 239–40; original italics).

Like Freud, most post-Freudian thinkers (including many object relations theorists) assume that dissociation is simply part of a pathological spectrum of disorders of which multiple personality is an extreme expression.

Jung, however, (like the dissociationists) saw multiple personality as an exaggerated form of the normally dissociable psyche (Haule 1992, p. 247). This difference in perspectives has important implications and Sonu Shamdasani argues that locating Jung as primarily a Freudian thinker who broke away misses the point of much of his work. Shamdasani (1998) traces Pierre Janet's influence on Jung (through Théodore Flournoy) and offers strong evidence that Jung's model was far closer to the French dissociationist tradition than it was to Freud's work.

In Jung's work the dissociationist heritage gives rise to the theory of complexes, a word whose use originates with Eugene Bleuler (Meir 1992, p. 202). Meir observes that '[m]any impressions are obliterated in the moment of perception on account of their incompatibility with the habitual attitude of the conscious mind; this seems to occur automatically and unconsciously' (1992, p. 205). These ego-dystonic impressions cluster together to create centres of 'not-I-ness', or inner Otherness – complexes – in the psyche.

The evidence for the existence of complexes comes from Jung's work on the word association test, which he was experimenting with between 1901 and 1904 at the Burghölzli Psychiatric Hospital in Zürich (Bair 2003, p. 66). Earlier scientists such as Kraepelin and Sommer had expected these kinds of tests to show up differences in intelligence, but Jung realized that they showed up differences in emotional terrain as the subject's consciousness was moved around their field of interiority by the impact of stimulus words (Leys 1992, p. 151).

**44** Sue Austin

What Jung found was that words whose associations took the subject into unconscious, emotionally charged internal spaces generated delays (whose duration correlated to the intensity of the emotion encountered), non-responses, perseverations, rhymes, self-references and so on. He argued that these interference phenomena occurred when the subject encountered within themselves a feeling-toned 'complex', and the key idea here is that of variations in the 'tone' or affective charge between different regions of the psychic landscape.

Hartman describes how Jung applied this dissociationist, complex-based understanding of the inner landscape to form a clinical approach which focused on centrifugal dynamics in the psyche and in the analytic process: 'First, he tried to recognize and attend to the aspects of the patient's personality which were "Not-I" and, second, he allowed the time necessary for the characteristics and personality of the "Not-I" to emerge (Hartman 1994)'. This acceptance of the psyche as inherently and normally dissociable offers the possibility of seeing the patient's 'symptoms' as potential carriers of fragments of unconscious communication.

### Centrifugal dynamics in Jung's view of the self – his doctoral thesis and his cousin Hélène's inner Other

Before exploring the implications of this view of the psyche through a clinical vignette I need to introduce a second element of Jung's early clinical thinking. This takes the form of his psychiatry doctoral dissertation in which he examined the supposed mediumistic talents of his young cousin, Hélène.

Jung's cousin Hélène had a reputation as a medium who could hold séances in which 'spirits' seemed to speak through her. In his 1902 dissertation Jung built on Flournoy's work to argue that Hélène's apparently mediumistic gifts were the product of the floodlight of her ego being switched off in her trance state (i.e., she entered a self-induced, hypnotic state).

Without her ego dominating, previously unconscious pockets of Hélène's personality would emerge seeming to 'speak through' her. Initially these included characters whose personalities ranged from dour to exuberant, reporting her many previous incarnations (which include having been seduced by Goethe), and having had numerous offspring through these incarnations. However, what eventually emerged was a serious and balanced personality called Ivenes (Ellenberger 1991, p. 43).

Haule summarizes Jung's reading of Hélène's behaviour saying that her:

> mediumistic fantasies played an important function in [her] adolescent development. The semisomnabulistic figure of Ivenes appeared to be her 'healthy personality' ... a kind of trial project for what she might become in twenty years' time. 'One cannot say that [Hélène] deludes herself into the higher state, rather that she dreams herself into it'. This recognition of a teleological component in fantasy, while foreign to Freud, had indeed been recognized by Paulham, Janet and Flournoy (Haule 1992, p. 249, quoting from Jung's thesis).

Here Haule is pointing to Jung's fascinating realization that pockets of the unconscious can contain seeds of who we can become. These unconscious pockets are, by their nature, split off from the ego and therefore cannot express themselves directly. Instead, their expression is necessarily more oblique and can include the production of psychological and somatic 'symptoms'. If these 'symptoms' are the expression of urgent, driven, unconscious communications they may be quite compulsive or have a strong semi-autonomous character.

What became apparent to me through the clinical vignette which I will describe shortly was that an eating disorder can be understood as an expression of such split-off psychological elements. And, although unconscious and unlived, these pockets of inner otherness can be crucial to a person's psychological development.

H.F. Ellenberger adds an important dimension to this perspective when he writes that:

> Whatever criticism could be made of Jung's dissertation, one major point is clear. He implied that [Hélène's] psychic growth was impeded by psychological and social obstacles and that her mediumistic utterances were a means resorted to by the unconscious to overcome these obstacles. (1992, p. 150)

Linking this to Haule's reading of Jung's thesis suggests that a 'symptom', such as an eating disorder, may also be a way in which a person's unconscious expresses itself because psychological and social obstacles leave it with no other choice.

## A clinical vignette: Jenny

In order to illustrate the clinical application of Jung's early explorations of these centrifugal dynamics in the psyche I will discuss my work with a young woman who I will call Jenny. About a year into analysis Jenny described her swings between periods of food restriction and non-vomiting bingeing as follows:

> It's as if I live in a glass room. While things are good with food, in other words, while I only eat fruit and yogurt, and not very much of those either, the glass walls hold, and I am safe. It may last hours, or days. It feels clean, ordered, sane. I am clean inside, acceptable. I can look people in the eye. I am not crippled with disgust at myself and what I do [with food]. Then, with no warning, I see a hair-line crack appear in one of the walls. Frantically, I try to tape it back together, hoping that I will be able to somehow make it unhappen. But I know I can't stop what happens next. It's only a matter of time before it all falls apart and I am eating whole loaves of bread, and all the food my flat mate has left in the fridge. I am awash with food madness. It is chaotic. And I have no idea if it will ever stop again. So far it always has, but I have no way of telling how or when it will happen. Maybe I will walk out of my front door and the sky will be just the right colour, and the wind touch me in some way. Maybe I will be on a bus and see an advert which somehow

**46** Sue Austin

clicks me back. Maybe I will wake up one morning and the glass room is back. Until next time. (Austin 2005, pp. 194–5)

## Initial reflections

My sense of Jenny was that she desperately wanted to create a safe, clean zone, where all desire was held in check by her glassy, fragile will, and where she felt she had a right to be a member of the human race. The only other place she could live from was somewhere where her will-power had failed, shattering her liveable sense of herself. That, in turn, dumped her into a tormenting state of chaos, desperation, shame and self-hatred. In sessions Jenny was often extremely distressed: she cried or sobbed and was desperate to stop bingeing. I frequently experienced a near-paralysing level of tension in the room and was often unable to feel or think very much at all. Arising as it did in the midst of this, Jenny's glass room image felt like an important breakthrough to a more reflective space and a different level of communication.

## Applying the notion of the Not-I: Jenny's goblin

Based on these ideas I had, for some time, been wondering about the kinds of (potentially unravelling) inner othernesses or Not-I elements of Jenny's personality which might be trying to express themselves through her bingeing. At this early point in our work together however, Jenny found any attempt to approach her own interiority very painful indeed. I imagined her predicament as like that of a turtle which, halfway through crawling up a beach, has had its shell ripped off, leaving all its insides exposed to any passing predator. Given this degree of vulnerability I saw my task as that of holding in mind the possibilities for greater psychological differentiation and growth contained in whatever part of Jenny was smashing up her glass room world and which she currently experienced as catastrophic. Again, what would emerge over time was how much conscious contact and engagement with these possibilities Jenny might (or might not) come to be able to bear.

Nonetheless, Jenny's glass room image depicted a powerful and potentially important aspect of that which was 'other' inside her and so when, eventually, her distress at talking about this image eased a little I asked her if she had any sense of what caused the crack in the wall of her glass room to start. Sobbing desperately, Jenny described a cruel, mocking, jeering goblin who hated her and tried to destroy her by smashing her glass room.

Seen in the light of Jung's early work on the Word Association Test and his understanding of his cousin Hélène's supposed mediumistic talents as dissociative phenomena, Jenny's monstrous goblin might:

- represent an unconscious element of her psyche which was expressing itself as a centre of intelligence which was acting independently of her ego;
- contain seeds of her future psychological growth, if she could bear to explore them.

## *Images of sitting with unbearable inner Othernesses*

An important question here is whether the growth offered by Jenny's goblin (as a pocket of ego-alien inner otherness) could be approached in any way: as she described the goblin's shattering attacks I got a sense of her world as lurching between an agonizingly anxious glass room configuration and a state of terrifying, devastated chaos. An image which conveys my experience of sitting with these dynamics is taken from a description I once heard BBC war correspondent Kate Adie give of covering the war in the former Yugoslavia.

Adie was trying to gain insight into what ordinary life was like in one of the cities caught in the conflict and had arranged to interview a civilian woman in her home. Adie climbed the stairs of an apartment block and knocked on her interviewee's door. The woman let her in and asked her to take a seat, apologizing for needing to finish the vacuum cleaning: she would then make them both a cup of tea and they could start the interview. All this made perfect sense, provided one ignored the fact that a whole wall of the apartment was missing, having been taken out by a bomb.

In practical terms, the conversation I am having with my patient may well be the equivalent of (for example) Adie discussing with her interviewee what it is like to live in a world where essential services such as water and power are only available intermittently and unpredictably. It is whatever conversation is possible in a place where thinking and feeling about the immediate situation are, at this stage, intolerable and overwhelming.

Such a conversation can be thought of as a response to the patient's need for a centripetal other. Over time, this other can offer a container within which the patient's distress and fragmentation may be held well enough for elements of ego strength and flexibility to start to return or develop for the first time. Reading Adie's image intra-psychically, this approach can, in time, support the patient's attempts to draw closer to her own experiences of having had structures and connections destroyed upon which she wholeheartedly depended, leaving her nowhere else to go.

Crucially, it can also offer the possibility (which is the focus of this chapter) of the patient being able to approach the parts of herself that need to explode and destroy structures upon which she depends.[1] Jenny's glass room and goblin images seemed to offer long-term possibilities for developing a vocabulary for exploring these needs, but meanwhile they also gave language to my own sense that this stage of our work was akin to sieving through the debris of her shattered glass room more and more slowly and carefully. My sense was that this enabled us to rerun the collapses of Jenny's glass room in slow-motion (as it were) until, at times, this became an almost still-by-still exploration. Again, I am drawing here on Hartman's observation that Jung allowed the time necessary for the characteristics and personality of the patient's 'Not-I' to emerge (Hartman 1994). Andrew Samuels translates this into clinical terms when he observes that Jung worked with the psyche by personifying its contents (Samuels 1989, p. 2) and Joseph Redfearn fleshes out this approach further in the following comment:

**48** Sue Austin

It seems to be a fundamental law of analysis, perhaps of parenting and of human relationships in general, that the individual (patient, infant etc.) can only yield up his pertinent bit of unconsciousness when this bit is given (or maybe feels it is given) enough recognition, value, sympathy (exactly which and what varies of course) by the analyst, parent etc. This is the essence of the effective countertransference attitude which has to be worked on by the analyst in connection with unconscious aspects of himself as well as of his patient. (Redfearn 1985, p. 111)

## *Slowing down and focusing on the detail of the worlds within the inner Othernesses*

In these 'stills' incongruent details began to become visible – for example, the way in which (prior to her last binge) Jenny's boss had ripped her off by not paying her at the end of her shift because business had been a bit slow. Jenny simply assumed that it was her responsibility to accept her boss's behaviour, rather than negotiate with him about it and question whether she should be loyal to a man who could afford the luxuries that mattered to him, while not paying her properly. She was determined not to be petty or disloyal, and thought her anger at her boss's behaviour 'mean'.

Sometimes the trigger was much more subtle, and only very close examination of the 'stills' gave us any clues about it. Often it had to do with something incoherent and deep down inside Jenny starting to scream with rage at what was happening to her. That scream and rage would terrify her, forcing her to identify with the 'don't make a fuss, don't put people out, I'm sure s/he didn't mean it' position, as she tried to cauterize her own response.

Bingeing was the one place where Jenny could 'let rip' with the raw, explosively aggressive energies that could not be experienced within her liveable sense of self[2] and her goblin was actually a part of her which (in addition to demanding that she learn how to use her own aggressive energies in clear ways) insisted that she start to learn about the experiences of coming undone. Butler offers a powerful insight into the central role these dynamics play in our capacity to draw close to inner and outer others when she writes '[l]et's face it. We're undone by each other. And if we're not, we're missing something' (Butler 2004a, p. 23).[3]

From this perspective, Jenny's bingeing can be seen as an expression of a healthy inner otherness which refused to lie down and die inside her glass, good-girl psychological coffin just as Jung's cousin Hélène's séances expressed a healthy inner otherness that refused to accept the deadening limits of bourgeois Swiss girlhood/womanhood.[4]

Drawing on these ideas I wondered whether Jenny's 'problem' was that her good-girl coffin was also her psychological container/skin. If so, I needed to proceed very slowly, concentrating primarily on her more overt needs for an experience of a centripetal other so that she could move beyond (what I imagined) as her shell-less turtle predicament and eventually start to approach the fascinating,

## Working with a woman with binge eating disorder  **49**

longed-for shatterings associated with her own capacities for intimacy and creativity, as expressed through her inner goblin.

### *Grief as a means of coming undone*

Over the years I've observed that grief can provide a means of engaging with the often highly charged field of tensions surrounding the seemingly irreconcilable need for a container and the (simultaneous) desire to be brought undone and bring the (containing) other undone. Again, Butler offers an insight into why this might be so when she points out that one of the reasons why we are so drawn to the unravelling, though potentially highly creative, edges of our liveable sense of self is that they are populated by the ghosts of our primary others which, as she puts it, 'live on in the fiber of the boundary that contains me, … [haunting] … the way I am, as it were, periodically undone and open to becoming unbounded' (Butler 2004a, p. 28).

By implication, as we come undone or become unbounded it may be possible to catch sight of the ways in which these primary others are entwined with the mechanisms that shape and police our experience of identity and our performance of it.

For Jenny an important insight into these dynamics came through the fact that, in spite of strenuous efforts, she cried in most sessions. She hated this, saying that it was pointless and that she needed to focus on stopping bingeing, or on a positive project in her life. Eventually, however, sometime after her glass room and goblin images had emerged, she was able to describe a family interaction from her adolescence which offered a glimpse of some of the ghosts that shaped her experience of coming undone. I heard Jenny's description of this interaction as indicating that she experienced anxieties about coming undone or bringing others undone as an important unconscious organizing factor in her family.

In the light of Butler's comment that 'grief contains the possibility of apprehending a mode of dispossession that is fundamental to who I am' (Butler 2003, p. 17) my sense was that Jenny had internalized these anxieties as a belief that feeling sad or lost for no apparent reason was not alright. This internalization meant that she was convinced that such feelings were self-indulgent and selfish, hence her distress at how much she cried in sessions (and, I suggest, hence the intensity of her need to cry). This internalization also meant that the modes of dispossession fundamental to Jenny's family's individual and collective lives were experienced as 'taboo'. Consequently, Jenny dared not get anywhere near her desire to be brought undone by experiences of excessive inner or outer othernesses through which she might encounter radical (but deeply unsettling) states of intimacy and aliveness.

Building on these understandings, I came to think of Jenny's tears and inner goblin as expressions of her need to explore what haunted the way she was periodically undone and open to becoming unbounded (Butler 2004a, p. 28). My understanding was that, like Jung's cousin Hélène, Jenny's dilemma was that 'recovery' (i.e., living the parts of her which had been split off and caused her

**50** Sue Austin

'symptoms') held fears that there might be costs and losses that were (at this stage) felt to be intolerable. Working with Jenny was very much about exploring these edges and the edgy question of how much 'recovery' she could bear to unravel into while retaining a liveable sense of herself.

Thus, in addition to offering a glimpse of the others who haunt how we come undone and experience undoneness, grief is one of the emotions which allow us to catch sight of what it is to live from a self that is organized around an emerging unconscious which, by its nature, we can never access or know.

Again, my experience is that this move from a will/ego-based experience of selfhood to something which is much more elusive and emergent can be essential for many people in analysis and especially so for women who have eating disorders.

## Self as an ec-static phenomenon

Having illustrated how the elements of Jung's early thinking about the centrifugal dynamics in the psyche can be used to think and work clinically, I will now return to the ideas themselves, drawing them into wider discussion of the self as an (as Butler calls it) 'ec-static' phenomenon and linking this to Laplanche's observation that the unconscious is organized around enigmatic signifiers.

This is the self that Stephen Frosh describes when he questions how our ideas of selfhood based on psychic integrity can be sustained 'when I have the feeling, always and everywhere, that something else is speaking within me – something over which I have no control (the defining feature of the unconscious), and the voice of which I cannot even properly hear' (2002, p. 397). This comment of Frosh's simultaneously points to Jacques Lacan's idea of the real *and* to the aspects of the Jungian and post-Jungian understanding of the unconscious in which I am interested.

Butler adds to this view of our relationship to the unconscious when she describes our experience of selfhood as follows:

> the 'I' repeatedly finds itself outside itself, and … cannot put an end to this repeated upsurge of its own exteriority. I am, as it were, always other to myself, and there is no final moment in which my return to myself takes place (2001, p. 23).

Butler's comment also resonates with Lucy Huskinson's reading of Jung's model as one in which the ego experiences the self as a violent other (2002), whose existence is known to the ego through repeated, disruptive upsurgings over which it has no control. From this perspective, the self is an inner otherness, a 'not-me' in me which (necessarily) remains alarmingly other to the ego.

Paul Kugler adds to this when he draws our attention to the central role of an irreducible inner otherness (out of which our consciousness arises) that lies at the heart of self-reflection (and by implication, the self) in the Jungian model. He writes:

Working with a woman with binge eating disorder **51**

[the] model of self-reflection found in classical psychology and philosophical epistemology works from the assumption that self-reflection is a mirror reflection. The subject-imago being objectively reflected upon is symmetrical (identical) to the subject doing the reflecting. This model of reflexivity adopts the logic of physical reflection. When applied to psychology, the process keeps the reflecting subject always caught in the solipsism of ego consciousness ...

Self-reflection in Jungian depth psychology is a process through which the personality turns back on itself in an asymmetrical fashion. This provides a way out of the philosophical solipsism and therapeutic narcissism inherent in the humanistic model. *The mirror at work in the Jungian hermeneutic does not reflect the self-same face. Rather it mirrors back the face of the Other.* (Kugler 1993; italics added)

Kugler's comments point beyond the emergent self towards how our experience of selfhood arises through encounters with inner otherness. In a paper in which she offers an important re-thinking of the main psychoanalytic models of selfhood and interiority, Butler offers an understanding of the self as 'ek-static' – in other words, our experience of selfhood is always outside us and beyond us. Butler develops this position out of her reading of Hegel and I will quote her at length as her argument is important and deserves to be given in detail. The following text is taken from the latter part of a discussion in which Butler is pointing out how her interpretation of Hegel is very different from Jessica Benjamin's:

When Hegel introduces the notion of recognition in the section on lordship and bondage in *The Phenomenology of Spirit*, he narrates the primary encounter with the Other in terms of self-loss. 'Self consciousness ... has *come out of itself* ... it has lost itself, for it finds itself in an *other* being ... One might understand Hegel to be describing merely a pathological state in which a fantasy of absorption by the Other constitutes an early or primitive experience. But he is saying something more. He is suggesting that whatever consciousness is, whatever the self is, will find itself only though a reflection of itself in another. To be itself, it must pass through self-loss, and when it passes through, it will never be 'returned' to what it was. To be reflected in or as another will have a double significance for consciousness, however, since consciousness will, through the reflection, regain itself in some way. But it will, by virtue of the external status of the reflection, regain itself as external to itself and, hence, continue to lose itself. Thus, the relationship to the other will be, invariably, ambivalent. The price of self-knowledge will be self-loss, and the Other poses the possibility of both securing and undermining self-knowledge. What becomes clear, though, is that the self never returns to itself free of the Other, that its 'relationality' becomes constitutive of who the self is ...

In my view, Hegel has given us an ek-static notion of the self, one which is, of necessity, outside itself, not self-identical, differentiated from the

**52** Sue Austin

> start. ... To be a self is, on these terms, to be at a distance from who one is, not to enjoy the prerogative of self-identity (what Hegel calls self-certainty), but to be cast, always, outside oneself, Other to oneself. (2004b, pp. 147–8; original italics)[5]

Like Kugler, I see the kind of ec-static, unsettling self which Butler describes as emerging from the exteriorities (inner othernesses) that surge up in us as the basis of the centrifugal aspect of the Jungian model. And if, as Butler suggests, selfhood is ec-static, working with our pockets of alien, inner otherness (as Jung did through the techniques he took from the dissociationist tradition and in his reading of his young cousin Hélène's supposed mediumistic talents) is a way of working with the field out of which experiences of ec-static selfhood can emerge. Indeed, privileging centripetal dynamics of coming together or wholeness in the analytic process actually *gets in the way* of creating the kind of environment in which the contradictory and unsettling (but inherently potentially more enlivening and relational) experiences of ec-static, centrifugal selfhood can emerge.

This idea that selfhood is entwined with our unravelling experiences of inner otherness also resonates with Laplanche's model of the unconscious and its formation which Allyson Stack summarizes as follows:

> ... those aspects of the adult message that the infant *cannot* translate, metabolize, or assimilate are *repressed* in the form of 'an internal foreign body' or 'psychical other ... Thus the unconscious is an 'alien inside me, and even one put inside me by an alien' .... (2005, p. 65; original italics)

Living with this alien unconscious, an unconscious put inside me by an alien (which feels both profoundly 'me' and 'not-me' at the same time), is my understanding of what is involved in coming to live from the mind-body-world field out of which ec-static self-experience can arise.

For Laplanche, the traumas which invade a child and become the signifiers around which they are organized are the complex communications which the child receives from the adult world. These (unconscious) communications cannot be assimilated by the child's still relatively unformed psyche, and the undigested/undigestable excess introduced by them is repressed by the child (Laplanche's primary repression). This process gives rise to enigmatic signifiers in the child's psyche which, being unconscious, are no longer knowable through direct means, but which nonetheless organize the child's (and later the adult's) inner and outer life. Laplanche describes these alien, internalized messages which structure our psyche as 'enigmatic' because they are 'not puzzles or riddles that can one day be solved by learning or applying the proper codes' (Stack 2005, p. 65). Crucially, these messages harbour 'an irreducible, interrogative kernel – a question neither sender nor receiver can ever completely answer' (p. 66).

From this perspective, individual development arises from the need 'to master, to translate these enigmatic, traumatizing messages', a process which continues for

Working with a woman with binge eating disorder   **53**

as long as we live (Laplanche 1999, p. 165). As Laplanche points out, however, the predominant response is to 'domesticate' the enigma of the other, so that 'the receiver of an enigmatic message is not translating the enigma of the message itself; rather she is simply translating her old translations' (Stack 2005, p. 68). In contrast to this, the enlivening, engaged response is a different form of repression: one which 'preserves the sharp goad of the enigma' (Laplanche 2002, p. 45).

## Conclusion: unravelling, fragmentation and working with the ec-static self

In this chapter I have suggested that the aspects of Jung's early work which provide ways of working with the centripetal dynamics in the psyche are, as Laplanche describes, potentially radically enlivening through the way they preserve the sharp goad of the enigmas around which the psyche is formed and is organized.

I have sought to describe a way of combining clinical techniques based on Jung's early work on the dissociability of the psyche with aspects of contemporary thinking about subjectivity, identity and the experience of selfhood. I have also described how the resultant analytic position can be used to access the seeds of recovery that can be found in the split-off, seemingly self-destructive energies which expressed themselves as (for example) a patient's binge eating disorder.

## Notes

1  This imagery parallels the 9/11 imagery discussed in relation to working with a chronically and severely anorexic patient in a previous paper (Austin 2009a). My use of images of explosions/war is deliberate and reflects my underlying interest in the question of how energies previously expressed as self- and/or other- destructive fantasies and actions can form the basis of a sense of agency, and the kinds of struggles that eating disordered women in particular have with these energies.
2  See also Redfearn's *The Exploding Self* (1992).
3  It is important that this comment is made in the context of grief in Butler's text.
4  Tragically Jung failed to disguise Hélène adequately in his thesis and Bair suggests that, as a result of this, rumours spread that Hélène's entire family were tainted with varying degrees of madness. Bair also comments that '[l]ater generations held Jung's dissertation directly responsible for the fact that many of the younger Preiswerk daughters in Helly's [Hélène's] generation did not marry' (Bair 2003, p. 64). This included Hélène.
5  I am aware that Jung disliked Hegel's work intensely. See Barbara Eckman (1992) for a discussion of the extent of this.

## *Acknowledgements*

This chapter is based on my 2009b and 2013 *Journal of Analytical Psychology* papers cited above (©2016, The Society of Analytical Psychology) and I would like to thank Giles Clark, Jill Welbourne, Michael Horne, Peter Fullerton, Ladson Hinton, Michael Lindner, Andrew Samuels, Michael Horne, Alison Clark, John Merchant and Leon Petchkovsky for their input into those papers – without their help neither would have been written, and nor would this chapter.

I would also like to thank *The Journal of Analytical Psychology* and its publisher, Wiley Blackwell, for their permission to use these two papers as the basis of this

**54** Sue Austin

chapter. My special thanks to Susanna Wright (joint editor-in-chief at The Journal) for arranging this permission.

Finally I would like to thank the North Pacific Institute for Analytical Psychology in Seattle and the Sydney Chapter of the International Association of Relational Psychoanalysis and Psychotherapy for opportunities to present earlier versions of my 2009 JAP paper 'Jung's Dissociable Psyche and the Ec-static Self'. My thanks also to Michael Lindner and Elisabeth Adametz for their invitation to give a re-written version of that paper at the Berlin Jung Institute in 2011. Additionally, I would like to express my appreciation to the New South Wales Institute for Psychoanalytic Psychotherapy for a similar opportunity in 2012.

## References

Austin, S. (2005) *Women's Aggressive Fantasies: A Post-Jungian Exploration of Self-Hatred, Love and Agency*, London and New York: Routledge.

Austin, S. (2009a) 'A Perspective on the Patterns of Loss, Lack, Disappointment and Shame Encountered in the Treatment of Six Women with Severe and Chronic Anorexia Nervosa' in *The Journal of Analytical Psychology*, 54, 1.

Austin, S. (2009b) 'Jung's Dissociable Psyche and the Ec-static Self' in *The Journal of Analytical Psychology*, 54, 5.

Austin, S. (2013) 'Working with Dissociative Dynamics and the Longing for Excess in Binge Eating Disorders' in *The Journal of Analytical Psychology*, 58, 3.

Bair, D. (2003) *Jung: A Biography*, Boston: Little, Brown and Company.

Butler, J. (2001) 'Giving an Account of Oneself' in *Diacritics*, 31, 4.

Butler, J. (2003) 'Violence, Mourning, Politics' in *Studies in Gender and Sexuality*, 4, 1.

Butler, J. (2004a) *Precarious Life: The Powers of Mourning and Violence*, London: Verso.

Butler, J. (2004b) *Undoing Gender*, New York: Routledge.

Eckman, B. (1992) 'Jung, Hegel and the Subjective Universe' in *Carl Gustav Jung: Critical Assessments*, Vol. 1, ed. Renos Papadopoulos. London: Routledge.

Ellenberger, H. F. (1991) 'The Story of Helene Preiswerk – A Critical Study With New Documents' in *History of Psychiatry*, 2, 5.

Ellenberger, H. F. (1992) 'Carl Gustav Jung: His Historical Setting' in *Carl Gustav Jung: Critical Assessments*, Vol. 1, ed. Renos Papadopoulos. London: Routledge.

Frosh, S. (2002) 'The Other' in *American Imago*, 59, 4.

Hartman, G. (1994) The Franco Prussian War or Jung as a Dissociationist, online at *The Jung Page* http://www.cgjungpage.org/learn/articles/analytical-psychology/139-the-franco-prussian-war-or-jung-as-dissociationist (accessed 24 May 2015).

Haule, J. (1992) 'From Somnambulism to the Archetypes: the French Roots of Jung's Split with Freud' in *Carl Gustav Jung: Critical Assessments*, Vol. 1, ed. Renos Papadopoulos. London: Routledge.

Huskinson, L. (2002) 'The Self as Violent Other: The Problem of Defining the Self' in *The Journal of Analytical Psychology*, 47, 3.

Jacobi, J. (1974) *The Psychology of C. G. Jung*, translated by Ralph Manheim, Yale: Yale University Press.

Kugler, P. (1993) 'The "Subject" of Dreams', online at *The Jung Page* http://www.cgjungpage. org/learn/articles/analytical-psychology/242-the-qsubjectq-of-dreams (accessed 24 May 2015).

Laplanche, J. (1999) *Essays on Otherness*, London, Routledge.

Laplanche, J. (2002) 'Sublimation and/or Inspiration', translated by Luke Thurston and John Fletcher in *New Formations*, 48.

Leys, R. (1992) 'Jung, and the Limits of Association' in *Carl Gustav Jung: Critical Assessments*, Vol. 1, ed. Renos Papadopoulos. London: Routledge.

Meir, C. (1992) 'The Theory of Complexes' in *Carl Gustav Jung: Critical Assessments*, Vol. 2, ed. Renos Papadopoulos. London: Routledge.

Nagy, M. (1991) *Philosophical Issues in the Psychology of C. G. Jung*, Albany: State University of New York.

Redfearn, J. (1985) *My Self, My Many Selves*, London: Karnac Books.

Redfearn, J. (1992) *The Exploding Self: The Creative and Destructive Nucleus of the Personality*. Asheville, NC: Chiron Publications.

Rowland, S. (2005) *Jung as a Writer*, London & New York: Routledge.

Samuels, A. (1989) *The Plural Psyche*, London: Tavistock Routledge.

Shamdasani, S. (1998) 'From Geneva to Zürich: Jung and French Switzerland' in *The Journal of Analytical Psychology*, 43, 1.

Stack, A. (2005) 'Culture, Cognition and Jean Laplache's Enigmatic Signifier' in *Theory, Culture and Society*, 22, 3.

Zinkin, L. (2008, reprinting 2001 paper) 'Your Self: Did You Find It or Did You Make It?' in *The Journal of Analytical Psychology*, 53, 3.

# 5

## EMMA JUNG'S PEN

### Jung, feminism and the body

*Cheryl L. Fuller*

> *Woman must write her self: must write about women and bring women to writing, from which they have been driven away as violently as from their bodies—for the same reasons, by the same law, with the same fatal goal. Woman must put herself into the text—as into the world and into history—by her own movement.*—Helene Cixous (1976)

Women and self-silencing have been much on my mind since reading Terry Tempest Williams' moving memoir, *When Women Were Birds: Fifty-four Variations on Voice*. Williams' mother died when she was 54, leaving to her daughter all of her journals. When she herself turned 54, she sat down with the journals planning to read them. But as she opened them, one after the other, what she found was blank page after blank page. Several shelves of journals and not a single word in any of them.

As I sat down to begin to write this chapter, a dream I had some 30 years ago came to mind. In the dream I was in Switzerland walking along a narrow street in Zurich. I came to a small stationer's shop. Inside I looked at the fountain pens and was especially drawn to one, a beautiful deep green pen. As I looked at it, the proprietor said to me that the pen was Emma Jung's and I should take it. Emma Jung's pen. I decided I needed to learn more about Emma, as most of what I knew of her was that she had remained with Jung despite issues of infidelity and that she herself left us very little writing of her own.

We have two essays written by Emma Jung and her work on the Grail Legend, published posthumously after Marie Louise von Franz worked on it. We learn from Irene Gaudissart's biographical essay about Emma, *Love and Sacrifice: The Life of Emma Jung*, that she instructed the people with whom she corresponded to burn her letters and, as very few survive, it seems they complied. In this sense, Emma Jung, like Terry Tempest Williams' mother, leaves us to discern what her silence means for us as Jungians and women.

Recently I have been thinking and writing about the intersection of depth psychology, feminism, the female body, and fat studies especially in clinical work. To my surprise I discover how little there is in the Jungian literature about body and most especially about the female body, yet another instance of women's silence. In the analytic encounter, body meets body, yet rarely is body spoken of. Without a body, we become like the nymph Echo, a voice without a body condemned to echo what she hears rather than speak her own experience.

The avoidance of the body is known and written about by a number of Jungians, among them Marion Woodman, Anita Greene, Gottfried Heuer, all of whom incorporate body work of various kinds into their analytic practices. In their work, it is most often assumed that issues of the patient's body warrant examination, but there is general silence about the body to body interaction of analyst and patient and the body issues present in such interactions. Other than a few pieces by Polly Young-Eisendrath and Marion Woodman, there is very little in the Jungian literature where we find discussion of the female body from the perspective of actual women. Of the many effects on women's lives and bodies of the stages of the reproductive cycle. Of the pregnant body. Of the deviant body. Of the mutilated body. Of the objectification of the female body and the fruitless quest for perfection that occupies the lives of so many girls and women. Of the aging body. This despite the reality that much of women's life experience involves changes in our bodies—menarche, menstruation, pregnancy, childbirth, menopause all marked by blood and changes in our bodies. Where are women's voices about women's bodies and psyches?

As Heuer (2005) notes, "Jungian psychology seems marked by a theoretical ambivalence towards the body, whilst mostly ignoring it clinically ... so the post-Jungians have only rarely engaged with the body in their theoretical and clinical work" (p.107). Or as Jung (1968) put it:

> We do not like to look at the shadow-side of ourselves; therefore there are many people in civilized society who have lost their shadow altogether, have lost the third dimension, and with it they have usually lost the body. The body is a most doubtful friend because it produces things we do not like: there are too many things about the personification of this shadow of the ego. Sometimes it forms the skeleton in the cupboard, and everybody naturally wants to get rid of such a thing. (p.23)

Rosemary Balsam (2012), a psychoanalyst, took up this problem of the absence of the female body in psychoanalysis in her book, *Women's Bodies in Psychoanalysis*. She begins by asking,

> How do we talk about bodies? How do we think about our analysands' bodies? How do we contemplate our own bodily presence in the office? How can we think more about our own bodies in relation to our patients? And those messages from past bodily experience that the mind holds in its

"jar"—how do we render them to another person to increase their comprehensibility? (pp. Kindle Locations 207–211)

Such important questions and so little discussed. We all have bodies. In every consulting room, body meets body. Why then the silence about the body, especially the female body?

Heuer (2012) suggests:

> body became Shadow because it renders us powerless vis-à-vis the vicissitudes of desire, ageing and death, and so was split off from the more valued mental and spiritual aspects of human experience. Thus excluded, that which is not valued becomes evil. This bias continues to flourish in analysis: in clinical practice the predominant aim is to touch the soul, never the body. Yet it is the body that constitutes our being in the world as matter, in that it forms the very basis from which we relate and interact with ourselves, with others and with the spiritual dimension of being. (p.12)

Like Jung, Heuer sees body as shadow, avoided because it inevitably brings into the room those aspects of life we most wish to avoid—death, aging, desire, greed, excess. Certainly the female body, and especially the fat female body carries this shadow and inevitably activates in both patient and analyst all of the anxieties attendant upon these shut off aspects of life.

Balsam (2012) sees another reason for avoidance:

> The silence in psychoanalysis about the female body—whether it is the patient's or the analyst's, and whether it manifests itself in a theory, in treatment, in a fin de siècle hysteria, or in a contemporary clinical presentation—suggests that this is yet another venue in which the internal and external aspects of bodily experience have not yet been integrated. Despite our clinical sophistication, it is difficult to sustain a mental integration of body and mind. How humanly eager we all are—analysand and analyst alike—to seek the transient but seductive comfort of dwelling with less anxiety in the mental spaces of splits, schisms, and rifts, where physical explanations and mental ones are kept in separate compartments. (pp. Kindle location 364–369)

We stay where we, both therapist and patient, can maintain the split of body from mind, where we can both see the body as something handy for transporting the head and the all important mind.

With friends I have somewhat jokingly speculated that the normative Jungian analyst is a slender, white, heterosexual male. Assuming for the sake of argument that this is true at least so far as determining the issues that analytical psychology concerns itself with, how does this relate to silence about the body? In 1975, Laura Mulvey published a paper in which she identifies for the first time what she called

Emma Jung's pen: Jung, feminism and the body **59**

"the male gaze" which she asserts is the film industry's assumption that the movie spectator is a man. Mulvey (1989) describes it this way:

> In a world ordered by sexual imbalance, pleasure in looking has been split between active/male and passive/female. The determining male gaze projects its phantasy on to the female form which is styled accordingly. In their traditional exhibitionist role women are simultaneously looked at and displayed, with their appearance coded for strong visual and erotic impact so that they can be said to connote to-be-looked-at-ness. (p.19)

Sharon Green (2010) takes from Mulvey and extends her insight:

> The phrase 'objectifying male gaze' emerged from this essay to designate the gaze from the point-of-view of the automatically assumed male perspective on an idealized female form. Through this gaze (which is active), the woman is seen only as an erotic (passive) object signifying patriarchal male fantasies about the female body and feminine identity. The norms of physical beauty and gender performance to which the woman is expected to aspire and comply are created and maintained through these fantasies. (p.344)

The power of the male gaze and its imperatives around attractiveness and appearance operates in and around us day in and day out. It operates in analysis regardless of the analyst's gender, as female analysts also operate under the male gaze and thus take on, unconsciously, the imperative for a woman to be attractive, the parameters for attractive being determined by that gaze.

I have been thinking about and writing about the essay "Fat Lady" in Irvin Yalom's (1990) book, *Love's Executioner*, since I first read it more than 25 years ago. The patient he writes about, "Betty," is a fat woman and Yalom confesses his very negative feelings about her body:

> I have always been repelled by fat women. I find them disgusting: their absurd sidewise waddle, their absence of body contour, breasts, laps, buttocks, shoulders, jawlines, cheekbones, everything, everything I like to see in a woman, obscured in an avalanche of flesh. And I hate their clothes, the shapeless, baggy dresses or, worse, the stiff elephantine blue jeans with the barrel thighs. How dare they impose that body on the rest of us? (p.94)

He does not even question that she or any patient should be expected to meet his standard of attractiveness in a woman. Male privilege affords to him the assumption that attractive means what is attractive to men. "How dare they impose that body on the rest of us?"

Yalom wrote about Betty in the mid-1980s. Surely things are different today? Sadly no. In mid-June of 2015, in a *New York Times* series about psychotherapy called "Couch," David Hellerstein writes about a patient of his:

Greta was not exactly alluring. It wasn't her looks, which were fine (I'm certainly no Adonis myself); it was her unfashionable dress and grooming. Which was a shame, not because I cared how she looked, but because Greta herself so deeply yearned for a romantic relationship ... One day, after a bit of hemming and hawing—I knew it would be a sensitive topic—I raised the obvious: Had she considered getting a makeover? One of her friends, as Greta herself had told me, had recently seen an "image consultant" who recommended a whole new wardrobe, new hairstyle, different makeup. Could that, I asked, possibly be helpful?

"After all," I added, "men tend to judge ... " (Hellerstein, 2015)

To the patient's credit, she became angry. They continued to work together for some time, she left and then years later, they connected again. She never did find the love she sought. Hellerstein counts his work with her as a failure. What he does not seem to consider is that her dress, her appearance was almost certainly not the cause of her failure to find the romantic relationship she desired. As attested to in the nearly 1,000 reader comments to the piece, many "dowdy" women—and men— find love. He seems never to have explored what other issues might be getting in her way. Because he sees whether or not she is attractive to him as indicative of what is important for her. Is it any wonder that male privilege and the male gaze enter the consulting room? Sharon Green (2010) reminds us of the world in which we all, especially Emma Jung, grew up:

a world in which all spectators were assumed to be adult men, all pronouns masculine, where the God of my family and church could only be imagined to be a masculine entity, and where 'the' masculine was conflated with activity and subjectivity, and 'the' feminine with passivity and objectification. (p.344)

In this world, of course Yalom and Hellerstein expect that their standards for what is attractive are if not universal, then very nearly so. Analytical psychology is rife with these gendered assumptions, which are often vigorously defended even by women.

Jung (1968) wrote in 1927:

But who, if it comes to that, has fully realized that history is not contained life of the past she can never come into conflict with history. But no sooner does she begin to deviate, however slightly, from a cultural trend that has dominated the past than she encounters the full weight of historical inertia, and this unexpected shock may injure her, perhaps fatally. (p.130)

Deviating from the cultural norm gets one tagged as pathological. It is no longer the case that a woman is expected to eschew ambition and stay at home raising children and caring for the home; that cultural trend has faded away for the most part. We are allowed, even encouraged to develop careers as well as tend to home and hearth. But it is still expected that a woman conform to the image of ideal femininity, that is be slender and visually appealing to men. Betty who was fat and Greta who was dowdy are both seen as failing in some way as women because their male therapists do not see them as attractive. As Young-Eisendrath (2012) puts it:

> female beauty dominates the lives of women and men through the formula that female beauty equals power. Wherever I am and whoever I'm with, I overhear evaluative comments about female appearances ... Both women and men evaluate women according to the shapes and sizes of their faces, legs, hips, and breasts. As a psychotherapist and a feminist, I frequently feel helpless to break the link between female appearance and power. (p.82)

Few of us realize that we do not see unmodified images of people, especially of women, in magazines, film, or television. The images of those we see as ideals, as possessing the looks we should aspire to, are not real. We do not see those women as we would see them were we to encounter them in the supermarket or on the street. As Susie Orbach (2009) points out:

> it is the photographic image—both the moving image on TV and film and the still photograph—that has created the new visual grammar. Its effects should not be underestimated. They are changing the way we relate to our bodies. John Berger's prescient statement that (bourgeois) women watch themselves being looked at has been transmuted into women assuming the gaze of the observer, looking at themselves from the outside and finding that they continually fail to meet the expectations our pervasive and persuasive visual culture demands. (pp.107–108)

We are bombarded with altered images—2,000–5,000 per week according to Orbach —images that "convey an idea of a body which does not exist in the real world" (p.109). Cosmetic surgery as a means to attain this non-existent ideal has flourished in this environment. Since 1997, the number of cosmetic surgery procedures has grown from 1,679,943 procedures (American Society of Plastic Surgeons, 2014a) to 15.1 million procedures in 2013 (American Society of Plastic Surgeons, 2014b). What is the result? As Orbach (2009) says,

> Cosmetic surgery as a consumer option is becoming normalised. The young discuss the procedures they will have. A rhetoric of empowerment supports and provokes their desires and suggests that not to alter themselves would be a sign of self-neglect ... The surgeon, both authoritative and solicitous, becomes the arbiter on female beauty. As he acknowledges the pain his patients feel, he demonstrates how he can change different aspects of their body for them, enabling them to reach the beauty standard he has himself set. In his engagement with them, he gives them the body they could never

imagine they would have. He is confident and persuasive. He responds to their wish with gravity but also as though they were choosing their dream holiday. (p.103)

The beauty industry and the diet industry reap profits in the billions of dollars each year as women pursue the hopeless quest of achieving the perfection of the images placed in front of us thousands of time each week, of sleek, flawless bodies which seem never to age. It is also worth noting that 90 percent of cosmetic surgeons, the "arbiter[s] on female beauty," are male (PR Leap, 2013) and 91 percent of patients seeking such surgery are female (American Society of Plastic Surgeons. (2014b).

Whether it is Hellerstein's dowdy patient or Yalom's fat lady or the Victoria's Secret model, we women are always under the scrutiny of the male gaze. And to deviate from the standard for attractiveness is to be deemed excluded from ordinary fulfillment, even from love. Sam Keen, in a brief anecdote, describes a fat woman he saw in an airport and his fantasies about her:

All by herself she was a parade of mammoth and grotesque proportions …

What happened to cause her to hide her loveliness, her dream, within the impenetrable mountain of her flesh? What pain? What betrayal? What disappointment? What lost love left her so hungry? (Keen, n.d.)

For Keen, it is unimaginable that a fat woman so far from the acceptable norm could have a love of her own, could even have a "classically handsome" man waiting for her at home. Because he sees her as mammoth and grotesque he imagines anyone would and it is even likely that she herself sees herself that way if she too has taken in the proscriptions against violating the norms for attraction.

Desirable as it may seem to be a beautiful woman, to be the object of desire, to find approval in the male gaze, Arlene Landau, a Jungian analyst, in her book, *Tragic Beauty: The Dark Side of Venus Aphrodite and the Loss and Regeneration of Soul* (2011) finds some of the hazards as well. Polly Young-Eisendrath (2012) uses the myth of Pandora's beauty box to indicate both sides:

From the Pandora story we can see that identifying with this "power" is a double bind – you're damned if you do and damned if you don't. If you identify with the image of female beauty, you put yourself into the Pandora box: beautiful but empty. Increasingly as a woman ages, she finds that identification with a beautiful appearance is a losing game. She will lose the game through aging when she no longer looks like Pandora, a "maiden" – youthful, slender, lovely. To identify with a beautiful appearance and to pursue that power leads to depreciation of her other strengths and ultimately to depression about falling short of standards. To disidentify with the power of appearance (and "let herself go") usually leads to feeling like an outsider, feelings of low self-confidence, and fears of failing to find a heterosexual partner or to be the object of a certain kind of male regard. (p.82)

Recently Bruce Jenner, winner of the 1976 Olympic gold medal in the decathlon, came out as transgender. His coming out as Caitlyn Jenner and the flurry of comment and interest around transgenderism that has followed has served to illuminate even further how the male gaze and female beauty dominate any discussion about women and their bodies. The discussions burst into the open as Caitlyn Jenner made her appearance on the June 2015 cover of the magazine *Vanity Fair*. In the cover image, Jenner appears tightly corseted in a strapless satin garment designed to highlight her waist and breasts. My first thought was that only the addition of bunny ears kept her from looking like the Playboy bunnies who once served as waitresses at Playboy Clubs. That immediate association was all the clue I needed to see that this image was made to appeal to men, to gain the approval of the male gaze as validation for her embrace of her woman self. Comedian Jon Stewart (Bradley, 2015) quipped, "It's really heartening to see that everyone is willing to not only accept Caitlyn Jenner as a woman but to waste no time in treating her like a woman. You see, Caitlyn, when you were a man, we could talk about your athleticism, your business acumen. But now you're a woman and your looks are really the only thing we care about." And as Ellen Goodman (2015) pointedly observed, "the silicon-cleavaged and made-over Olympian is now the sweetheart of the Twittersphere and cable chatteratti where people are talking about nothing but her glam girl status." No one was talking about her athletic achievements, that she was an Olympic athlete, that she has parlayed that athletic success into a fortune in the tens of millions of dollars. All the talk was about how good she looked, how "feminine" and "hot" she was, as if her appearance were all that mattered. And of course, in her new image, she appears far closer to 30 than to her actual age of 65. To become a woman, Jenner started taking hormones well before the physical transition was completed. He had hair on his body and facial hair removed. He had what is known as "facial feminization surgery" which involves such procedures as hairline correction, forehead contouring, jaw and chin contouring, Adam's apple restructuring and other procedures to make the face conform more closely to that of a female (Anon, 2015).

He also had surgery to augment his breasts. According to press accounts, he/she has not had sexual reassignment surgery to alter genitalia. The cover photo and images in the article within the magazine gave us insight into Jenner's idea of a woman, and perhaps unsurprisingly it aligns well with the view of most men and is greeted with approval by the male gaze.

It is not surprising that when Elinor Burkett (2015) in an opinion piece, "What Makes a Woman?", in the *New York Times*, dissented from the general praise given Jenner, she was met with considerable criticism. For dissenting, she was called a crotchety feminist and roundly criticized because she objected to Jenner's claim to knowing what it is to be a woman. Having lived his life benefitting from male privilege and his status as an elite male athlete, she believed his female identity to be very different from hers and that of females like her.

At the same time that the discussion was swirling around Jenner and transgenderism, a similar issue appeared around race when Rachel Dolezal, who had long

**64** Cheryl L. Fuller

self-identified as black and passed as African American was outed by her parents, igniting outrage over her claim to being black while having two white parents. The major criticism leveled against her was that she had not "walked the walk," not had to grow up on the receiving end of all the difficult experiences that accrue to African Americans living in our racist culture. That she had worked effectively for civil rights, was employed by the NAACP, had studied and was teaching African American studies mattered not at all. The consensus arrayed against her was that as a white person she could not choose identity as a black person, no matter how strongly allied and identified with African Americans she felt; only African Americans can authorize that identity.

While the parallels are not exact and the issues involved are complicated and go beyond the scope of this paper, there is enough similarity here to help illuminate the reality that women and women's experiences are apparently insufficient to determine who is a woman. One of the issues raised by Burkett is that at least a very vocal faction of the trans community objects to focusing on reproductive rights as not a valid women's issue because it excludes trans women. Granted these objections along with objections to the use of "vagina" and performances of *The Vagina Monologues*, the play by Eve Ensler, as exclusionary come from extremists in the trans community. But it is often from the extremes that we can see broader issues, in this instance the pervasive power of the male gaze as determinative of what is or is not legitimately woman.

What does it mean when a person says she is in the wrong body? We hear this from transgender people—this feeling they have of being in the wrong body. And in a less direct way it is what we hear when any of the legions of women unhappy with their weight go on diet after diet in a largely fruitless quest to release the thin woman they believe lives inside them, a thin woman trapped in the wrong body. What does that mean? The effort to find "the right body" leads to all manner of surgical solutions, ranging from the cosmetic procedures, which as noted earlier have become so common, to removal of most of the stomach in order to lose weight, to facial feminization surgery, to sexual reassignment surgery, most often performed on male-to-female transsexuals and involving removal of the penis and testes and insertion of breast implants. In other words, the quest for the right body easily leads to mutilation of the existing body. Both sexual reassignment surgery and bariatric surgery have an unexpected consequence of significantly elevated risk of suicide post-operatively. Dhejne *et al.* (2015) found the suicide rate for post-operative transsexuals is around 20 times higher than for a control group matched in terms of age and sex. And Moskowitz (2010) reports that 41 percent of transgender people have attempted suicide. Among patients who have undergone bariatric surgery, the suicide rate is six to seven times higher for people who have had the surgery than those who did not (Alexander, 2008; *New York Times*, 2007). This alarming elevation of suicide risk in these two groups, both of which are people desperate to obtain and inhabit "the right body," suggests that in at least a significant percentage of them, the body itself is not the problem. But in a society that finds efforts to pursue perfection through surgery acceptable if not admirable, there is little critical examination of what taking that pursuit to such dramatic lengths means nor of the inherent danger of the entire notion of the perfect body. As Orbach (2009) notes,

> the very problems the style industries diagnose are the same ones the beauty industry purports to fix. They are handmaidens in the process of deconstructing and reconstructing our bodies. And the purported fixes are offered as solutions which we can't help but wish to take advantage of. The solutions entice us. We do not see ourselves as victims of an industry bent on exploiting us. In fact we are excited to engage with and reframe the problem: there is something wrong with me that with effort—exercise, cash and vigilance—I can repair. I can make my offending body part(s) right. (p.112)

Or, as Wilchins (1997) asks:

> What kind of system bids us each make of our bodies a problem to be solved, a claim we must defend, or a secret we must publicly confess, again and again? … The question really should be … whose agenda is it that demands your hips must be gendered with a particular meaning or to even have any meaning at all? (p.39)

It is clear that the depth psychologies tend to avoid issues of body, whether male or female. Balsam (2012) beautifully states the vital importance of body in the work of analysis:

> All of us have bodies; we can see them, recognize their outlines; touch them, smell them even. We can tell our own bodies apart from other people, at the same time that we know that we are more alike than different. We all eat, extracting in a complicated fashion from the world around us the life-giving elements that we need, and eliminating the waste of that process. We have skin, nerves, blood vessels, and muscle and organ sensations; we walk, talk, see, and hear. We feel pleasure, anger, fear, and pain. We cry. We live cooperatively or we war, or are isolated. All born of females … whether we like it or not, we are identified by our genitals as male or female in almost every culture on the globe. We mature as sexual beings. We choose mates; most of us procreate and take care of our young. Once young ourselves, we grow older. Our organs fail; we die. The next generation takes over and mourns loss. All of this raw physicality, with its average-expectable patterning as we live and observe it over the span of our lives, exists somewhere within us. It contributes richly to our private thinking, and serves as a backdrop to all of our interactive dealings with others. (pp. Kindle Locations 226–230)

And so I return to Emma Jung and my dream of her pen. In her biography, Gaudissart finds in Emma's choices—to remain with Carl, to make her peace with

Toni Wolff, to make supporting Carl her major life's work—an admirable path. Indeed viewed from a certain point of view it is. Gaudissart (2015) describes it:

> How many such women, in bygone ages and in modern times, have remained faithful to a vocation, to some frequently mysterious vow? How many have shared the destiny of a particular man, a figure to whom they offered their support and encouragement, apparently setting aside any legitimate ambitions or aspirations of their own in order to devote their lives to becoming the spiritual womb and the crucible of his fulfilment? Is such behavior to be regarded as proof of weakness? Is it a search for glory or for perfection? Should we not see it rather as the manifestation of a gift, of a particular form of talent, of a sacred path through life? Numerous examples of these special and out of the ordinary lives can be called to mind. In many cases they were weighed down by suffering, doubts, or uncertainty; at the same time, they represented a testimony of joy. Can there be any doubt that such lives are archetypal representations of a certain form of womanhood that finds its fulfilment in the experience of supporting a fellow human being in the realization of his or her potential and destiny? (pp. Kindle Locations 2128–135)

As Gaudissart indicates, most of the women who were drawn to Jung and analytical psychology were unmarried and without children. Emma's situation as Carl's wife and the mother of their five children made her position more complicated than most; developing her own interests required her to deviate more from the traditional roles than was customarily supported.

If Carl Jung is the father of analytical psychology—and there is no question that he is —then we might consider Emma Jung and Toni Wolff the mothers. As they gave their lives over to supporting, nurturing, inspiring Jung in his work, they effectively subsumed their own separate interests to serve his. Occupying this position took its toll on both women. Toni and Emma were both younger than Carl— Emma by seven years, Toni by thirteen—yet both of them died before he did. Toni Wolff had rheumatoid arthritis, an autoimmune disease which is in effect an attack on the self by the body's own immune system, and one might wonder if this was in part a price she paid for her sacrifice of her own ambitions to foster Carl Jung's work. Neither woman leaves behind much of her own work in writings. Both came to be known largely through her association with Carl rather than by dint of her own work.

Building on the foundation provided by Emma Jung and Toni Wolff, their lives and their devotion to Carl Jung become, consciously or not, the model for how to be a woman and a Jungian. Though there have been a number of important women Jungians in the years since the Jungs and Toni Wolff—among them certainly Marie Louise von Franz, Esther Harding, Irene Claremont de Castillejo, Marion Woodman, Ann Ulanov, as well as Jean Shinoda Bolen, Clarissa Pinkola Estes, and many others—for the most part, they have stayed within the basics of analytical psychology and avoided criticizing its shortcomings and sexist elements. Gaudissart

Emma Jung's pen: Jung, feminism and the body **67**

tells us that "[t]he powerful aura surrounding Jung scarcely allowed anyone to dream of criticizing him or taking him down from his pedestal. This was the reality with which Emma's day-to-day life was imbued" (pp. Kindle Locations 2600-2602), an aura that has apparently persisted well past Jung's death. As a consequence ordinary parts of women's lives like what menarche meant for them or their struggles about how they look and their efforts to police their own bodies or childbirth, infertility, sexual desire have been seldom if ever considered in the Jungian literature, in case studies or theory. As Balsam (2012) says,

> How rarely do past or contemporary case reports of women even briefly refer to experiences of childbirths, for example, unless written up as a special focus? Yet, these are common but momentous physical events that most women experience even in life-changing ways, for better or worse. More attention is given to a female's medical history, her choice of lovers, or an account of all the places she lived or her separation anxieties. (pp. Kindle Locations 252–254)

It was these very elements of women's lives that Jung did not give notice to, not surprising as of course they are not an experience of his or any man's life. It was left to women to develop these aspects of our psychology, a psychology that is deeply embedded in our bodies.

One would hope that feminism would have brought awareness of women's issues into Jungian consciousness, as Young-Eisendrath (2012) indicated:

> When feminism informs psychology, it reveals the gaps, blindspots, and deficits that color female subjectivity within the history of patriarchy. When feminism is incorporated into psychology, it releases girls and women to speak. (pp. Kindle Locations 252–254)

Search the archives of *Quadrant* or the *Journal of Analytical Psychology*; two of the major Jungian journals and missing are papers on the impact of the pregnant analyst, issues relating to other aspects of the analyst's body such as weight. Surely I am not the only Jungian psychotherapist or analyst who is fat but other than writing I have begun to publish, there is nothing to be found about this in Jungian literature. Yet there are several such papers in the psychoanalytic literature including one published as I was writing this paper. In fact there has been but one article in Jungian literature on the topic of obesity published since Marion Woodman published her books *The Owl Was a Baker's Daughter* and *Addiction to Perfection* in the 1980s, this despite near daily articles and papers published in the popular and in the scientific press on the subject.

I have often told the story of when I first visited the state of Maine. It was in 1963 when I came on vacation with my brother and his family. As we drove up the Maine Turnpike past Waterville I saw a large sign advertising a restaurant called "The Silent Woman." The sign depicted a decapitated woman serving refreshments on a tray. Though I knew nothing about feminism, I viscerally understood what a

**68** Cheryl L. Fuller

horrible image that was—a headless woman performing her service function with the implication that this is perhaps the highest and best form of woman, woman without a voice. Both sign and the restaurant are long gone but that image remains for me a powerful one reminding me of how much we need to keep our heads and our voices. No psychology, including analytical psychology can be said to be complete without women's voices about women's bodies and women's experience. Or as Helene Cixous (1976) urges:

> By writing her self, woman will return to the body which has been more than confiscated from her, which has been turned into the uncanny stranger on display—the ailing or dead figure, which so often turns out to be the nasty companion, the cause and location of inhibitions. Censor the body and you censor breath and speech at the same time. Write your self. Your body must be heard. Only then will the immense resources of the unconscious spring forth. (p.880)

## References

Alexander, C. (2008). Depression after Bariatric Surgery: Triggers, Identification, Treatment, and Prevention. *Bariatric Times*. [online] Available at: http://bariatrictimes.com/depression-after-bariatric-surgery-triggers-identification-treatment-and-prevention/ [Accessed 26 Jun. 2015].

American Society of Plastic Surgeons. (2014a). Plastic Surgery Procedures Continue Steady Growth in U.S. [online] Available at: http://www.plasticsurgery.org/news/2014/plastic-surgery-procedures-continue-steady-growth-in-us.html [Accessed 21 Jul. 2015].

American Society of Plastic Surgeons. (2014b). Plastic Surgery Statistics Report. [online] Available at: http://www.plasticsurgery.org/Documents/news-resources/statistics/2013-statistics/cosmetic-procedures-national-trends-2013.pdf [Accessed 21 Jul. 2015].

Anon. (2015). [online] Available at: https://en.wikipedia.org/wiki/Facial_feminization_surgery [Accessed 22 Jun. 2015].

Balsam, R. M. (2012) *Women's Bodies in Psychoanalysis*. New York and London: Taylor and Francis. Kindle Edition.

Bradley, B. (2015). Jon Stewart Calls Out Media for Coverage of Caitlyn Jenner's Looks. *Huffington Post*. [online] Available at: http://www.huffingtonpost.com/2015/06/03/jon-stewart-caitlyn-jenner_n_7501734.html [Accessed 21 Jun. 2015].

Burkett, E. (2015). What Makes a Woman? *New York Times*. [online] Available at: http://www.nytimes.com/2015/06/07/opinion/sunday/what-makes-a-woman.html [Accessed 20 Jun. 2015].

Cixous, H. (1976). The Laugh of the Medusa. *Signs*, 1(4), 875–893. [online] Available at: http://links.jstor.org/sici?sici=0097-9740%28197622%291%3A4%3C875%3ATLOTM%3E2.0.CO%3B2-V [Accessed 17 Mar. 2015].

Dhejne, C., Lichtenstein, P., Borman, M., Johansson, A., Långström, N. and Landén, M. (2015). Long-Term Follow-Up of Transsexual Persons Undergoing Sex Reassignment Surgery: Cohort Study in Sweden. *PLOS ONE*. [online] Available at: http://journals.plos.org/plosone/article?id=10.1371/journal.pone.0016885 [Accessed 23 Jun. 2015].

Gaudissart, I. (2015). *Love and Sacrifice: The Life of Emma Jung*. Asheville, NC: Chiron Books. Kindle Edition.

Goodman, E. (2015). Caitlyn Jenner's Vanity Fair Cover a Display of Ageism, Not Just Sexism. *The Boston Globe*. [online] Available at: https://www.bostonglobe.com/opinion/2015/06/10/caitlyn-jenner-vanity-fair-cover-display-ageism-not-just-sexism/nzfrBvHSnxAGZDf3gwe9lK/story.html [Accessed 22 Jun. 2015].

Green, S. R. (2010). Embodied Female Experience Through the Lens of Imagination. *The Journal of Analytical Psychology*, 55, 339–360.

Hellerstein, D. (2015). The Dowdy Patient. *New York Times*. [online] Available at: http://opinionator.blogs.nytimes.com/2015/06/12/ [Accessed 20 Jun. 2015].

Heuer, G. (2005). In My Flesh I Shall See God: Jungian Body Psychotherapy. In N. Totton (Ed.), *New Dimensions in Body Psychotherapy*. New York: Open University Press.

Heuer, G. M. (2012). 'In My Flesh I Shall See God': Body and Psyche in Analysis. London: Guild of Pastoral Psychology.

Jung, C. G. (1968). *Analytical Psychology: Its Theory and Practice*. New York: Vintage Press.

Keen, S. (n.d.). Till The Fat Lady Sings. [online] Available at: http://samkeen.com/mini-stories/till-the-fat-lady-sings/ [Accessed 22 Jun. 2015].

Landau, A. (2011). *Tragic Beauty: The Dark Side of Venus Aphrodite and the Loss and Regeneration of Soul*. New Orleans, LA: Spring Journal Books.

Moskowitz, C. (2010). High Suicide Risk, Prejudice Plague Transgender People. *Live Science*. [online] Available at: http://www.livescience.com/11208-high-suicide-risk-prejudice-plague-transgender-people.html [Accessed 27 Jun. 2015].

Mulvey, L. (1975). Visual Pleasure and Narrative Cinema. *Screen*. [online] Available at: http://imlportfolio.usc.edu/ctcs505/mulveyVisualPleasureNarrativeCinema.pdf [Accessed 20 Jun. 2015].

Mulvey, L. (1989). Visual Pleasure and Narrative Cinema. In *Visual and Other Pleasures*. Bloomington: Indiana University Press.

New York Times (2007). A Tragic Risk of Weight-Loss Surgery. [online] Available at: http://well.blogs.nytimes.com/2007/10/17/a-tragic-risk-of-weight-loss-surgery/ [Accessed 23 Jun. 2015].

Orbach, S. (2009). *Bodies (BIG IDEAS//small books)*. New York: Picador. Kindle Edition.

PR Leap. (2013). Why Are All the Plastic Surgeons Men? [online] Available at: http://www.prleap.com/pr/207181/why-are-all-the-plastic-surgeons-men [Accessed 20 Jul. 2015]

Wilchins, R. (1997). *Read My Lips: Sexual Subversion and the End of Gender*. New York: Firebrand Books.

Yalom, I. D. (1990). *Love's Executioner and Other Tales of Psychotherapy*. New York: Harper Perennial.

Young-Eisendrath, P. (2012) *Jung, Gender and Subjectivity in Psychoanalysis*. Abingdon: Taylor and Francis. Kindle Edition.

# 6

# IN SEARCH OF THE HEROINE

*Coline Covington*

The archetypal image of the hero is familiar and has been described extensively in analytical psychology (Campbell 1949; Jung 1912; Kerenyi 1959; Neumann 1954). There is, however, no reference in these works to 'heroine' nor any description as to who she might be or what characterises her. We are left to assume, along with the Oxford English Dictionary, that 'heroine' is the feminine form of hero, or in other words, a female hero. The concept of the 'heroine' is relatively recent as compared with that of the 'hero', and the term 'heroine' was not used in Homeric or classical Greek literature until it appears for the first time, used ironically, in Aristophanes' play, *Clouds*. Even more remarkably it was not used in English and French medieval literature. 'Heroine' appears to have come into regular use first in French and then in English classical language, where it evokes a classical world in which the concept would have been unknown.

As a female hero, the heroine shares the characteristics of the hero and is principally recognised by her heroic feats, through which she acquires the status of a demi-goddess or saint. Her heroism may also transform her into a symbol of state or nation, such as Boudicca and Jeanne d'Arc. The female hero is essentially the woman warrior whose battles take place within the male world. Although she is unusual in this one respect, her sex is nevertheless incidental. She might as well be a hero.

The female hero is also characterised by sacrifice. She is not to be confused with the Gothic and romantic heroine so often portrayed as a social victim. This is the heroine, as exemplified by Medea and Antigone, who sacrifices her life to uphold patriarchal authority and a higher moral order. These are women ruled by the masculine principle, the purpose of whose sacrifices is the preservation of the old order and protection against chaos. It is their actions which make them heroic.

Another role assumed by the heroine is that of partner, or partner-to-be, of the hero. In this guise we find women such as Odysseus' Penelope, who waits faithfully

In search of the heroine **71**

for her husband's return, and Sleeping Beauty, who waits to be brought to life by her prince. These are women who play a waiting role, resisting the flow of time, and whose aim is to be united with the hero. We would normally consider this form of heroine as representing the feminine aspect of the hero: that is, the anima, who plays an integral part in the hero's quest. But what happens when we look at these women more closely in their own right? And what in particular is happening during this waiting process, which seems such an important element in these stories and which stands out in marked contrast to the phallic activity of the hero and the female hero? This heroine is distinguished from her heroic brothers and sisters by what are in effect *anti-heroic* qualities.

In my attempt to identify the heroine, I would like first of all to return to her counterpart, the hero, and ask a basic question, 'Why is the hero represented as male?' An answer would give us the most important clue as to who the heroine is. The hero's story is one of individuation, a striving towards self-determination, and the struggle to know the world, to become conscious. This is the treasure to be gained. The hero is required to leave home, to set out on a journey in search of the treasure. According to Jung, 'The heroes are usually wanderers, and wandering is a symbol of longing, of the restless urge which never finds its object, of nostalgia for the lost mother' (Jung 1912, para. 299). The impetus for the hero is the need to break free from the mother and his wandering is an oscillating path between a desire for recognition of and connectedness to the mother and the wish to be independent of her.

The fact that the hero is male can be shown to be no accident. From the standpoint of the archetype of separation (Strauss 1964), he represents the first separation of the infant from the mother at birth, and so he assumes the form of something other – a male. While the hero derives from and is produced by the maternal nexus, he is not an opposite to the mother. As an archetype of separation and differentiation, the hero introduces an opposite constellation, necessary for psychic balance. What then is the opposite of the hero? Is it simply the anima? As Redfearn points out, 'The archetypes of hero and anima belong to the phase of separation from the maternal matrix, and are developed out of experiences of separation, frustration, and weaning …' (Redfearn 1979, p. 202). If we see the hero's opposite as the anima, it brings us back full circle to the maternal nexus and we are no nearer to understanding how the hero can ever, as it were, develop beyond the mother. Is the opposite to the hero rather the heroine and, if so, can we locate her origins in the paternal nexus? Is hers a struggle to break free from father? And what is her role in the individuation process?

## 'The Handless Maiden'

One story which sheds light on the heroine as anti-hero and her role in the individuation process is Grimm's fairy tale of the 'The Handless Maiden':

There was once a miller who had fallen into poverty and had nothing left but his mill and an apple tree, which stood behind it. One day he met an old man, called

**72** Coline Covington

Evil One, who offered to make him rich in return for what was behind his mill. Thinking he was only giving away his apple tree, the miller readily agreed and received his first payment on the understanding that Evil One would return in three years to make his claim. The miller went home with his riches and told his wife what had happened. She threw up her hands in horror for she knew that it was their daughter, who had been sweeping behind the mill, whom Evil One wished to claim.

Three years passed, and Evil One returned to claim the maiden. But she washed herself clean and drew a circle of chalk around herself so that Evil One could not touch her. Evil One ordered the miller to keep his daughter away from water and said he would come again to claim her. The miller did as he was told and his daughter sobbed into her hands, washing them clean so that Evil One was once again unable to possess her. Enraged, Evil One told the miller to cut off the maiden's hands. The miller explained his dilemma to his daughter and she willingly gave him her hands to cut off. Evil One came a third time and, although the maiden had lost her hands, she had cried so much that her arms were clean.

Defeated, Evil One gave up his claim and in return for what she had given him, the miller offered to look after his daughter for the rest of her life. But she refused, saying she must leave home and live on the mercy of others. The maiden left home and walked some way until nightfall when she came upon a royal garden on the other side of a stream. She saw an orchard of pear trees and was consumed with hunger. Without her hands, however, she could not cross the stream and in despair she fell on her knees and prayed to God. A light shone and the maiden saw a break in the stream and crossed into the garden, where she ate one of the pears. The king's gardener had seen the maiden in the moonlight and, taking pity on her, had decided to let her be. The next day the king noticed that one of his pears was missing and asked the gardener if he had seen anyone. The gardener confessed that he had seen a young woman, without hands, enter the garden and eat the pear. The king was intrigued by this and waited the next night to see if she would return. The maiden came back and the king approached her and heard her story and gave her shelter. They soon fell in love and married and the king had some silver hands made for the maiden and with these she was able to function.

They lived happily for a time and then the king was called away to war. While he was away, his wife gave birth to a baby boy and her mother-in-law sent news to the king. But Evil One managed to intercept the messenger and alter the letter to say that the queen had given birth to a monster. The king received the message and was very distressed and sent word back to his mother to take care of his wife and the child until his return. Evil One again intercepted the messenger and changed the letter, asking the king's mother to kill his wife and child and to keep his wife's tongue and eyes as a sign that she had fulfilled his order. The king's mother could not bring herself to do this and instead warned her daughter-in-law of the king's murderous intentions, begging her to leave with the baby at once. The queen fled, taking refuge in a large forest. In anguish, she fell on her knees and prayed to God again for guidance and a light shone on a path leading to a small cottage in a clearing in the woods. She knocked on the door and a young maiden

In search of the heroine **73**

in white welcomed her and took care of the queen and her child for seven years. During this time, the queen's hands miraculously grew back.

When the king returned home, his mother showed him the tongue and eyes of a calf, saying that they were the queen's. The king wept bitterly and, seeing his grief, his mother explained that the queen had in fact left for safety with her baby. The king spent the following seven years searching for his wife and finally came upon the cottage in the woods where he found them, although at first he did not recognise the queen because she had real hands. They returned home and re-married to celebrate.

As the title of the story indicates, the maiden's identifying feature is her hand-lessness – a plight suffered in fairy tales, according to von Franz (1972, p. 70), only by heroines. The maiden falls primarily in the category of the heroine who waits, although prior to this she follows an eventful course. She starts out, like the hero, compelled to leave home; she must separate from her father who has offered to keep her, handicapped as she is, for the rest of her life. Following this initial sacrifice and separation, the maiden undergoes a process of individuation resulting in repara-tion and eventual reunion. At the same time the hero/king is undergoing a parallel process which entails the typically heroic ingredients of going out into the world, fighting battles, and searching for something precious which has been lost, in this case the maiden. The king wanders while the queen rests – it is this juxtaposition that epitomises the dynamic relation between hero and heroine.

The activating force of the story is the problem of deprivation – the miller's poverty has made him eager to get rich quickly. His greed gets the better of him and he exchanges his apple tree – that which nourishes him and which also requires his care – for riches which demand no work on his part. What he also sacrifices is his own child, whom he regards as expendable. The daughter is used to obtain riches and power and the miller's relationship with her is not valued for itself. As the wish to possess an ever-flowing source of food, with no strings attached, leads to his severing the relationship with his child and with the real potential source of nourishment within, the child in turn becomes helpless.

For her part, the daughter is compliant and passive; her only actions are those of self-defence as she protects herself from being claimed by Evil One through main-taining her purity and innocence. While the miller has become possessed by Evil One, his daughter reacts defensively in denying her own needs; she does not assert herself, as she must above all ensure the interests of her father.

Although she avoids being claimed by Evil One, the daughter's failure to hold on to what she needs allows her to become a willing victim, attracting the exploita-tion of others. She loses her hands and becomes genuinely incapacitated, unable to do anything for herself. The greediness from which the maiden is trying to protect herself is embodied by Evil One, who represents the archetypal devouring mother, usually depicted in fairy tales as the wicked stepmother, mother-in-law or witch.

The incident which brings about the maiden's rescue is her eating of the pear in the king's garden. By this act, she acknowledges her dependency on the fruit of the earth which she needs to survive. Her eating without the use of hands serves here as a regressive symbol of orality. The womb or breast-shaped pear reconnects the maiden to a good, nourishing mother and this enables the king to come on the scene, representing a new position or attitude. The king, as opposed to the miller, values what is in his garden and attempts to make reparation by providing the maiden with silver hands. This allows the maiden to regain some functioning, although in an artificial manner. All continues well until the king has to go away to war. His departure is linked with the queen's pregnancy, and the birth of the child precipitates Evil One's intervention yet again with the resurgence of jealousy, possessiveness and murderous feelings. It is the coming of the child, the product of the maiden's new relationship, and the dawning of a new consciousness, that brings with it the old fears of the devouring mother, once again projected on to Evil One, who in turn describes the child as a monster.

Evil One tries to get his revenge for failing to possess the maiden by plotting the death of both her and her child. He advises the mother-in-law to preserve the queen's tongue and eyes – those parts of the body which, like the hands, are used for taking in and grasping the world as well as relating to it. In the king's absence, the queen becomes a victim for the second time and in her attempt to escape the wicked plotting of Evil One, she is cast out and becomes helpless. But the queen's persecution is the vital component in forcing her to withdraw from the world, to retreat to a place hidden in the depths of the forest where her hands can grow back so that she is able to function properly. The queen's stay in the forest is a time of inactivity and incubation, in which inner processes are at work. The forest is synonymous with the unconscious, which contains what is unknown and mysterious; it symbolises the maternal source from which the individual emerges as the tree is born within the forest. Dieckmann refers to this solitary period in the forest as corresponding to 'a deepened state of introversion' and quotes Hedwig von Beit:

> This retreat into forest solitude, a religious motif, is the act of a medieval penitent, and in the history of culture it goes back to the ancient anchorite practices in which influences from India played a part. The purpose of such behaviour is to bring about the greatest possible degree of introversion and to remove all attachments to the external object. Thus there arises a corresponding enlivening of the inner world, intensified to the point of auditory hallucinations, visions, and states of ecstasy. (Dieckmann 1986, p. 94)

The queen, however, is not entirely alone. She has fled with her infant into the caring hands of the woman in the cottage whose presence is vital. She performs the task of the transcendent function and enables the queen to experience connectedness to a primal mother and to resolve an inner split.

## Case illustrations

The maiden's withdrawal into a maternal nexus in reaction to the paternal nexus in which we first find her has particular relevance to clinical work. The position of the

In search of the heroine **75**

two mothers in the story is worth noting in this regard. Both the mother and the mother-in-law have the maiden's interests at heart, yet they are ruled by paternal authority, and the bad mother is conspicuously absent. Instead we find the ruthless father who falls under the influence of Evil One. Badness is personified by Evil One, who is outside the family and unrelated to it. The splitting off of badness, and the bad mother, is somatised in a splitting off of the body, as the maiden's hands are cut off. Hands are used to grasp, to touch and to discriminate; they are also linked to our ability to express anger, as the muscles used to grip are the same as those used in anger. Our heroine survives initially by having clean hands; she remains innocent, unconnected to her anger, i.e. shadowless, and is consequently persecuted.

This splitting is recognisable in many of our patients. A young woman, Ana, was tragically caught in the plight of the heroine. When she first started therapy Ana had only partial use of her arms and hands, and they were also painful. She had seen several doctors, and all had told her there was nothing physically wrong with her. Throughout her childhood she had survived the family psychodynamics by her superhuman efforts to be independent and to do everything herself. In this way she had managed to avoid acknowledging her dependency on her depressed mother, whom she insisted she had taken care of as a child and not vice versa. Ana could describe her mother only as good, kind and suffering. She was a mother who tried her best, especially in the face of Ana's tyrannical father. Ana seemed similar to her mother when she told me, uncomplainingly, of the attacks she suffered at the hands of her employers, friends and family. After the course of a year she began to be aware of her angry feelings towards me. The pains in her arms increased disturbingly and, after searching for many months, Ana finally found a surgeon who agreed to operate, with the result that she lost all feeling in her hands. The denial and splitting off of the bad mother and the feelings attached to her was achieved for Ana, as in the case of the maiden, through an encircling of innocence which left her literally incapacitated.

Another woman, Elizabeth, came to see me because she felt she was surrounded by cotton wool, unable to feel or move. Although she felt comfortable, enclosed in a 'circle of safety', she was also frightened of becoming paralysed. She complained that whenever she was with people their lives and feelings took possession of her; they passed through her, making her feel empty inside, as if she had no inner life of her own. At the start of her analysis she brought a picture she had drawn of herself in which her head and shoulders were surrounded by a white halo, her eyes looked as if they were closed, and the rest of her body was wrapped so that it looked like a cocoon. There was a red bolt of lightning in the background. Elizabeth commented on her hands, which looked as if she was wearing mittens. She remembered that she had been swaddled as an infant and remarked that she had never felt her body and had no memory of physical sensation. She felt her mother had supervised her every action.

Elizabeth later described a scene she had observed on a bus of a large pink baby, just over a year old, sitting on its mother's lap. Whenever the baby reached for her toes, or started to play with something, its mother's hands followed and guided the

**76** Coline Covington

baby's, with the result that the baby could never follow through with its own actions. The baby stared at Elizabeth with a blank expression on its face. Like the large pink baby, Elizabeth's picture of herself seemed to be of a baby wrapped up in herself who could not reach out and make her needs known without a mother's anticipation and intrusion. It is a picture of a baby closed up in an autistic-like cocoon, unable to discover its separateness.

In Elizabeth's analysis, the difficulty was in starting and sustaining some degree of involvement. Each session was punctuated by starts and stops. At times anything I said was felt by Elizabeth to be an impingement and her expression went blank like that of the baby. My words cut her off and myself at the same time. Elizabeth said she felt like a small child, absorbed in playing, who is suddenly whisked away by her mother before she has finished. She had internalised this controlling mother who persistently interrupted her thinking and prevented her inner thoughts from developing of their own accord.

The problem of making do with artificial hands, of being cut off from feeling, and of feeling half-alive, is a common reason for seeking therapy – where at some level the patient has recognised the need to retreat into the forest. Peter, a middle-aged man, stated at the outset of his analysis that he could afford treatment for only one year. His business was going rapidly downhill and he complained that those around him were taking advantage of him. He described them as ruthless and greedy, while he prided himself on his impeccable and honest work. He had been divorced some time previously and could remember little about his wife or marriage, explaining that he had felt only half-alive and had not really known what he had been doing. Following his divorce, he became a playboy – he was the life of every party, he had women running after him, his business flourished, and he saw himself as a kind of golden boy or hero. But the women he met soon began to be unfaithful, he felt deceived by his friends, and his business faltered. He could not understand what had been the cause of his downfall, although he admitted that it was a relief not to have to be the playboy any longer.

During his first few months of analysis, Peter thrashed about, desperately trying to make plans for his business and his personal life, asking my advice about what he should do. Realising that I could not tell him what to do, he lapsed into silence. For months he would arrive, talk for a while, and then sink into silence. At first, his silence seemed angry and resentful, making me feel like the useless and helpless one. Gradually the quality of the sessions changed and Peter's depression became more manifest as he contracted 'flu and complained of feeling lifeless and having no energy. After some time this too changed and he seemed more relaxed, even to the point of falling asleep, which he did on a few occasions. He began to tell me that his business was improving and he had been able for the first time to confront a former colleague who had cheated him in the past and to speak up for himself in other situations. He seemed to be coming back to life bit by bit, as he found he could reach out for what he wanted without feeling the shame of a fallen hero. He could begin to see his own needs and regain his appetite. At the end of the year, Peter left, saying he had renewed contact with his daughter, from whom he had

In search of the heroine **77**

been estranged for the last ten years, and that in reconnecting with his past he could begin to feel hopeful.

## Discussion

### *Deintegrative and integrative processes*

Peter came to life after a period in which it seemed as if nothing was happening. Fordham refers to a 'steady state' which tends to be sterile and in which new components can therefore be incorporated (Fordham 1985, p. 102). Fordham notes that both 'the studies of creative activity undertaken by Marion Milner (1957) in her book *On Not Being Able to Paint*, and in Ehrenzweig's (1957) paper "Creative surrender" contain this idea, which we have also seen illustrated in the episode in the forest' (p. 102). Fordham explains that 'the steady state represents one phase in a dynamic sequence; integration is followed by deintegration, which in turn leads to a new integrate. The sequence is conceived to repeat throughout life and lies at the root of maturational development' (p. 102).

It is important to differentiate the 'steady state', which is often reached through regression, from a regressive state. Fordham suggests that 'one object of regression could be to realise steady states' (p. 106). While regression may be a forerunner of the 'steady state', it is within the 'steady state' that the bridging between opposites occurs and is realised. It is in its very nature something which is known or achieved only after the moment has passed, and it cannot be observed while it is occurring; it is an unconscious process. In this way, it is similar to the period of growth in which the heroine regains a bodily state of wholeness – the process of which is hidden from sight in the depths of the forest. The hero's moment of glory – that moment which turns man into a hero – is, on the other hand, constituted by an action which derives its powers from being clearly visible.

While for the heroine, regression precedes the 'steady state', for the hero it follows the heroic activity and serves the purpose of bringing him back to earth. The hero strives towards consciousness and self-determination. Like a toddler learning how to walk, he has to think himself into walking and put mind over matter in order to achieve this. But at some point the toddler, who has joined the gods, will inevitably stumble in order to be reminded, sometimes quite painfully, of his human stature. From this experience of helplessness and dependency, the heroine is activated.

The heroine cannot truly act for herself until she is able to internalise her experience of matter (mater or mother). What marks her out is not simply her state of dependency, but how her dependency is transformed. Her capacity to form an inner connection with mother is manifest in the re-growing of her hands. This process is one of symbolisation and hence imagination. Just as the hero has to be able to imagine something other or different in order to be able to separate, the heroine must imagine what is within, to reintegrate matter, and in this way to regain her connection to the world outside. Without the capacity to imagine, the split cannot be resolved and no integration can take place.

**78** Coline Covington

Although I have indicated a fairly simple association between hero and independence and heroine and dependence, each constituting an imaginative process which is nevertheless different in intent, there are, of course, countless exceptions to this rule. We can think of many heroes who have had to withdraw from the world and undergo a period of isolation and dependency – Jonah in the belly of the whale, Christ in the desert, Achilles in his tent – all withdrew in order to become heroines, and this is what ultimately humanises the hero. Similarly, heroines are not only passive, they also have to undergo superhuman struggles, to say nothing of suffering; they also have to become heroes. The inevitability of the exceptions underscores the link between hero and heroine, mirror images of each other.

## Psyche and gender

If we accept that heroes can be heroines and heroines can be heroes, it raises certain questions regarding the psychology of men and women and whether, for example, the actual process of separation and individuation differs between the sexes. The concept of hero and heroine – and their different struggles – cannot be applied exclusively and respectively to men and women. Men can be under the influence of the heroine just as women can follow the path of the hero. The anatomical difference between hero and heroine does not indicate a basic difference in the psychology of men and women; it is a metaphor of otherness. Samuels makes the point that from our discovery that little boys build towers and little girls enclosures when given bricks, we can see a *similar* psychological process at work (Samuels 1986, p. 8; 1987, p. 27). Both boys and girls are interested in their own bodies and in exploring what is different in each other. What is striking is the universality of anatomy as a metaphor in the psyche. This similarity is also apparent in the process of separation; while the relationship to mother is inevitably different for boys and girls, because of their sexual identity, both share a basic need to separate and must achieve this by exploring how they differ and how they are similar – through opposition and identification.

The danger in failing to recognise the concept of hero/heroine as metaphorical is that of making the symbolic actual, or identifying with the archetype, resulting in both an inflation and a deflation. The anatomical differences of hero/heroine are only too often taken to apply literally; the qualities associated with the heroine of passivity, receptivity and renewal have been regarded as intrinsically 'feminine' and therefore innate in women, while the active, penetrating qualities of the hero have been seen as intrinsically 'masculine' and therefore innate in men. Apart from the false dichotomy this creates between men and women, it encourages within us the tendency to emphasise one aspect at the expense of the other.

## In search of the heroine

A further question arises as to why we cannot simply equate the hero with the 'masculine' (or masculine principle) and the heroine with the 'feminine'

In search of the heroine **79**

(or feminine principle). The problem in using these terms is that they connote not only a specific gender relationship but the very existence of such categories as 'masculine' and 'feminine'. The importance of hero/heroine is that it can be understood only within a spectrum, the aspects functioning in dynamic inter-dependence. Both aspects must be valued together. So rather than, for example, following the appeal that what we need is more of the 'feminine's to counteract what is regarded as an imbalance of 'masculine' consciousness, I am suggesting that instead we need to incorporate the hero/heroine spectrum.

## Conclusion

Hero and heroine counterbalance one another and form a typically reactive psychological process. Because we see the impetus to separate from mother as the beginning of individuation, it does not mean that hero is more primary than heroine or that one is more essential than the other. Within a developmental framework, the interchange between hero and heroine constitutes a way of imagining the dynamics of deintegration and reintegration in the process of individuation. In this respect, the hero is symbolic of the process of deintegration and the heroine of the process of reintegration. The two necessarily go hand in hand.

While the hero represents the first separation as effected through independence, the cutting of the umbilical cord, the heroine represents a subsequent dependency, in which a new attachment is discovered which can then enable further separation to occur. Autonomy for the heroine is achieved not through doing, or making things happen, or going out into the world. It is during her period in the forest, when nothing appears to happen, that things change and her plight is resolved. It is for this reason that we sometimes fail to recognise her.

### *Postscript to 'In search of the heroine'*

In re-reading this chapter, written over 25 years ago, what strikes me most is the number of women patients I have worked with who are desperately waiting for a prince to rescue them, to make them feel the love and acceptance they did not have from their families and, in particular, from their mothers. Early traumas, negligence and emotional abuse have left these women handicapped, unable to take care of themselves and to fight for what they want in life. They are handless maidens who feel helpless and inadequate. Even if they find a prince to love them, this relationship can only provide them with a prosthetic. They still lack their own agency.

What is apparent in the fairy story is that the maiden's mother fails to protect her; she is unconscious of the father's pact with the devil and seems unable to do anything but comply with the situation. The maiden remains pure thanks to her tears of suffering, although she is cut off from her feelings of rage, signified by the loss of her hands. She becomes the archetypal masochistic victim, following in the footsteps of her passive mother. The implication in the story is that she chooses to leave home rather than be a burden to her father. Her wanderings lead her to the king's garden and, enticed by his fruit trees, she is eventually discovered by him. Their marriage signifies the maiden's rescue and she is given mechanical hands that allow her some degree of autonomy. All seems to go well until the maiden becomes pregnant and the king goes off to war; she is then left unguarded at the mercy of her wicked mother-in-law. Seeing the danger she is in, the maiden manages to escape with her life – and her child.

It is only when the toxic mother figure emerges clearly in the narrative that the maiden takes action to protect herself. This is the psychological turning point in the story and reflects the point at which masochistic patients begin to be aware of their destructive mothers and how they have internalized their destructive relationships with their mothers. It becomes clear that no prince can truly rectify the fundamental damage caused by the mother's sadism – a destructiveness that threatens to repeat itself in the maiden's new role as a mother.

In clinical work, the recognition of toxic elements in the mother's relationship with the patient is a vital part of the healing process insofar as it enables the patient not only to learn how to protect herself but also to feel free to hate the mother who has failed or actively harmed her. The devaluation of the feminine can only be healed through an acknowledgement of rage and hatred and the loss of innocence. This is when the maiden's hands are restored within her psyche; she is able to transform herself from victim to agent and take charge of her life with her own hands.

## References

Aristophanes. *Clouds*. L1. 314–15. Loeb Classical Library. London. Heinemann.

Campbell, J. (1949). *The Hero with a Thousand Faces*. Princeton. Princeton University Press.

Dieckmann, H. (1986). *Twice-Told Tales*. Wilmette, Illinois. Chiron Publications.

Fordham, M. (1985). *Explorations into the Self*. Library of Analytical Psychology, Vol. 7. London. Karnac Books.

Jung, C. G. (1912). "The origin of the hero." In *Symbols of Transformation*. Col. Works, Vol. 5. Princeton. Princeton University Press.

Kerenyi, C. (1959). *The Heroes of the Greeks*. London. Thames & Hudson.

Neumann, E. (1954). *The Origins and History of Consciousness*. London. Routledge & Kegan Paul.

Redfearn, J. W. T. (1979). 'The captive, the treasure, the hero and the "anal" stage of development'. *Journal of Analytical Psychology* 24, 3: 185–205.

Samuels, A. (1986). 'Beyond the feminine principle: a post-Jungian viewpoint'. (Unpublished).

Samuels, A. (1987). 'Gender and the borderline'. (Unpublished).

Strauss, R. (1964). 'The archetype of separation'. In *The Archetype*. Ed. A. Guggenbühl-Craig. Basel. Karger.

Von Franz, M.-L. (1972). *Problems of the Feminine in Fairy-Tales*. New York. Spring Publications.

**PART III**
# Theme: Literary Landscapes

# 7

# FEMINISM, JUNG AND TRANSDISCIPLINARITY

## A novel approach

*Susan Rowland*

## Introduction

In "The Carrier Bag Theory of Fiction," Ursula K. Le Guin offers what amounts to an archetypal theory of Western culture in Jungian terms (Le Guin 1986). Moreover it is one distinguished by a primal division of gender, not in sexual or somatic structures, but rather based on formal distinctions arising from labor. While prehistoric hunters, not slowed down by suckling infants, had exciting adventures shooting spears at nimble prey, the gatherers were forced to multitask. Typically, they were searching for berries while taking care of children. Given that the earliest cultural artifact surviving from these times is a spear point, it seems organically linked to the earliest extant literature of heroic adventures. The spear-point stories of combat suggest the primacy of "epic," a genre characterized by male heroes and splendid weapons fashioning a sense of linearity and phallic potency.

Epic's high cultural status propels it into modernity where its heroic quest for supremacy over the "other," be that other a monster, an opposing city, nature or the other gender in its binary logic, becomes a *forming* influence on modern science and its propensity to develop pointed missiles as weapons of war. So far so patriarchal in the historical imagination of a Western modernity that privileges the durable quality of flint arrowheads as indicative of where we come from. But what if the spear point is not the first cultural artifact?

> A leaf a gourd a shell a net a bag a sling a sack a bottle a pot a box a container. A holder. A recipient. (Le Guin 1986: 150)

If we measure a significant development of the human psyche by the first "thing" groups of humans probably used to enable their communal lives, then the first cultural object must have been a container, something used to drink from, cook with,

**84** Susan Rowland

or carry water, or food. The first cultural artifact was probably the proto carrier bag! In this sense, the "container" is at least equally significant as a founding structure of human consciousness. Here Le Guin proposes another crucial descendant of the primal gourd in the art form that is the well-populated novel as opposed to the epic's focus on a single testosterone-fuelled hero. The novel *contains* heterogeneous elements forced into a relationship.

> That is why I like novels: instead of heroes they have people in them. (Le Guin 1986: 153)

Recognizing this probability enables a shift of perspective from a sense of inevitability about masculine or epic dominance of cultural structures. Taking the lead from Le Guin here, such a shift is where I would position feminism. Whatever feminism is in the twenty-first century, it can be posited as a carrier bag that contains the radical shift of perspective *engendered* by perceiving such archetypal structuring operating over the centuries. This is not to suggest that these are the only two archetypal dynamics, nor to imply that C. G. Jung—not mentioned by Le Guin—identified them in this way. Rather I want to suggest in this chapter that extending Le Guin's identification of the founding carrier bag with the novel form into Jungian and Archetypal Psychology, opens up a feminist space for making and critiquing knowledge. In particular, such a *novel* environment can be grounded in adherence to feminist principles of respecting difference and, partly for that reason, be offered to multiple disciplinary locations via the new paradigm of transdisciplinarity.

First of all it is worth looking at Jung's own turn from epic transcendence into novelistic immanence. For his writing in *The Collected Works* provides two contributions to this chapter's feminist transdisciplinarity: the embodied presence of archetypes and his textual capaciousness to other voices. He is provoked, of course, by the feminine.

## C. G. Jung as Feminist Novelist

> The anima has an erotic, emotional character, the animus a rationalising one. Hence most of what men say about feminine eroticism, and particularly about the emotional life of women, is derived from their own anima projections and distorted accordingly. On the other hand, the astonishing assumptions and fantasies that women make about men come from the activity of the animus, who produces an inexhaustible supply of illogical arguments and false explanations. (Jung 1954: 338)

In this quotation we see the delightful slippage between Jung the epic pioneer of psychological concepts and Jung the novelist whose carrier bag writing contains "other" voices. For these three succeeding sentences begin by offering a binary notion of psychic gender only to have this humorously grounded in an obviously partial perspective. First of all, "anima" and "animus," those properties of the other gender in the unconscious, are polarized between "emotion" and "irrationality" in a sentence positing an objective, detached view. Then the voice switches to a masculine position affirming the impossibility of detaching anima-generated emotionality from an understanding of women. The third sentence is charged with just such anima distortions indicted in the second. Is Jung falling into a trap he has just announced, or might this be a net for the unwary reader? If it is the anima and not the ego who speaks of the "inexhaustible" irrationality of women, has this writer noticed it and does he expect his reader to?

The assumption we might make about Jung's authorial position here is indeterminable. We cannot know whether this is a conscious or unconscious trickster at work. Is he deliberately setting a trap for the reader, or unthinkingly falling into it himself? What is apparent is the dual voices at play in this so-called theoretical writing. In fact we have both a lofty assertion of opposing concepts of anima and animus, and a very *situated* demonstration that both reinforces and simultaneously challenges such transcendent epistemology. A feminist approach here can take a hint from the title of this volume and see this proposal of gender theory as *from somewhere* as well as purporting to be from nowhere and everywhere.

My suggestion is that Jung's writing needs to be read as just such an intervention into a feminine epistemology as critical, multiple and grounded, whether deliberate or not on his part. For I argue that his whole *Collected Works* amounts to an attempt to rebalance the gendered psyche of modernity in a way that can be further illuminated by first a structuralist and then a transdisciplinary paradigm; moves that themselves are mythically described by James Hillman on Jung as Dionysian. Jung too, turns out to prefer people to heroes.

## Jung's turn to the feminine

Three moves in Jung's overall project characteristically enact Jung's attempt to re-orient consciousness to end exclusion of the feminine. They are his adoption of Eros and Logos as gendered styles of consciousness, the ambivalent figure of the gender-fluid trickster, and his far-reaching idea of synchronicity. All three bear the marks of his own psychic resistances to a portrayal of female equality. In effect, Jung summons a powerful feminine, the "mater" of the Goddess, in order to shore up the fragile signifying of the masculine in modernity. His innate conservatism nevertheless has truly revolutionary properties.

First of all, Eros and Logos appear as essentialist designations of a male's consciousness determined more by discrimination and disembodied spirit, Logos. This is mirrored by a female's intrinsic orientation to feeling and relatedness or Eros (Jung 1959: 29). So far so binary. However Jungian individuation, the process of becoming more individual, more whole, by an ever-growing relationship with the unconscious, counters essentialism. It is not only desirable but inevitable that Eros, associated with a male's unconscious anima, be integrated through individuation.

**86** Susan Rowland

So too a woman's animus will bring Logos alive in her psyche, even if Jung was at times skeptical of its success (Jung 1959).

What is suggestive here is how Eros and Logos, as inhabitants of the human psyche that *require* mutual accommodation, evoke a structuralist notion of myths of consciousness proposed by Jungians, Ann Baring and Jules Cashford in *The Myth of the Goddess* (1991). They describe the building of the modern western psyche as resulting from the unequal relationship of monotheism's Sky Father who succeeded an animistic Earth Mother. Prior to the arrival of the three great monotheisms of Judaism, Christianity, and Islam, religions centered on the reverence of the Earth as alive, sacred, generative, and the source of all being. This Earth *Mother* was not a woman as opposed to a man because she existed prior to gender division. She gave birth to women, men, animals, rocks, and plants equally. For her matter and spirit are one being. Most often she was figured through animistic cultures which saw nature as animated, full of individual and articulate spirits.

Monotheism drove animism to the margins and installed a dominant dualism because its Sky Father gods created nature as separate from himself, so non-divine, non-embodied. Separation and disembodiment characterized Sky Father religions in structuring a dualism between God and nature/matter that became mapped into human culture as hierarchical divisions between spirit or mind and body, human and nature, men and women. Here Jung's Eros and Logos consciousness can be seen as a stark attempt to re-orient the founding creation myths of the Western psyche. For Earth Mother never disappeared of course. She became marginalized to re-appear in the animated matter of art in painting and sculpture as well as the multiple in-spirited characters of the non-"hero" driven novel, as Le Guin showed.

Earth Mother also lived on, I suggest, in the figure of the trickster and as such found a place in Jungian psychology.

> Even [the trickster's] sex is optional despite its phallic qualities: he can turn himself into a woman and bear children ... This is a reference to his original nature as a Creator, for the world is made from the body of a god. (Jung 1959: 472)

Capable of either gender or multiple variations of same, the trickster is the embodied, amoral, protean psyche itself. In "his" infinite variety we see the seedbed of an animistic vision of matter as sacred. Trickster is all feeling and no logical or rational separation from what *matters*. Of course he demonstrates the core principle of *The Myth of the Goddess*, the need for both types of consciousness without one dominating over the other.

Later in his career Jung found the goddess again in a perspective upon creation itself that is Earth Mother. For in his notion of synchronicity is an alternative to the narrative of Genesis when God creates then steps back from his creation. Union with the creator can come only with death or the end of this created world. By contrast, synchronicity is described by Jung as "*acts of creation in time*" (Jung 1960: 965).

Synchronicity is meaningful coincidence such as when the psyche and material reality come together in a way that forges meaning rather than a causal connection.

Feminism, Jung and transdisciplinarity: a novel approach **87**

It is a vision of reality from within his depiction of the psychic quality of Eros, the "feminine" function of relationship, as opposed to (inevitably) the "masculine" Logos principle of conscious discrimination. So nature is to be investigated because and *by means of* the human psyche that is part of it. True knowledge here is that which takes account of the psyche. By contrast, rational ego-lead enquiry is a form of "knowing" that is constructed out of the repression of relating to unconsciousness; it is knowledge as separate and transcendent of the matter to be investigated. Logos knowledge relies upon the hero myth as the sole arbiter of what is to be valued as "science."

> For [experimental science] there is created in the laboratory a situation which is artificially restricted to the question and which compels Nature to give an unequivocal answer. The workings of Nature in her unrestricted wholeness are completely excluded .... [W]e need a method of enquiry which ... leaves Nature to answer out of her fullness. (Jung 1960: 864)

Perhaps here is Jung's Earth Mother most completely because "she" is Nature as wholly creative, divine. This is the animistic universe in which dreams inform about momentous events otherwise unknown, feeling and somatic archetypal images prove prophetic and meaningful beyond the rational understanding of a mechanistic or causal approach to reality.

Synchronicity forced Jung to reassess the fundamental Logos orientation of modernity that separated psyche from non-human nature. He proposed an animistic universe in which archetypes extend beyond the human psyche to its union with matter in the psychoid. In so doing, his entire project fulfills what James Hillman described as his treatment of the myth of Dionysus. It moreover indicated Jung the feminist novelist may have Dionysus as his archetypal foundation!

## Hillman on Jung and Dionysus

In "Dionysus in Jung's Writings," Archetypal Psychologist James Hillman points out that C. G. Jung stresses "dismemberment" as his key narrative in the many myths of the god Dionysus (Hillman 1972/2007). In Jung's treatment of the dismemberment of the divine being, Hillman discerns a possibility of psychic rejuvenation in the corporeal breaking apart of an aging god. He calls Christian modernity too Apollonian, seeing in Apollo the emphases of Sky Father dualism taken to excess. So in Hillman's analysis, an era dominated by one god defined by distance and disembodiment is to be followed by dismemberment and multiple stories of being in Hillman's preferred polytheistic approach to psyche. However, I shall show that Jung's dismembering of Dionysus has possibilities unexplored by Hillman.

According to Hillman, Jung sees a two-stage dismembering process: first comes a separation into opposites, such as the very notion of Apollonian and Dionysian itself. This separation satisfies Jung the lover of polarities who is reluctant to truly integrate the feminine. Yet Jung the rebalancing psychologist of the modern western psyche

**88** Susan Rowland

needs Earth Mother animism in the form of bisexual, embodied, ecstatic Dionysus. In the second stage of Dionysian dismemberment, the god is scattered in pieces.

Opposition is then transformed into multiplicity, with a wider dispersal of the divine in matter, which both Jung and Hillman call archetypal. To Jung, archetypes are inherited potentials in the human psyche for certain sorts of images and meaning (Jung 1960: 352–3). They represent the possibility of many different modes of psychic functioning; or as Hillman later puts it, a polytheistic psyche in which the gods are diverse ways of being in the world (Hillman 1972/2007). Hillman also points out that this second stage of Dionysian dismemberment entails an entry into a different type of consciousness. We enter a new cosmos with the dispersed fragments of the body of the god (p. 26). Distance from the divine becomes interiority and animistic multiplicity within the domain of the god.

> The movement between the first and second view of dismemberment compares with crossing a psychic border between seeing the god from outside or from within his cosmos. (p. 26)

Here we find ourselves in Jung's realm of synchronicity, of "*acts of creation in time*" or as Eros knowing, connected, feeling, relational, embodied. Second stage Dionysian dismemberment is the synchronous universe, Eros, trickster and the feminine mode of knowing and being. Symptomatically, Hillman notes that *zoe*, the life force of the body in Eros is awakened by this process of divine dismemberment (p. 29). This new consciousness or *zoe* is an intimation of wholeness that does not erode differences. The new enlivening *zoe* is animistic in a particular way of awareness of its own *partial* consciousness, aware of itself as *parts*.

> Rather the crucial experience would be the awareness of the parts *as parts* distinct from each other, dismembered, each with its own light, a state in which the body becomes conscious of itself as a composite of differences. The scintillae and fishes eyes of which Jung speaks … may be experienced as embedded in physical expressions. The distribution of Dionysus through matter may be compared with the distribution of consciousness through members, organs, and zones. (Hillman 1972/2007: 28)

So I suggest that in this way, Earth Mother consciousness returns again in Jung's work as dismembered Dionysus, the fragmented divine body seeding the universe with its archetypes. It is time to look at other returns of Earth Mother in order to see how her offspring, the literary form that is the novel, may be an *in-forming* participant in feminist knowing and being.

## Earth Mother evolution: complexity and transdisciplinarity

Frequently hidden in plain sight is the return of the Earth Mother as the mythical narrative of the theory of evolution first proposed by Charles Darwin in *On the*

*Origin of Species* (1859/2006). Fundamental to Darwin's thought was that the world came into being of itself without an exterior divine creator. He therefore needed to portray nature as supremely generative and found himself forced to personify "her" as primal source and maternal matrix of everything. In effect, Darwin re-animates Earth Mother mythical narrative as the story of creation that is whole (posited to encompass all) but not complete (because Darwin knew his scientific approach and language resources could not rationally account for all). Earth Mother in *On the Origin of Species* is profoundly alive as myth in a Jungian sense as a narrative creating and finding the border between the knowable and the unknowable.

Darwin's divinely created earth is succeeded in evolutionary science by another theory of generation that is well aware of its limitations in producing a complete and rational account of the fabrication of our world. Tacit knowing and complexity evolution are also Earth Mother and potentially "Jungian" notions through his feminine practices such as synchronicity.

Jung's synchronicity is the notion of an ordering in nature accessible to the human psyche. A parallel perspective is to be found in the work of Michael Polyani, in *The Tacit Dimension* (1967), and Wendy Wheeler, in *The Whole Creature* (2006). Wheeler brings Polyani's depiction of "tacit knowledge" into her imaginative construction of new work in evolutionary science of complexity. She finds in his work an understanding of nature that is significantly oriented around the body as a knowing organ, not unlike Hillman on Jung's consciousness of the dismembered Dionysian body.

Polyani's "tacit knowledge" is the kind of embodied, partly unconscious knowing that we acquire by body and psyche working together at levels not accessible to ego (separation) consciousness. Effectively, tacit knowledge is knowledge based on body and connection where consciousness of the parts as dismembered parts can be mutually activated. So tacit knowing cannot be captured in words abstracted from embodied acts. Mythically, tacit knowledge is constellated in the *zoe* or body life force of the Earth Mother.

> Tacit knowledge is creaturely skillful phenomenological knowledge. Human creatures *know* they have it ... which cannot be put into words, but which is experienced in all creative artisanship and art, and in creative and skillful living generally. This is language as semiosis which is not reducible to words, but which is embodied in acts. (Wheeler 2006: 47)

Tacit knowledge is potentially meaningful because it is ordered and communicated. What makes it "tacit" is that it is always part of an intimated order that is far greater than can be articulated just as a dismembered body cannot simply be stuck back together as one physical being (Polyani 1967: 50). In effect, tacit knowledge bridges humans and nature in the new complexity science, as Wheeler clarifies. Furthermore, tacit knowledge, in its deep rootedness in nature through the human body, is the feminine origin of newness in art and culture.

**90** Susan Rowland

Whereas the West's adherence to the dominance of Sky Father values emphasized disembodied abstraction as the proper basis for knowing (Logos), tacit knowledge is the psyche and the body working together at their psychoid interface or Eros.

> When we make a thing function as the proximal term of tacit knowing, we incorporate it in our body – or extend our body to include it – so that we come to dwell in it ...
>
> It is not by looking at things that we understand them, but by dwelling in them. (Wheeler 2006: 63)

I suggest that Wheeler's "dwelling in them" as the better form of knowing is both Earth Mother and Dionysian, invoking consciousness as *zoe*. Wheeler uses Polyani's tacit knowledge to re-situate the body in nature as an organ of knowing indivisible from the psyche. Both exhibit the profound desire to re-animate and *re-embody* Earth Mother consciousness in her dispersed yet carnal mode. Art and culture flourish through tacit knowledge, Wheeler argues. It is through the incarnated creative and multiple psyche that the "new" happens. Moreover, what is crucial is that tacit knowing infers a complexity greater than can be measured by rational methods. Such complexity is not confined to cultural change. Rather, "complexity" is now regarded as key to evolution Herself.

The recognition of a definitive role for unmappable complexity marks a significant development in the theory of evolution after Darwin. Evolved nature is not so much a competition between wholly separate species as Darwin originally envisaged, but is more like successive, ever more complexly interpenetrating environments.

> Complex systems evolve via the emergence of strata of increasing complexity. Biological evolution proceeds in this fashion, as, we have now seen, does human culture and human knowledge. Human discovery and invention – human creativity – proceeds via tacit knowledge and our sense that we are in contact with a complex reality of which there is more to be known ... (Wheeler 2006: 67–8)

Culture is therefore nature *creating through the tacit, unarticulated knowledge of human beings*. Tacit knowledge is *realizing* (making "real" by articulating into human language) the synchronous nature of nature! Tacit knowing invokes *zoe* and thereby has implications for the whole project of our traditional disciplines of knowledge as I shall demonstrate.

Similarly to complexity evolution, Jung calls synchronicity *"acts of creation in time,"* specifically associating these meaningful coincidences with "nature" as mother (Jung 1960: 965). Jung's unconscious psyche, like Wheeler's and Polyani's, is also embodied. His "synchronous events" are apprehended through/as tacit knowledge in the body as somatic intuition. Effectively, he too embraces the creativity of nature through tacit *significance* into culture.

Feminism, Jung and transdisciplinarity: a novel approach **91**

To sum up. What is being argued here is that nature has an underlying rationality too complexly entangled for human objective measurement or the abstracted ego to grasp. This intricate rationality is part of a constantly evolving complexity of totalities. Such complexity is arguably another way of describing the consciousness engendered by Earth Mother or dismembered Dionysus: it is tricksterish, archetypal, and synchronous. Fascinatingly complexity theory is also effective in accounting for how *culture* evolves in the sense of how societies and groups creatively interact and mutate beyond the capacity of rational analysis. In this sense, animistic Earth Mother is alive and her *zoe* is the life force wherever creativity is generated in ways too complex to calculate, predict, control, or consciously measure.

Nature's "complex" totalities include human cultures, which is where the signifying potential of nature flowers into human language. Semiotics becomes what Wheeler calls "biosemiotics," the signifying of animated life (Wheeler 2006: 139). Although Wheeler does not make use of Jung's archetypal sense of animism, nor myths of Dionysus, nor Earth Mother, this consciousness, what Jung called "synchronicities" are moments where tacit embodied Earth Mother knowledge grasps just a little more of nature's creativity as she portrays it.

> Creativity is in many ways a word for describing autopoeisis as biosemiotic life: all nature and culture is creative becoming and change. In human complex systems, creativity is semiotic liveliness: liveliness in language and liveliness in the processes via which tacit knowledge can emerge in concepts which can be articulated or, rather more accurately, *are* articulated as the process of such emergence. (Wheeler 2006: 139)

Everything said here about nature is also appropriate to Jung's view of the unconscious. Jung's unconscious is embodied and so embedded in our nature as continuous with the non-human. Synchronicity is one aspect of Jung where he *grounds* his unconscious as in meaningful semiotic *interconnectedness* with nature as Nature.

The psyche is not only inside our corporeal being. To be more precise, the psyche shows "inside" *and* "outside" to be powerful cultural metaphors. Language shapes our relation to the world; it is not a neutral medium. So it is time to look at a way of dealing with the "animistic" multiplicity of academic disciplines with their different languages. How can such a dismemberment of knowledge find its *zoe*, its Dionysian animation? For we seek disciplines that manifest *realization*, the making real of their plurality *as parts*.

## Transdiciplinarity and Dionysus

First appearing in 1970, from Jean Piaget in the sense of "a total system," "transdisciplinarity" has been most helpfully theorized by Basarab Nicolescu (Nicolescu 2002). He gave a valuable overview in his talk at the Congress of Transdisciplinarity in Brazil in 2005, later published as "Transdisciplinarity – Past, Present and Future"

**92** Susan Rowland

(Nicolescu 2005). Nicolescu rejects the totalizing project inherent in Piaget's definition and dismisses any possibility of a hyperdiscipline, one capable of subsuming all disciplines of human knowing into a system of perfect knowledge or ultimate truth. Rather Nicolescu prefers to stress what he calls "beyond disciplines" in his transdisciplinarity, which appears to mean beyond the pretensions of any one epistemological construct to encompass all meaning.

Where Nicolescu is particularly persuasive is his building transdisciplinarity on the post-quantum human subject and his move to embrace the implications of complexity theory for human knowing. Arguing that quantum discoveries end the primacy of the traditional scientific method of repeatable experiment, Nicolescu posits a new human subject for *all* research. Quantum physics discovered that some reality cannot be judged by the criteria of objectivity or absolute separation between the observer and the observed because the way phenomena are measured changes the results radically.

Transdisciplinarity aims for a sense of human knowledge as a unity but an "open" unity by which Nicolescu means accepting that humans live on several levels of reality at the same time and it will never be possible to rationally know all of them. These realities cannot be eroded or simplified (Nicolescu 2005: 4). Such a recognition of irreducible differences indicates that transdisciplinarity must be considered as theoretical, phenomenological and as experimental. Nicolescu proposes three axioms of transdisciplinarity to replace those of traditional science that go back to Gallileo.

Hitherto, many scientific disciplines adhered to the following axioms or fundamental principles:

i) The universe is governed by mathematical law.
ii) These laws can be discovered by scientific experiment.
iii) Such experiments, if valid, can be perfectly replicated. (p. 5)

As Nicolescu points out, such privileging of "objectivity" has the unfortunate effect of turning the human subject into an object by stripping out feeling and values (p. 5). The problem lies in the positing of *one* level of reality as foundational to all others. This single way of structuring knowing then subsumes realities like the social or psychological to its objectivizing paradigm.

By contrast, Nicolescu's transdisciplinarity explicitly disavows mathematical formalism because of the human subject's complexity in both simple and theoretical senses, as we will see. Nicolescu's fundamental principles, or three axioms for the methodology of transdisciplinarity are as follows.

i) The ontological axiom: *There are, in Nature and in our knowledge of Nature, different levels of Reality and, correspondingly, different levels of perception.*
ii) The logical axiom: *The passage from one level of Reality to another is insured by the logic of the included middle.*
iii) The complexity axiom: *The Structure of the totality of levels of Reality or perception is a complex structure: every level is what it is because all levels exist at the same time.* (p. 6)

Feminism, Jung and transdisciplinarity: a novel approach **93**

This approach to what we know and how we know it amounts to a transformation of approach to the universe as multidimensional. Reality is now complex. So are human beings. Nicolescu insists that no one level of reality, such as sight perception, for instance, can constitute a dominant position for knowing. No sense organ or academic discipline is capable of understanding all the other levels of reality in total. Knowledge in any of its forms is necessarily incomplete or "open" (p. 7). Academic disciplines cannot pretend to a hierarchy where one is privileged above all the others. Moreover, such an approach does away with the interior/exterior boundary of knowing.

> Knowledge is neither exterior nor interior: it is simultaneously exterior and interior. The studies of the universe and of the human being sustain one another. (p. 8)

As Nicolescu reiterates, his transdisciplinarity crucially undoes the classical subject/object division in favor of the ternary: subject, object, hidden third that is both subject and object (p. 8). This "included middle," explicitly prohibited by the previous rational paradigm where A could not be also non-A, does not, he notes, eradicate those types of logical knowing that do insist that A cannot be non-A. Rather, it shows them to be incomplete: they are one level of reality, not a primal truth framing all of them. Traditional objective science has its place as one *part* of the dismembered body of academic knowing that we call "disciplines."

"Complexity" too needs a context for its inclusion in Nicolescu's transdisciplinarity. Some theorists are looking for a mathematical rendering of complexity, which would, in this notion of transdisciplinarity limit the levels of reality that it could encompass. So Nicolescu offers the structure of horizontal and vertical axes.

> It is therefore useful to distinguish between the horizontal complexity, which refers to a single level of reality and vertical complexity, which refers to several levels of Reality. (p. 13)

Symptomatically Nicolescu notices the ancient lineage of complexity theory as interdependence, everything really is connected to everything else (p. 13). He sees his three axioms as innately values generating. The hidden third or included middle emphasizes the interdependence of the model. Where humans and the universe are regarded as interdependent, then we either have values or chaos.

For this reason, higher education needs to convert to transdisciplinarity so that it can develop the three main types of intelligence: rational analytical, feeling, and of the body (p. 15). These intelligences demand complexity on the question of meaning. So here "horizontal meaning" is what most traditional academic disciplines do; they situate meaning at one level of reality. By contrast, a transdisciplinary education would provide meaning vertically, at several levels of reality with none privileged over all the others. Nicolescu suggests poetry, art, or quantum physics as providing vertical or multiple levels of meaning (p. 17).

**94**  Susan Rowland

Interestingly for Jungian studies, Nicolescu rejects attacks on psychoanalysis from those preferring chemical interventions into the mind. Scientist and medics who reject the taking cure are guilty of simplifying different levels of reality to one, the biochemical (ibid.). To illustrate his revolutionary vision of knowledge, Nicolescu contrasts traditional academic disciplines providing fragments of one level of reality to cultures and religions which anticipate transdisciplinarity by spanning multiple realities. What he calls "technoscience," the alliance of instrumental technology with traditional science of repeatable experiments, is confined to the zone of the "object" in his tripartite vision of subject, object, and hidden third (p. 17). He calls for technoscience to become a "culture" by entering a dialogue with religion that would expand its zones of reality to all three (p. 17).

For the world of education in disciplines, I will argue that Nicolescu's vision is remarkably similar to the ethos of Earth Mother consciousness and its *articulation* into dispersed Dionysus.

> The transdisciplinary education, founded on the transdisciplinary methodology, allows us to establish links between persons, facts, images, representations, fields of knowledge and action and to discover the Eros of learning during our entire life. The creativity of the human being is conditioned by permanent questioning and permanent integration. (Nicolescu 2005: 14)

Here is education in the framework of complexity theory that positions the human *within and part of* the creativity of non-human nature. Nicolescu's Eros is Earth Mother in knowing and synchronous in epistemology. Symptomatically, Nicolescu betrays his core concern with traditional science in his persistent yet helpful motif of subject, object, and hidden third that is both. However, his insistence that knowing is both interior and exterior unites complexity theory with transdisciplinarity's challenge to the atomization of education in discrete disciplines. For far from acknowledging dismembered Dionysus, separate academic disciplines are all too used to rejecting any consciousness of each other as viable, yet different levels of reality. In the modern university, our mutually indifferent, or even antagonistic disciplines have no consciousness of themselves as dismembered parts. They therefore have no *zoe*, no dynamic life force in their separate incompleteness.

It is transdisciplinarity, I suggest, united with complexity theory that embraces Jung and Hillman's vision of dismembered Dionysus. Moreover, this transdisciplinary ecstatic god has followers well before the hysterics of early psychoanalysis identified by Hillman (Hillman 1972/2007: 17). I propose that those early wild women of Dionysian rites include the sedate Jane Austen in the female dominated rise of the novel. For example, her *Sense and Sensibility* (1811/1990) demonstrates the clash of values over contrary relations to nature that is also different realities coming into contact.

> Edward: "I like a fine prospect, but not on picturesque principles. I do not like crooked, twisted, blasted trees. I admire them much more if they are tall,

Feminism, Jung and transdisciplinarity: a novel approach **95**

straight and flourishing ... I have more pleasure in a snug farmhouse than a watch-tower – and a troop of tidy, happy villagers please me better than the finest banditti in the world.

Marianne looked with amazement at Edward, with compassion at her sister. Elinor only laughed. (Austen 1811: 122–3)

Edward and Marianne reveal their very different adoption of Eros in knowing the countryside where Marianne's once privileged family is living in comparative poverty. She is "Romantic" in espousing the ideals and excited sensibility of cultural Romanticism in regarding nature as a source of ecstatic feeling. Totally at odds here is Edward whose disposition draws back from the implications of Romantic philosophy. His temperament finds a home in religious beliefs (he wants to be a clergyman) that to him entail a pastoral care for the poor. He therefore celebrates the prosperous farming landscape as an extension of religious and social principles.

The novel brings both highly complex constructions of reality into a relationship without negating either, nor suggesting that either is complete: the conditions of transdisciplinarity. Marianne has vertical axes of psyche, poetry, and the freedom-loving culture of Romanticism. Edward possesses the vertical axes of religion, its extension into the social with pastoral care and even a proto-scientific vision of successful farming and interest in trees as "flourishing."

Taking a cue from Le Guin's novel as carrier bag, the novel genre is, I propose, Earth Mother in its animism, and also specifically Dionysian in its *zoe* of life force generated in its *complex*, skilful articulation of different parts of reality in conversation. The novel fosters such conversation that promotes, as here, awareness of these perspectives as *partial*, as *parts*.

Perhaps Nicolescu's included middle should be seen as feminist and novelistic as well as importing as non-marginal the intelligences of feeling and the body?

## Feminism and the included middle: Jung's symbols, archetypes, and novels

As argued above, Jung's *Collected Works* are closer to novels than to conventional scientific writing. They are feminist novels in the sense that their animistic nature serves his project by turning to what has been marginalized in modernity as feminine. Such a feminine includes what he calls feeling and connection as Eros as opposed to discrimination and separation as Logos, the trickster androgynous plurality of Earth Mother and "her" complexity creativity that he named synchronicity.

Jung the feminist novelist is also Dionysian as Hillman diagnosed in his two-stage dismemberment. First of all there is dualism, a rending into oppositions that pepper Jung's terminology. More profound and more feminist-friendly is Jung's second stage Dionysian dismemberment into parts, aware of themselves as parts with an emphasis on Earth Mother, embodied consciousness. Jung's trickster and animistic writing is here the dispersed corporeality of the ecstatic god.

**96** Susan Rowland

Taking this unlikely push of Jung into feminism further is to consider his writing as proto-transdisciplinary. Crucially, Jung's stress on the impossibility of complete knowledge given the indigenous mystery of the psyche is one factor that his work shares with Nicolescu. Jung has the potential to be a significant stabilizing force in Nicolescu's transdisciplinarity where the latter repeatedly warns against the trap of erecting some hyperdiscipline, as a pretension to control all meaning.

This is one instance of how Jung might contribute to the transdisciplinary project. There are many more as we start to perceive psychoanalysis and Jungian studies as intrinsically transdisciplinary in their acceptance of multiple levels of reality. Dreams, for example, are real. They are also necessarily of a different order of reality than social engagement, historical events (no longer present to senses), bodily perception, or cultural representations. Depth psychology of Freudian and Jungian persuasions has a particular expertise in working with multiple levels of reality as simultaneous and *complex* forms of knowing.

As an example of taking Jung's Dionysian feminism a stage further into transdisciplinarity, I want to consider the Jungian symbol as an instance of the hidden third, here to be brought into knowing as the included middle. Jung writes about the symbol as a specific type of image, which is itself a manifestation of the unconscious as imag[e]-ination, the psyche as intrinsically image-making. Looking primarily at images in words, Jung called "signs" those images standing for a relatively known or stable meaning while "symbols" are pointers to something relatively unknown or not yet known (Jung 1966: 105).

Symbols connect the conscious ego to the archetypal collective unconscious. They therefore are prime examples of Nicolescu's "vertical" or multiple levels of reality, being at one level perceptual and on another intuitive, and on yet another "spiritual" in the sense of pertaining to the immaterial unknown. Here I want to emphasize that Jungian symbols are far from icons of disconnection to the embodied world. Given that Jungian archetypes are inherited potentials, they have a bodily as well as spiritual pole (Jung 1960: 367). In transdisciplinary terms, symbols derived from archetypes operate vertically to manifest realities of body, feeling, and spirit.

In this way symbols can activate all Nicolescu's intelligences of body, feeling, and analytical intellect. They are the *third* term between the different levels of reality evoked. The symbol of a rose in a love poem can be felt somatically and erotically as well as analytically as an idea about love in ways that are profoundly human and connecting as well as divine and transcendent. A Jungian symbol connects the psyche to what matters. It does so because it is the third that is both matter and psyche in the Sky Father binary logic that there is the human psyche *inside* us and matter *outside*. The symbol is the included middle.

Finally we must notice that this symbol as included middle is an engine of complexity in the sense that it is a portal between human and non-human nature. Jungian symbols are scraps of the dismembered Dionysian body. They materialize *zoe*; they are the animated sparks that embody Earth Mother, the creatures that make the feminine texture of the novel. A symbol for Jung is an image of the deep psyche that stitches us into the cosmos as an act of feminine knowing. Such symbols

Feminism, Jung and transdisciplinarity: a novel approach **97**

are necessarily fragments aware of themselves as parts. To end this chapter I want to give an example of a Jungian symbol in/as a literary form. Modern detective fiction, I suggest, provides a healing integration of the wilder aspects of Dionysian dismemberment.

## From Dionysian trickster to Athena containing the furies in detective fiction

Earth Mother is not a "woman" for she is prior to gender division into dualism. Much of her divine abilities occur in bisexual Dionysus, a complex trickster. In *The Ecocritical Psyche* (2012), I argued that the ancient trickster myth sponsors the modern detective narrative, a form distinguished by its deceptive qualities *vis-à-vis* the reader. However, there are other archetypal energies in detective fiction that become visible once we see this trickster novel through a Dionysian lens.

For Dionysian dismemberment, as Hillman intuits in Jung, has to move beyond oppositions that would posit Apollonian Sky Father as all rational matched by Dionysus as total un-reason. Maenads tearing men to pieces inspired by the ecstatic god is not the ideal, nor indeed necessary consequence of divine dismemberment. Literal rending of bodies may be one possible consequence of replacing one dominant archetypal structure (Sky Father, Apollo) with its opposite (Earth Mother, Dionysus), but it is not the desired aim of animistic and transdisciplinary creative multiplicity. Put another way, multiple archetypes require polytheistic solutions. So the possibility of trickster detective fiction going too literally Dionysian invokes a very different type of god(dess): Athena.

For Athena is not only the goddess of the city but of what makes communal life possible. We see her at work in Aeschylus's play, "The Eumenides," persuading the Furies not to tear apart guilty Orestes who has murdered his mother to avenge the slaughter of his father (Aeschylus 458 BCE). Athena stops the cycle of revenge. The Furies are incorporated into the city as aliens but as great sources of its fertility. They become zoe, *contained* by Athena as city goddess who is also the divine bringer of weaving and pottery.

Athena *contains*. She exists in detective fiction in tension with Dionysus and mitigating his more literal bodily qualities of tearing apart. Detective novels are Athena in containing and integrating the Furies in us that threaten chaos at the crime of murder, the crime that makes human community impossible if it is not solved. In this sense, detective fiction as a literary form is a symbol in the Jungian sense. It is a temple of Dionysus and Athena (and other gods too). Detective fiction is the included middle between psyche and matter, not least because it deals with what *matters*.

I began with the feminine nature of the novel and so end with its variously gendered gods. The novel is a powerful location for marginalized and feminine energies, a model for multiple and transdisciplinary knowing, and a trickster stealing her way into Jung's *Collected Works*. She is novel, news from somewhere from within the fragmented body of the goddess.

**98** Susan Rowland

## References

Aeschylus. (458 BCE) "The Eumenides," in *The Oresteia*, trans. Robert Fagles, New York: Penguin Books, 1966, pp. 227–77.

Austen, J. (1811/1990) *Sense and Sensibility*, Oxford and New York: Oxford University Press.

Baring, A. and J. Cashford (1991) *The Myth of the Goddess: Evolution of an Image*, New York and London: Vintage.

Darwin, C. (1859/2006) *On the Origin of Species; By Means of Natural Selection*, New York: Dover Thrift Editions.

Hillman, J. (1972/2007) "Dionysus in Jung's Writings," first published in *Spring: A Journal of Archetype and Culture*, in *Mythic Figures: Uniform Edition of the Writings of James Hillman, volume 6.1*, Putnam C.T.: Spring Publications Inc., pp. 15–30.

Jung, C. G. (1953–91) *The Collected Works of C.G. Jung*, eds. H. Read, M. Fordham, and G. Adler, trans. R. F. C. Hull, London: Routledge, Princeton N.J.: Princeton University Press.

Le Guin, U. (1986/1996) "The Carrier Bag Theory of Fiction," in C. Glotfelty and H. Fromm (eds.), *The Ecocriticism Reader: Landmarks in Literary Ecology*, Athens and London: The University of Georgia Press, pp. 149–54.

Nicolescu, B. (2002) *Manifesto of Transdisciplinarity*, Albany, N.Y.: State University of New York Press.

Nicolescu, B. (2005) "Transdisciplinarity – Past, Present and Future," paper presented at Second Congress of World Transdisciplinarity, Brazil, Sept 6–12, 2005, published in *Cetrans: Centro Educacao Transdisciplinar*, pp. 1–24; www.cetrans.com.br accessed February 7, 2015.

Polyani, M. (1967) *The Tacit Dimension*, London: Routledge & Kegan Paul.

Rowland, S. (2012) *The Ecocritical Psyche: Literature, Evolutionary Complexity and Jung*, Hove and New York: Routledge.

Wheeler, W. (2006) *The Whole Creature: Complexity, Biosemiotics and the Evolution of Culture*, London: Lawrence & Wishart.

# 8

## FIERCE YOUNG WOMEN IN POPULAR FICTION AND AN UNPOPULAR WAR

*Elizabeth Eowyn Nelson*

The moment a woman of any age thinks that power is masculine, the natural prerogative of males but not females, she relinquishes an essential element of her human endowment. This erroneous thought impoverishes women psychologically by limiting their imagination of how to be vital, effective, thoughtful people in the world. It impoverishes culture by undermining the many important ways in which women can, should, and already do exercise social, economic, and political power.

For Jungians, viewing power as masculine is antithetical to the theory of individuation because it effectively truncates the possibility of a woman's wholeness. For feminists, adopting a limited view of woman's aptitude for power, including her actual capacity for aggression, violence, and warfare, is naïve. It may be sentimental, a vestige of the nineteenth-century notion of the woman as "the angel in the house," morally superior to males and charged with upholding the purity of society and culture—a charge that is unfair to both women and men. A further question arises from thinking that power is masculine: it indicates a monolithic idea of power—power as domination—as opposed to a finely differentiated understanding of the many kinds of power indigenous to human beings regardless of sex, a biological distinction, and gender, a sociocultural distinction?[1] So long as domination dominates our idea of power, Hillman warns (1995, p. 98), we will remain dangerously ignorant. Thus exploring how women express their power can encourage any of us to think with subtlety and precision about a topic that is central to human life.

In this chapter, I propose to focus on expressions of power found in young women in their late teens and twenties growing toward adulthood. The sources for the analysis may seem, at first glance, to be strange bedfellows: what could popular novels possibly have in common with an unpopular war? Let's begin with uncanny timing, nearly too precise to be credible. Beginning in 2005 and ending in 2013, four bestselling works worth billions of dollars—the *Twilight* saga, the *Millennium* trilogy, the *Hunger Games* trilogy, and the *Divergent* trilogy—centered upon fierce young women protagonists who are aggressive, armed, and dangerous.[2] As a Jungian attuned to activated archetypal patterns in culture, this abrupt, unprecedented shift in modern fairy tales seizes my attention. During the same period, for the first time in American history female soldiers were attached to all-male units engaged in direct ground combat in Iraq and Afghanistan. Two Marine Corps programs in particular, the Lioness program and Female Engagement Teams (FETs), are noteworthy. The skill, strength, and dedication of the recruits, many in their twenties, astonished some of their deeply skeptical (male) instructors. Though the deployment of women began winding down with force reduction in the Middle East, the idea is not going away. The success of these historic programs is so great that the Marine Corps announced in August 2015 that FETs would be reinstituted (Seck, 2015). Perhaps the Marines were prompted by an historic development in a rival branch of the military, the U.S. Army. On August 21, two young women graduated from the Army's Ranger School, "the absolute toughest, most demanding course in the military," according to Command Sgt. Major Curtis H. Arnold Jr. (Mallin, 2015). Though military policy still prohibits their participation in direct ground combat, the graduation of First Lieutenant Kristen Griest and Captain Shaye Haver "is a significant crack in the wall keeping women formally off the battlefield" (Thompson, 2015, n.p.). What kind of young woman leaps at such an opportunity?

That is not a question that can be fully answered within the scope of this chapter, but exploring the fictional works alongside the experience of women in combat situations may generate ideas for discussion and further research. In the four novels, for instance, the protagonists are vital, passionate, and intensely committed. They discover and develop a distinctive form of power symbolized by their weapon of choice. They are eager to use their power on behalf of someone or something they love and, over time, develop a strong affiliation with their pack. Their prowess includes clear strategic thinking, physical strength, toughness, and skill. Their confidence in themselves rises as they undergo arduous training to nurture their innate capacities. In the end, they emerge as bold, aggressive young women who are not "animus-possessed" distortions of some sort of "true" femininity. I explore these themes and consider how they might illuminate the experience of real-life women in the military, particularly those who are eager to enter combat. The precise simultaneous fluorescence of fierce young women in fiction and reality indicates the activation of an archetypal pattern, the *female warrior*, long unrecognized in patriarchy. The spirit of the times, in Jung's own phrase, is clearly calling attention to this pattern in a most dramatic way. It needs to be met with the spirit of the depths, the long history of armed, ferocious women dating back at least 5,000 years. In this chapter, I will argue that we are remembering something that patriarchal cultures have mostly forgotten: the original powers of the ancestral feminine. I wonder, in fact, if fierce young women in fiction and reality are seizing our attention, quite dramatically, because they are ready to step onto a battlefield of their own choosing.

Fierce young women **101**

I didn't recognize my concern for fierce young women until I saw, in retrospect, the pattern in my research and writing. For instance, my fascination with *Psyche's Knife* (Nelson, 2012) reveals a deep commitment to the complex young woman at the center of the second-century Roman fairytale *Eros and Psyche*. When we underestimate Psyche, we diminish ourselves. I stepped in as her advocate, as I continue to step in and advocate for young women who are viewed in disrespectful and naïvely reductive terms, put in their place for the comfort and convenience of a culture that prefers well-behaved women. I am not a well-behaved woman. I speak as a second-wave feminist educated in the 1970s and 1980s who welcomes third-wave feminism. My heart and mind go out to those who are navigating the treacherous terrain of adolescence and young womanhood. They are the beneficiaries of the first and second feminist movements, yet many struggle with the label *feminist* or, if they are receptive to it, struggle with *how* to be feminist in the twenty-first century. Jungian feminists in the twenty-first century can offer such young women a nuanced understanding of the complexity of gendered life while remaining fully committed to protesting the ways in which they subtly diminish themselves, or each other, or the feminine.

An archetypal Jungian approach can additionally explain the cross-generational allure of young warriors. Rather than treating girlhood as a stage of life that one enters and exits, archetypal psychology views it as a *pattern of experience* that occurs biologically during youth but also re-arises in response to various stimuli over the course of a woman's life. (The focus on young women has matured into its own discipline known as Girls' Studies in works by scholars such as Gilligan (1982), Hancock (1981, 1989), Pipher (1994), Harris (2004), McRobbie (2004), and Jensen (2009).) Within a mature woman, the pattern of experience can be reactivated and remembered: one's *girl* is an inner figure who can have quite a lot to say to the 50-, 60-, or 70-year-old. In fact, the key finding of Hancock's dissertation research at Harvard is the aliveness of the girl in women. One's girl can deeply identify with, and become wholly involved by, contemporary tales of young women in novels and in combat. I conjecture that these fierce young women expand our imagination of femininity and satiate a hunger for role fluidity that subverts any patriarchal or rigid notions of gender.

## The significance of popular culture

Noting the activated images within culture at any moment in time, while also attending to how those archetypal images evolve, is a potent means to explore what is alive in the collective psyche. For example, Baring and Cashford (1993) used this approach to trace the evolution of the divine feminine across time and cultures, and it is part of Singer and Kimbles' 2004 work on the cultural complex. Finally, as Hillman (1983, p. 12) argues, paying attention to "all culture, all forms of human activity" is at the heart of archetypal psychology's move beyond the four walls of the therapy room. This is especially pertinent when the cultural event attracts the critical attention of serious mainstream media. For instance, NPR's John Powers,

#### 102 Elizabeth Eowyn Nelson

commenting on the allure of Lisbeth Salander from the *Millennium* trilogy (2005–2007) and Bella Swan from the *Twilight* saga (2005–2008), argues that these works represent a "sweeping change" in popular culture (Powers, 2010, n.d.). Two additional protagonists Powers did not discuss have proven equally alluring and marketable: Katniss Everdeen, the central character in the *Hunger Games* trilogy (2008–2010) and Tris Prior in the *Divergent* trilogy (2011–2013). Lest anyone imagines that this trend has begun to fade, I would add two more names: Arya Stark and Daenerys Targaryan, pivotal and very fierce characters growing into womanhood in the HBO miniseries *Game of Thrones*, based on George R. R. Martin's fantasy saga (1996–).

Feminists generally as well as influential Jungians recognize popular culture as a "critical site" for studying issues of gender and power. Contemporary media, including novels, film, television, and music, are enormously influential, "defining emergent sexual codes of conduct. They pass judgment and establish the rules of play" (McRobbie, 2004, p. 7). Harris asserts an important "relationship between popular cultures, material conditions and gendered identities" (2004, p. xix). In Frankel's 1998 study of the adolescent psyche, he observes that adolescents who are "hungry for experience" feed themselves in part on the media (p. 49). To attend to them,

> we must attend to how the adolescent's imagination is fed through the music, movies, television, literature, and poetry that adolescents are attracted to and actively seek out. From an archetypal perspective, we might ask: How do the songs, poems, dances and stories resonate with pre-existing patterns in the adolescent psyche that actively demand expression? (pp. 49–50)

Frankel urges us to "focus a psychological eye" on such media, "taking heed of the powerful cultural forces impacting adolescence" (p. 224). Jensen (2009) agrees, noting that Jung wrote about high and low art since both offer insights into social, political, and economic forces shaping the psyche. "If interpretation evolves from context, as Jung certainly believed, then all context is important, including popular culture" (p. 2).

The four heroes prominent in popular culture from 2005 to 2013—Lisbeth, Bella, Katniss, and Tris—exhibit the ferocious, instinctual strength and deep loyalty to their "pack" reminiscent of the "wild woman archetype" described by Pinkola-Estes in *Women Who Run with the Wolves* (1992). They are forced to navigate treacherous worlds, whether it is a supernatural landscape as in Meyer's *Twilight* series (2005–2008), or a dystopian world featured in Collins' *Hunger Games* trilogy (2008–2010) or Roth's *Divergent* novels (2011–2013). Indeed, the intensity of their existence—the high stakes for which they risk their lives and the deep moral issues they must decide—may in part explain their appeal to readers of all ages. In these fantasy worlds, the emotional situations each protagonist faces are realistic, moving, and relatable. Such worlds may be no more fantastic than the mythic stories from remote religious and cultural traditions that fascinate Jungians beginning with Jung's *Symbols of Transformation*, first published in 1912, which marked his intellectual independence from Freud.[3] Stories that move readers need not be literally true to offer contemporary women and men imaginative possibilities in feeling, thought, and action beyond what is supposedly "natural" in any given sociocultural context. As Rowland (2002) argues, readers of fantasy literature "have deep responses to it without regarding it as objectively 'true'. Such stories have feminist value by attempting to show readers what it might be like to live outside traditional patriarchal religious structures and conventional gender roles" (p. 150).

## Archetypal feminism

Numerous scholars have pointed out that turning to Jung to expand our understanding of gender may be a deeply problematic start. "Androcentrism and misogyny distort Jung's discussions of women, the anima and animus, and the feminine," states Wehr, to such an extent that "analytical psychology, as a body of theory, does not contain an adequate definition of women and the feminine" (1987, p. 99). To Jung's credit, Wehr notes, "Jung's valuing of what he called the 'feminine' has pointed to what is lacking, undervalued, misunderstood, and feared in the Western world" (p. 125). Moreover, Jung's method of working with images—mapping one's inner world and seeing its correspondences to the outer world—has a great deal to offer both women and men (p. 126). Wehr insists on contextualizing women's experience, as do Lauter and Rupprecht (1985), who argue that archetypes manifest as "a tendency to form and re-form images in relation to certain kinds of repeated experience" and thus may "serve to clarify distinctively female concerns that have persisted throughout human history" (pp. 13–14). As Rowland points out (2002, p. 83), Lauter and Rupprecht hint at essentialism—what is a distinctively female concern?—yet I appreciate their close attention to the sometimes obscure, sometimes overlooked, lived experience of women. "The archetype becomes a feminist tool for re-examining and re-evaluating patterns in women's experience as they are revealed in psychotherapy, studies of the arts, myths, dreams, religion, sociology, and other disciplines" (p. 16). Simply put, these scholars point out that Jungians cannot be in dialogue with feminism, or any liberationist theory, so long as it rests on a universalizing ontology and epistemology in which the psychology of the individual is deprived of its social, historical, and political context—studied without full credit given to the impact of prevailing culture. The spirit of the times must discourse with the spirit of the depths. One without the other is incomplete.

## Kinds of power in fiction

The spirit of the times is offering us fierce young women with impressive kinds of power that are essential to the narrative drive of the stories. The central conflict hinges on their effectiveness, which includes skill, focus, and perseverance used on behalf of a well-articulated set of values. Entire books have been written about each one, so it is impossible to do full justice to the characters in one chapter.

## 104 Elizabeth Eowyn Nelson

Here I want to discuss two important characteristics shared by Bella, Katniss, Tris, and Lisbeth: they are armed and they consciously use their power to protect their pack—in all cases actually forming a pack out of disparate subgroups through the intensity of their devotion. Power serves a tribal goal rather than a self-aggrandizing one. They share one additional trait I want to consider: in part because they are women and in some instances physically diminutive "little girls," they are frequently underestimated by friend and foe alike. The friends learn quickly. The foes often die.

The range of specific skills each fierce young woman exercises is quite broad, already demonstrating a variegated idea of power. It is possible to array the stories on a spectrum from traditional heteronormative texts with more-or-less conventional gender roles to socially and culturally subversive depictions. I will first look at the extreme ends of the spectrum, Bella Swan from the *Twilight* saga and Lisbeth Salander from the *Millennium* trilogy, which commenced their American debut in the same year, 2005. Next I will examine the heroes from the two dystopian trilogies: *Hunger Games* (2008–2010) and *Divergent* (2011–2013). Finally, I will use the themes discovered in fiction to explore how female soldiers, through arduous preparation for armed combat, become protagonists of their own lives.

### Bella Swan: traditional is not trivial

From a feminist perspective, easily the most traditional story of the four is the *Twilight* saga (Meyer, 2005–2009), which is teen romance fiction with supernatural elements, set in a remote corner of the Olympic peninsula. Feminist scholars have soundly criticized the sagas for many reasons, including that 18-year-old Bella chooses marriage and motherhood over education and a career (Donnelly, 2001; Mann, 2009; Mukherjea, 2011). In a snarky yet accurate comment, NPR columnist Powers says its plot "could hardly be more conservative. From beginning to end, the supposed 'outsider' Bella is defined by her romantic yearnings—love for a man that's so strong she'll turn into a vampire to be with him" (2010, n.p.).

Though this journalist and many, many other readers find nothing to redeem Bella Swan as a role model, I will risk disagreement. Almost no one is what they appear to be in the *Twilight* saga, including Bella. It is a mistake to read her reductively. Yes, she is a vulnerable and loving young woman who remains a virgin until marriage and immediately gets pregnant, refuses to abort the child even when her life is seriously at risk, and, in fact, dies giving birth. (She comes back to life with a transfusion of vampire venom, becoming a poised, lethal predator.) So far, there is little for any stout-hearted feminist to admire. However, Bella shows impressive focus and determination in numerous situations, most dramatically in her desire to become vampire in spite of the active opposition of her boyfriend Edward and in her refusal to banish anyone she loves from her "tribe" even when pressured to do so. She develops over time and through adversity a surprising core of resilience. In fact, it is her particular skill that makes it possible for her new blended family to prevail in the final deadly battle of the saga.

Stephenie Meyer cleverly subverts the nineteenth-century novels she assiduously reads, admires, and even invokes in the *Twilight* saga by, among other things, continuing Bella's story beyond the wedding day. Marriage and motherhood end Bella's human life, but they accelerate her individuation. When Bella becomes one of the undead, her human "quirk"—an ability to shield her thoughts even from the extraordinary mind-reading capacity of Edward—is finally recognized and, through rigorous training, developed into a formidable power. Shachar (2011, p. 153) describes it as "essentially the power to 'extend' herself as a shield to protect her family," a role traditionally allowed to women as mothers, implying that Bella's new-found power is less impressive than a more aggressive, targeted, and presumably male or masculine form. True, Bella's power may be considered traditional but it is not trivial. She clearly imagines her shielding capacity as a potent offensive weapon, a javelin that she can hurl from her body and shape to her will. Second, when Bella measures her skill against an adversary with a similar ability, she describes her as "panicky and weak" and "no warrior" because it is "not her job to fight but to protect. There was no bloodlust in her. Raw as I was, I knew that if this were a fight between her and me, I would obliterate her" (Meyer, 2008, p. 693). Third, Bella can become an invulnerable shield only by learning to see, taste, and direct her rage, an emotion that patriarchal texts—from Greek myths to nineteenth-century novels—disallow to women or punish them for. Once she does feel her rage, Bella credits it with bringing "every aspect of my being into sharper focus" (p. 620). Last, and possibly most important, Bella keeps secret the full extent of her new-found skill. No one in the final battle of the *Twilight* saga, friend nor foe, realizes the size, strength, and precision of the energetic shield Bella can extrude. When Bella's entire way of life is at stake, she privately exults in her new power.

> My fury peaked … I could taste madness on my tongue—I felt it flow through me like a tidal wave of pure power … I threw the shield with all the force in my mind, flung it across the impossible expanse of the field—ten times my best distance—like a javelin… I could feel it flex like just another muscle, obedient to my will. I pushed it, shaped it to a long, pointed oval. Everything underneath the flexible iron shield was suddenly part of me— I could feel the life force of everything it covered like points of bright heat, dazzling sparks of light surrounding me … Barely a second had passed … Everything had changed absolutely, but no one had noticed the explosion except for me. (pp. 690–691)

Bella's own view of her power is critical: she is a warrior who understands bloodlust and intends to obliterate her foe to protect what she loves. She has shaped a natural gift into a potent weapon and exults in her triumph on the battlefield.

Bella ultimately comes into her own though a protracted struggle with her beloved and on behalf of what she loves, a wildly diverse family consisting of vampires, shape-shifters, half-breeds, and a couple of humans. Most importantly, this sphere still affords her the opportunity to become powerful, effective, and

## 106  Elizabeth Eowyn Nelson

self-confident. I propose that the supernatural elements of the saga may serve as metaphor for ill-fitting blended families. Perhaps the ultimate fantasy portrayed in the novels is not the "happily ever after" ending of a traditional romance, but that natural enemies can live together harmoniously. Considering the violent sectarian warfare around the globe, this is indeed a compensatory fiction for the twenty-first century.

### Lisbeth Salander: gender outlaw and lone wolf

The opposite end of the spectrum is the *Millennium* trilogy, Swedish mainstream novels translated into English and published the same moment as the *Twilight* saga, beginning with *The Girl with the Dragon Tattoo* (2005). It offers "a liberal fantasy of perfect justice" instead of "a conservative fantasy of romance" (Powers, 2010, n.p.) but it is no less a fantasy, which is part of the visceral appeal. Though the story's predators are not literally vampires they are far more horrifying because Lisbeth navigates a gritty, believable contemporary world in which powerful, wealthy men can and do successfully track, torture, and kill women.

Lisbeth Salander is a marvelous creation, as unnerving as she is alluring. The popularity of the novels has been attributed largely to readers' fascination with her (Hook, 2011; Steiner, 2011; Yingling, 2011; Rutledge, 2011), which includes the important fact that Larsson endows his female lead with qualities that might have passed unnoticed if she were male. As Yingling states, "a brilliant, monosyllabic, arrogant male computer hacker with little emotional expression who has a plan to put old-guard authority figures in their place is a familiar stereotype in fiction" (p. 196). But a female? No. That draws attention. Lisbeth illuminates "the fallacies involved in rigid gender roles" says Hook (pp. 52, 58), confronting us with this question: "Why are we so interested in limiting our range of behavior?"

Lisbeth defies conventional gender roles in many ways, most notably by possessing a pitiless, strategic intellect aided by photographic memory. She is a brilliant self-taught computer hacker, a respected member of an international elite group of hackers who know her by the pseudonym *Wasp*. This skill gives Lisbeth a predatory edge. She can, through downloading specialized software, watch the digital life of her prey. But who falls into the category "prey"? The short answer is anyone who annoys her, or appears to threaten her freedom or even question it, or who wants to get close. "Lisbeth often appears remote and self-contained, as if making her way through a world of obstacles rather than a world filled with people" (Yingling, 2011, p. 202). Lisbeth's quality of unrelatedness may be, for many, the most obvious way in which she challenges conventional gender expectations. Certainly Lisbeth would contradict the basic findings of Gilligan's research at Harvard, in which the individuation of young women emphasized affiliation and morality arose "from the experience of connection" (1982, p.160). As Gourguechon states, "we could almost say that [Lisbeth] fails to remember that she is connected to people, and has to work consciously to overcome the instinctive tendency to behave as if she is not" (2011, p. 88).

Lisbeth probably would find the heartbreak of Bella Swan wholly unimaginable, even repugnant. But it would be a mistake to confuse Lisbeth's limited sociality with a lack of eros. As a young girl, she risks her life to defend her mother Agneta, who is systematically brutalized by Lisbeth's father until Agneta suffers irreversible brain damage. As a young woman, Lisbeth becomes a tireless crusader against what she hates: the men like her father who prey on women with seeming impunity. Her father survives Lisbeth's attack and uses his old boy's network of venal men, which includes the corrupt psychotherapist Teleborian, to imprison his 13-year-old daughter in a psychiatric hospital. Strapped to a bed for more than a year, Lisbeth is well aware that her psychiatrist's gaze was sexual, not clinical, medical, or caring, and she is physically powerless to defeat him. So she resorts to the only weapon she can use: her mind. Already remote from the world by force of habit, Lisbeth willfully chooses to focus her attention on something else; that is, she intentionally uses dissociation as a defensive weapon to prevent a known enemy from penetrating her mind *while simultaneously recording every detail for future retribution.* Although Lisbeth remains incarcerated, the novel portrays her strategy as a triumph, one that is particularly unnerving to a corrupt psychiatrist whose primary offensive skill is mental assault.

Lisbeth's skill, like Bella Swan's, is the ability to create and deploy a mental shield. Surviving the incarceration at St. Stephen's is only one example of Lisbeth's impressive focus, determination, and willpower, qualities she shares with Bella. She is able to achieve the privacy often craved by adolescents even when deprived of her freedom. Thus I agree with Anderegg (2011) who argues that "she is the teenager we all thought we were but, because of her great gifts, she is able actually to defeat the authorities over and over (unlike ourselves, who eventually had to capitulate)" (p. 75). Her "great gifts" include a razor-sharp, pitiless mind, at once both logical and strategic. She nonchalantly hacks the computers of many people, including allies, yet targets her predation at "men who hate women," the original Swedish title of the first novel. When pressed, Lisbeth is also a physical threat, despite her diminutive size, in part because she coldly assesses this potential weakness in herself and does something about it. Through relentless effort—again exemplifying her focus and determination—Lisbeth becomes a skilled martial artist who earns the deep admiration of the man who trains her. As several characters in the story learn, it is best not to disturb, provoke, or annoy her.

If Lisbeth surprises some traditionalists through her dress, makeup, sexual appetite and preferences (she prefers both men and women, on her terms), she would very likely surprise Jung and some Jungians through the quality of her mind. As Wehr pointed out nearly 30 years ago, "one of the most wounding messages of patriarchy to women is that they do not think clearly" (1987, p. 120), which Jung's animus theory does nothing to dispel. In fact, the notion that a woman who thinks clearly does so because she has a well-integrated animus "colludes with a patriarchally encouraged tendency to see only the male as rational, logical, and dependable" (p. 122). I imagine Lisbeth would find this idea annoying. Then she would do something about it.

**108** Elizabeth Eowyn Nelson

## Katniss and Tris: rebel leaders with a cause

Less traditional than Bella, but not quite gender outlaws, the fierce young women in the *Hunger Games* and *Divergent* trilogies grow up in bleak, dystopian worlds that reflect the actual fears of political, economic, and environmental collapse among young people today. Shiffman (2014) described *The Hunger Games* as "the novel of their generation" because it "depicts adolescents rigorously trained by adults for desperate but meaningless life-or-death competitions. Its dark emptiness resonates with students' latent unease and dissatisfaction. ... They're driven by fear" (n.p.). The *Divergent* trilogy portrays an equally dark emptiness, not because children are forced to fight to the death for the amusement of the glittering inhabitants of the capitol, but because the population is segregated into strictly defined factions, none of which offers a whole life, only partial existence. Moreover, a political revolution is underway in which the pitiless leader of one faction deploys mind control technology among the members of another faction to create an army obedient to her will.

Katniss Everdeen, the protagonist of *The Hunger Games*, is forced to become the family's provider at a young age. She has no illusions about the political, economic, and spiritual oppression the inhabitants of District 12 face every day. To keep her family fed, she travels beyond the supposedly electrified fence (which no longer has any current, a sign of the community's endemic disrepair) and hunts game with her ally Gale, who also supports his impoverished family. Thus Katniss is portrayed as a natural predator—agile, strong, and highly skilled with a bow and arrow—for the purpose of survival not sport. Her pack is clearly her family, her friends, and the wider community of District 12—all the world she knows as the trilogy begins. Katniss' knowledge of the oppression deepens as the story progresses. She volunteers in place of her 12-year-old sister for the annual "Hunger Games," which pits a pair of children from each district against one another in a fight to the death. Groomed for success, which has less to do with physical survival in the arena and more to do with her entertainment value, Katniss sees widespread squalor, a grotesque contrast to the wealth of the capitol. In *The Hunger Games* trilogy, Collins has held up a mirror to the growing economic divide in contemporary America.

Although she may be focused, tough-minded, and driven, Katniss is neither unfeeling nor indifferent. "Katniss is allowed what we so seldom see in books or movies: the freedom to be a person first, and anything else, which may include her gender, second" (Skinner and McCord, 2012, p. 111). As "the girl on fire" and ultimately "the Mockingjay," she becomes the symbol of the rebellion, succeeds in uniting populations that the capitol was eager to keep divided. The overarching imperative to survive the bleak dystopian surround endows Katniss with the realistic, pitiless cast of mind, intense focus, and disciplined willpower reminiscent of Lisbeth Salander. Both fierce young women are strategic thinkers and relentless fighters, occasionally allied to the males in the stories but not passively awaiting rescue or direction from them.

Tris Prior, the protagonist of the *Divergent* trilogy, is an interesting blend of *The Hunger Games'* Katniss and *Twilight's* Bella. Her character arc is a journey from the self-sacrifice and social modesty once unambiguously proscribed for women toward the adept, aggressive, confident stance of a warrior. Tris is born into the Abnegation faction, the silent, grey-clothed group in this post-apocalyptic world that eschews sociopolitical gamesmanship and is devoted to service. When the moment arrives for Tris to choose her own faction—a ritual allowed all children verging on adulthood—she chooses Dauntless, the faction that prizes physical strength, courage, and audacity to the point of recklessness. Dauntless also are filled with an élan that is unmistakable and seductive. For Tris, awakening to her own daring is awakening to her original, authentic self, a move that also connects her more fully to her mother who was born into Dauntless and is a capable warrior in her own right. Though Tris is not associated with a particular weapon as is Katniss (bow and arrow), the trilogy dramatizes the development of her courage, stamina, and toughness, which is portrayed as both a mental and physical feat. Like Katniss, Tris is pivotal in uncovering the tyrannical political plot at the heart of the story and defeating its leader.

The broadly political implications of a personal choice for Tris, Katniss, and Bella is one of the subtle ways in which these fierce young women are painted in feminist hues, whether the authors intended this or not. Who and what they love are deeply interfused, the foundation for being-in-the-world that actively shapes their sphere of influence. In contemporary female-centered fiction, this sphere extends well beyond the home to include the pack they run with (and frequently lead), to borrow Pinkola-Estes' archetypal imagery. Lisbeth is the outlier, in part because she is deeply traumatized and understandably wary of relationship, but primarily because her sexual proclivities are never constrained by heteronormativity or monogamy, and least of all by the sociocultural institution of marriage. Yet Lisbeth's impact in the realistic world of corruption is as great as Katniss' or Tris' role in defeating tyranny. Lisbeth is not the visible symbol of rebellion Katniss is, but instead works behind the scenes with stealth, determination, and skill. Oddly, she shares this proclivity for stealth with Bella, whose predatory skill is consistently underestimated. The shield Bella can extrude and use as an offensive or defense weapon may be invisible to others—as Lisbeth's hacking is invisible to her prey— but it is not invisible to herself. Both young women know their own power and enjoy using it.

## Kinds of power in combat

Are the protagonists in contemporary novels reflected in contemporary life? Based on the evidence of American women in the military, the answer is yes. The female warrior is a potent activated archetype in fiction and reality. Before examining the war in Iraq and Afghanistan, it is important to note that the historical record is filled with examples of women in combat (Goldstein, 2001, p. 403). Though women always have been a tiny minority, clearly "they can fight; they can kill" but only after overcoming "stubborn resistance from men" or resorting to disguise (p. 127). Moreover, when the war is over, states have assiduously returned to "normal" by

**110** Elizabeth Eowyn Nelson

forgetting the women's contribution and reinforcing their "natural" domestic sphere (Goldstein, 2001; Miles and Cross, 2008[4]).

Jones (1997), who draws examples from history as well as myth and legend, argues that "women's martial history is much richer and deeper by far than is commonly understood in the West" (p. 249). In fact, there is

> no martial domain exclusive to either males or females. Both attacked enemy strongholds, defended castles, laid sieges, and led expeditionary forces. Both built military empires, dueled for honor with sword and pistol, and designed military strategy. Spying, terrorism, banditry and piracy, assassination, demolitions, aerial combat, guerilla warfare, hand-to-hand combat—all boast expert women practitioners. (p. 249)

Nonetheless, warfare continues to be almost entirely a male enterprise, even after three waves of feminism. Goldstein, who published his scrupulous research in 2001, states that "designated combat forces in the world's state armies today include several million soldiers (the exact number depending upon definitions of combat), of whom 99.9 percent are male" (p. 10). He offers several fascinating reasons for gendered warfare,[5] including the need to draw a "sharp dichotomy of hellish combat from normal life" in which "normal life becomes feminized and combat masculinized" (p. 301). This idea closely resembles the thesis of Miles and Cross: "The reality of women at war challenges a profoundly held fantasy in both women and men," they say, "that men make war to protect and defend women; that women are too weak to fight and unsuited to warfare; and that all women have to do in wartime is to keep the home fires burning" (2008, p. *xv*).

For some women, tending the home fires is not enough. They long to train for direct combat as legitimate members of a military unit: soldiers who happen to be female. As an archetypal psychologist, I envision this desire as the influence of their *daimon*. Such women are following the telos of their lives, in which individuation includes the full expression of martial spirit. The question is not why these fierce young women want to fight, but why shouldn't they? As liberal feminist, I uphold their right to individuate through military experience, eschewing the temptation to judge them as "animus possessed" due to some congealed notion of gender that assumes that a martial daimon is a masculine daimon, unsuited to women. In fact, I applaud their willingness to subvert pre-scripted roles and become the central character in their own life story. Moreover, I recognize that their battlefield is not limited to direct ground combat in war; it also is a symbolic battlefield at the heart of society and culture. As Jones (1997) puts it, women "are often believed to have no biological connection and therefore no deep understanding of the warrior tradition," which is "the baseline of the rules played by state leaders." Without this, "men and women will never reach a common consciousness of their equality as humans until both accept that women have a claim on the title 'Warrior'" (p. *xii*).

There is one obvious difference between fiction and reality. None of the works depict state-sponsored combat, though the *Twilight* saga, the *Hunger Games* trilogy,

Fierce young women **111**

and the *Divergent* trilogy do portray something approximating guerrilla warfare. When women "have participated in combat during guerrilla wars," says Goldstein (2001), "they have done so with good results. They have added to the military strength of their units, and sometimes fought with greater skill and bravery than their male comrades" (p. 83). The *Millennium* trilogy is probably best considered an espionage novel, as Lisbeth works covertly to track and destroy her enemies. Espionage, like guerrilla warfare, is another arena in which women have typically excelled, primarily because male combatants consistently underestimate their cunning, courage, and capacity for violence. Thus the novels are conservative in that martial women have, historically, played a more prominent role in guerrilla warfare and espionage than in conventional military units.

In the aftermath of the state-sponsored war in Vietnam, military recruitment of women began to rise under a combination of two pressures: feminist political activity, including the heated battle to pass the Equal Rights Amendment, and the end of mandatory military service for males. The ever-conservative armed forces was faced with a pressing need for bodies to fill roles and female bodies would do—as long as they were kept far from the battlefield. However, by the time the Gulf War commenced, combat zones could no longer be easily defined. "More than half the 375 US soldiers killed were support personnel, not 'combat' troops" (Goldstein, 2001, p. 95), an issue that continued in Iraq and Afghanistan, and a likely feature of future warfare.

Also an ongoing issue was what to do with the increasing number of women who enlisted in the military. There is little question that some saw the military as a way out of a life they were eager to discard and never imagined themselves in combat. Michele, one of the young women profiled in *Soldier Girls* (Thorpe, 2014) who joined the National Guard and ended up in Iraq, fits this description. Oddly, for a person who eschewed combat, Michele loved "the gunfighter phase" of her training; her gun became a constant companion. She "slept with her gun, did push-ups with it lying it across her hands so that her lips kissed it when she bent toward the ground … and spent hours and hours firing it" (p. 19). Other women in the National Guard, such as Debbie who "worked on howitzers, mortars, and the large guns in the rotating turrets of tanks" and "found the big guns romantic" (p. 35), were eager to deploy. Certainly a thorough depth psychological analysis must take into account the variety of women who joined the National Guard never expecting to depart for the Middle East. However, a better measure of the activation of the archetypal female warrior focuses on young women who intentionally sought direct combat—or as close to it as they could get.

In 2004, the Marine Corps introduced an experimental program that gave a few enlisted women this opportunity. Ironically, their deployment with all-male combat units occurred because the military was stymied by the deeply patriarchal Islamic culture. American men could not search Muslim women; even looking at them is considered culturally insensitive. As a result, 50 percent of the population was off-limits and potentially dangerous. The military began to understand they were fighting "half-blind. Only female soldiers would ever have access to women

## 112 Elizabeth Eowyn Nelson

in these societies—and these women often knew everything the men in their families and neighborhoods were up to" (Callahan, 2015, n.p.) The Lioness Program attached "female Marines to combat units to search Iraqi women and children who [might have been] trying to smuggle money or weapons through security checkpoints in Iraq" (Dunn, 2009, n.p.). Though manning checkpoints is not the same as joining a special ops team for a night-time assault, the women were serving "directly alongside combat units" with the result that it "inadvertently provided women with more equality on the frontlines" (n.p.). Nikole Estrada, describing her experience as a Lioness in 2008, says "this was our opportunity to serve a more direct role in this war ... a rare opportunity to work outside the wire, away from our desk jobs" (n.p.). It was also an enormous risk, since "news of female suicide bombers was everywhere" (n.p.).

The surprising success of the Lioness program led to the creation of Female Engagement Teams (FETs) in 2009, which deployed to Afghanistan "in small detachments with male infantry units in order to collect information from families and communicate with women without breaking cultural taboos" (Seck, 2015, n.p.). Given the innocuous name "Cultural Support Teams," the young women who signed up were nonetheless trained for lethal combat and worked with both conventional and special operations units. They share the traits depicted by fierce young women in popular fiction: they are vital, passionate, and intensely committed to a cause and eager to exercise their prowess, which includes physical strength, mental toughness, courage, and skill. Their self-confidence rises as they undergo arduous training and, over time, develop a strong affiliation with their pack.

This constellation of traits is readily apparent in *Ashley's War* (Lemmon, 2015), an in-depth profile of the women who first leaped at the chance to join Female Engagement Teams. Most of the applicants "had been itching all their lives to go to war—not as nurses or typists or machinists or any of the other jobs that gradually, over decades of struggle, came to admit women, but as special operations soldiers" (p. 25). One woman said, "all my life, all I ever wanted was to belong to a group of ass-kickers battling on the front lines" (p. 25). Another said "I know in my bones this is what I'm supposed to do. ... And these are the people I'm supposed to be working with" (p. 84). Most of the recruits were well aware that their predilection for combat was unusual. "Women found them weird for wanting to go to war. Men found them threatening" so they "forged a bond based on friendship and respect," a sisterhood "cemented by the fact that they had never before known people like themselves" (p. 145).

First Lieutenant Ashley White, for whom the book is named, was equally convinced that she had found a band of sisters and her purpose. One of her instructors said the petite soldier was "sweet enough to be a Disneyland greeter" (p. 125). Scottie Marks, a veteran Ranger who was in charge of CST training, quickly realized how intense, focused, and committed the women were and knew this group would eventually dispel the recalcitrant myths about female soldiers. Though Marks, too, recognized Ashley's sweetness and natural humility, he dubbed her "the megaton quiet blonde" for her exceptional physical stamina, skill, and mental

Fierce young women **113**

focus (p. 125). Lieutenant White was the first CST to earn the coveted Combat Action Badge. While attached to a Ranger unit, she was the first CST to die.

Some months earlier, during their training, Marks had warned the young women "at the end of the day, our world lives and dies by a gun" (Lemmon, 2015, p. 116). He made it clear that they were "not a part of the Ranger assault team" but would be placed "in situations where you will have to flip that switch from 'CST' to killer in a heartbeat. No matter how nice and quiet and even safe the moment feels, you are always in the middle of a fight" (p. 117). Two (male) Rangers died alongside Ashley, killed by an IED. At the funeral, the head of Army Special Operations Command Lt. General John Mulholland, said this:

> Make no mistake about it, these women are warriors; these are great women who have also provided enormous operational success to us on the battlefield by virtue of their being able to contact half of the population that we normally do not interact with. They absolutely have become part of our Special Operations family. They absolutely will write a new chapter in the role of women soldiers in the United States Army and our military and every single one of them have proven equal to the test. (p. 257)

The fierce young women serving in direct combat in the American military deserve far more attention from depth psychologists and feminists; this brief excursion barely scrapes the surface. At the end of the day, I find it deeply ironic that the misogyny of Iraqi and Afghanistani society helped to break down one more misogynist barrier in America, the military's opposition to officially trained and sanctioned women warriors. It is also ironic, but not unprecedented, for women to have the opportunity to serve in direct combat in part because of gendered assumptions that they are less aggressive or violent, with a "natural" aptitude for relationship. Future feminist psychological analyses of female warriors must be nuanced, paying close attention to the ways that organizations like the military reinforce and undermine gender conventions.

## Conclusion

*Women Who Run with the Wolves* (1992) rehabilitated the word "wild" that has typically been used pejoratively when describing a woman's behavior. "In its original sense," Pinkola-Estes says, wild "means to live a natural life, one in which the *criatura*, creature, has innate integrity and healthy boundaries ... a force that women [and men] cannot live without" (p. 8). The fierce young women discussed in this chapter dramatize the journey toward wildness—and the wildness of the journey toward becoming adult. Equally important, their lives are characterized by great vitality, passion, and role fluidity that often challenges congealed ideas about traditional femininity. In struggling to find what they belong to, they carry "stories and dreams and words and songs and signs and symbols" (p. 12) for millions of people around the world, young and old, male and female. Such stories, Pinkola-Estes says,

**114** Elizabeth Eowyn Nelson

"sharpen our sight so that we can pick out and pick up the path left by the wildish nature," reassuring us that "the path has not run out, but still leads women deeper, and more deeply still, into their own knowing" (p. 6). I hope more fierce young women move deeply into their own stories, their own knowing, and their own wildness, so that they develop and use their power on behalf of what they love.

## Notes

1 Postmodern feminists hotly debate both sex and gender as stable categories of meaning. See for example Butler, 1990/2006 and McKinnon, 1987.
2 As of January 2015, the value of the various franchises, which includes a combined revenue from books, film tickets, and DVD sales and rentals, are staggering. The *Twilight* franchise is valued at $5,736,100,000 and the *Hunger Games* franchise, $3,782,000,000 (www.statisticbrain.com). In August 2014, Amazon announced that the *Hunger Games* trilogy "had officially surpassed J.K. Rowling's *Harry Potter* as its best-selling book series of all time" (www.fool.com). The *Divergent* series, which includes three books and as yet only two films, occupied three of the top six spots in bestselling titles for 2014, grossing close to $5,000,000 (www.publishersweekly.com) and more than $600,000,000 in film and DVD revenue (www.the-numbers.com). When the third book in the series, *Allegiant*, was released, "it promptly demolished HarperCollins' first-day sales record by moving an incredible 455,000 copies" (www.fool.com). The *Millennium* trilogy by Steig Larsson sold 75 million books as of December 2013, and film revenues for the Swedish productions exceeded $2,000,000 (www.boxofficemojo.com). The American 2011 remake of the first film, directed by David Fincher, earned in excess of $320,000,000 (www.the-numbers.com).
3 Other notable texts include Baring and Cashford (1993), Campbell (1968, 1988), Downing (1981, 1988), Hall (1980), Hillman (1972), Emma Jung (1970), Perera (1981), von Franz (1970, 1974, 1996), and dozens of others.
4 Miles and Cross point out that "the decline of fighting woman has gone hand in hand with the progress of 'civilization,' which in every age has insisted on women's weakness and inferiority through a battery of religious, biological, social, and cultural constraints that have kept women out of public life and in the home" (2008, pp. 4–5).
5 I highly recommend Goldstein's (2001) work and his persuasive conclusions. "The omnipresent potential for war causes cultures to transform males, deliberately and systematically, by damaging their emotional capabilities (which biologically resemble those of females). Thus manhood, an artificial status that must be won individually, is typically constructed around a culture's need for brave and disciplined soldiers" (p. 283). Though there are "small, innate biological gender differences in average size, strength and roughness of play" that are used to physically prepares males for war, this would not be enough without the psychological preparation, the "cultural molding of tough, brave men, who feminize their enemies to encode domination" (p. 407).

## References

Anderegg, D. (2011). "What to say when the patient doesn't talk." In *The psychology of the girl with the dragon tattoo*. (67–79). Rosenberg, R. and O'Neill, S. (Eds.). Dallas, TX: BenBella Books.

Baring, A. and Cashford, J. (1993). *The myth of the goddess: Evolution of an image*. New York: Penguin.

Benioff, D., Weiss, D. B., Doelger, F., Caulfield, B., Strauss, C., and Martin, G. R. R. (Executive Producers) (2011–2015). *Game of thrones* [television series]. HBO.

Butler, J. (1990/2006). *Gender trouble: Feminism and the subversion of identity*, 2nd ed. New York: Routledge.

Callahan, M. (2015, April 19). Inside the military program that put women in combat. *New York Post*. http://nypost.com/2015/04/19/inside-the-military-program-that-put-women-in-combat/ Retrieved July 27, 2015.

Campbell, J. (1968). *The hero with a thousand faces*, 2nd edition. Bollingen Series XVII. Princeton, NJ: Princeton University Press. (Original work published in 1949).

Campbell, J. (1988). *The power of myth*. New York: Doubleday.

Collins, S. (2008). *The hunger games*. New York: Scholastic.

Collins, S. (2009). *Catching fire*. New York: Scholastic.

Collins, S. (2010). *The mockingjay*. New York: Scholastic.

Donnelly, A. (2011). Denial and salvation: The *Twilight* Saga and heteronormative patriarchy. In *Theorizing Twilight: Critical essays on what's at stake in a post-vampire world*. (178–193). Parke, M. and Wilson, N. (Eds.). Jefferson, NC: McFarland & Company.

Downing, C. (1981). *The goddess, mythological images of the feminine*. New York: Crossroad.

Downing, C. (1988). *Psyche's sisters: reimagining the meaning of sisterhood*. New York: Harper & Row.

Dunn, N. [Lance Cpl. ]. (2009, March 13). Lioness Program 'pride' of the Corps. http://www.usmc.mil/units/mciwest/29palms/Pages/LionessProgram%E2%80%98pride%E2%80%99oftheCorps.aspx Retrieved July 27, 2015.

Estrada, N. (2008, May 2). First person account of Iraq's Lioness Program. *The North Shore Journal*. http://northshorejournal.org/first-person-account-of-iraqs-lioness-program Retrieved July 22, 2015.

Frankel, R. (1998). *The adolescent psyche: Jungian and Winnicottian perspectives*. New York: Routledge.

Gilligan, C. (1982). *In a different voice: Psychological theory and women's development*. Cambridge, MA: Harvard University Press.

Goldstein, J. (2001). *War and gender: How gender shapes the war system and vice versa*. Cambridge: Cambridge University Press.

Gourguechon, P. (2011). "Mistrustful." In *The psychology of the girl with the dragon tattoo*. (81–98). Rosenberg, R. and O'Neill, S. (Eds.). Dallas, TX: BenBella Books.

Hall, N. (1980). *The moon and the virgin*. New York: Harper & Row Publishers.

Hancock, E. (1981). *Women's development in adult life*. (Doctoral dissertation, Harvard University).

Hancock, E. (1989). *The girl within*. New York: Fawcett Columbine.

Harris, A. (2004). "Introduction." In *All about the girl: Culture, power, and identity*. (xvii–xxv). Harris, A. (Ed.). New York: Routledge.

Hillman, J. (1972). *The myth of analysis: Three essays in archetypal psychology*. Evanston, IL: Northwestern University Press.

Hillman, J. (1983). *Archetypal psychology: A brief account*. Woodstock, CT: Spring Publications.

Hillman, J. (1995). *Kinds of power*. New York: Doubleday.

Hook, M. (2011). "Lisbeth Salander as a gender outlaw." In *The psychology of the girl with the dragon tattoo*. (47–64). Rosenberg, R. and O'Neill, S. (Eds.). Dallas, TX: BenBella Books.

Jensen, G. (2009). "Introduction to the puer/puella archetype." In *Perpetual adolescence: Jungian analyses of American media, literature, and popular culture*. (1–11). Albany, NY: SUNY.

Jones, D. (1997). *Women warriors, a history*. Washington, DC: Brassey's.

Jung, C. G. (1990). *Symbols of transformation*, 2nd edition. [The Collected Works of C. G. Jung, vol. 5]. Bollingen Series XX. Princeton, NJ: Princeton University Press. (Original work published 1912).

Jung, E. and von Franz, M.-L. (1970). *The grail legend*, 2nd edition. Dykes, A. (Ed.). Princeton, NJ: Princeton University Press.

Larsson, S. (2005). *The girl with the dragon tattoo*. New York: Alfred A. Knopf.

Larsson, S. (2006). *The girl who played with fire*. New York: Alfred A. Knopf.

Larsson, S. (2007). *The girl who kicked the hornet's nest*. New York: Alfred A. Knopf.

Lauter, E. and Rupprecht, C. S. (1985). *Feminist archetypal theory: interdisciplinary re-visions of Jungian thought*. Knoxville, TN: University of Tennessee Press.

Lemmon, G. (2015). *Ashley's war*. New York: HarperCollins.

Mallin, A. (2015, August 18). Inside ranger school: What the first female graduates had to beat. http://abcnews.go.com/US/inside-ranger-school-female-graduates-beat/story?id=33156246 Retrieved August 22, 2015.

Mann, B. (2009). Vampire love: The second sex negotiates the twenty-first century. In *Twilight and philosophy: Vampires, vegetarians, and the pursuit of immortality*. (131–145). Housel, R. and Wisnewski, J. J. (Eds.). Hoboken, NJ: John Wiley and Sons.

Martin, G. (1996). *A game of thrones*. New York: Bantam Books.

McKinnon, C. (1987). *Feminism unmodified: Discourses on life and law*. Cambridge, MA: Harvard University Press.

McRobbie, A. (2004). "Notes on postfeminism and popular culture: Bridget Jones and the new gender regime." In *All about the girl: Culture, power, and identity*. (3–14). Harris, A. (Ed.) New York: Routledge.

Meyer, S. (2005). *Twilight*. New York: Little, Brown.

Meyer, S. (2006). *New moon*. New York: Little, Brown.

Meyer, S. (2007). *Eclipse*. New York: Little, Brown.

Meyer, S. (2008). *Breaking dawn*. New York: Little, Brown.

Miles, R. and Cross, R. (2008). *Hell hath no fury: True profiles of women at war from antiquity to Iraq*. New York: Three Rivers Press.

Mukherjea, A. (2011). Team Bella: Fans navigating desire, security, and feminism. In *Theorizing Twilight: Critical essays on what's at stake in a post-vampire world*. (70–83). Parke, M. and Wilson, N. (Eds.). Jefferson, NC: McFarland & Company.

Nelson, E. (2012). *Psyche's knife: Archetypal explorations of love and power*. Williamette, IL: Chiron.

Perera, S. (1981). *Descent to the goddess: A way of initiation for women*. Toronto: Inner City Books.

Pinkola-Estes, C. (1992). Women who run with the wolves: Myths and stories of the wild woman archetype. New York: Ballantine Books.

Pipher, M. (1994). *Reviving Ophelia: Saving the selves of adolescent girls*. New York: Riverhead Books.

Powers, J. (2010, July 19). Two ladies: Are you Team Bella, or Team Lisbeth? National Public Radio. http://www.npr.org/templates/story/story.php?storyId=128518742 Retrieved March 10, 2015.

Roth, V. (2011). *Divergent*. New York: HarperCollins.

Roth, V. (2012). *Insurgent*. New York: HarperCollins.

Roth, V. (2013). *Allegiant*. New York: HarperCollins.

Rowland, S. (2002). *Jung, a feminist revision*. London: Routledge.

Rutledge, P. (2011). "Resilience with a dragon tattoo." In *The psychology of the girl with the dragon tattoo*. (213–231). Rosenberg, R. and O'Neill, S. (Eds.). Dallas, TX: BenBella Books.

Seck, H. (2015, August 5). Marine Corps revives Female Engagement Team mission. *Marine Corps Times*. http://www.marinecorpstimes.com/story/military/2015/08/05/marine-corps-revives-female-engagement-team-mission/30796519/ Retrieved August 7, 2015.

Shachar, H. (2011). A post-feminist romance: Love, gender, and intertextuality in Stephenie Meyer's *Saga*. In *Theorizing Twilight: Critical essays on what's at stake in a post-vampire world.* (147–161). Parke, M. and Wilson, N. (Eds.). Jefferson, NC: McFarland & Company.

Shiffman, M. (2014, November). Majoring in fear. *First Things.* http://www.firstthings.com/article/2014/11/majoring-in-fear Retrieved May 4, 2015.

Singer, T. and Kimbles, S. L. (2004). *The cultural complex: Contemporary Jungian perspectives on psyche and society.* New York: Routledge.

Skinner, M. and McCord, K. (2012). The Hunger Games: A conversation. In *Jung Journal: Culture and Psyche* 6:4 (106–113). DOI: 10.1525/jung.2012.6.4.106

Steiner, H. (2011). "If Lisbeth Salander were real." In *The psychology of the girl with the dragon tattoo.* (153–167). Rosenberg, R. and O'Neill, S. (Eds.). Dallas, TX: BenBella Books.

Thompson, M. (2015, August 20). America: Meet your first female Rangers. *Time.* http://time.com/4005578/female-army-rangers/ Retrieved August 25, 2015.

Thorpe, H. (2014). *Soldier girls: The battles of three women at home and at war.* New York, NY: Scribner.

Von Franz, M.-L. (1970). *An introduction to the psychology of fairy tales.* New York: Spring Publications.

Von Franz, M.-L. (1974). *Shadow and evil in fairy tales.* Zurich: Spring Publications.

Von Franz, M.-L. (1996). *The interpretation of fairy tales,* revised ed. Boston, MA: Shambhala. (Original work published 1970).

Wehr, D. (1987). *Jung and feminism: Liberating archetypes.* Boston, MA: Beacon Press.

Yingling, S. (2011). "The magnetic polarizing woman." In *The psychology of the girl with the dragon tattoo.* (191–210). Rosenberg, R. and O'Neill, S. (Eds.). Dallas, TX: BenBella Books.

# 9

# EXPLORATIONS IN THE POETICS OF THE FEMININE PRONOUN

*Leslie Gardner*

> ... *[stylistic technique] represents the sacrifice of the legislating subject itself ... the poetic movement unsettles the category of meaning*
> — Theodore Adorno (1992 p. 114)

What does depth psychology bring to rhetorical considerations of grammar? Looking into this question will bring us close to the underlying assumption of that question – that grammar makes a difference – and that depth psychology is engaged with pronominal issues as I am proposing here.

Jacqueline Rose alludes to issues around the idea of the unspeakable, which, she argues, might even become speakable. This is potentially achieved by the awareness and contemplation of the unconscious which depth psychology is wholly engaged with, making analytical psychology a crucial element in this consideration of gender.

'Unspeakable' is about being off the grid, not articulating in the dominant ways of the culture and so inexpressible, but what is unspeakable is also deep within us, unattainable by language or conceptual thought. This is the source/place of what critical feminist theorists like Alcena Davis Rogan call 'deviancy': perhaps the inevitable deviancy of feminism.

In effect, my inquiry points the way to a *topos* of deviancy, a *topos* of what Vico would perhaps call *vera narrativa* – 'truth speaking' with implied underlying assumptions of individuality/particularity and irrationality that join up in the universal by necessity. For him this was gestural, pre-conceptual, pre-cognitive communication. In light of Vico's remarks, we can see that several feminist writers explore linguistic levels of communication that even a radical feminist in her examinations of objectivity and materiality, Karen Barad, find acceptable. Her background in quantum physics makes her a nuanced commentator on such scientific matters as psychology. The visceral presence of the communicating subject factors in heavily in an enquiry

Explorations in the poetics of the feminine pronoun **119**

into the nature of gender. She acknowledges Judith Butler's contributions but moves on. The attention to *soma* in my argument may seem a truism but it is contentious especially in light of current transgender issues.

Barad begins with the importance of means of communicating, referring to Foucault, and picking up from Butler, but disputes the narrow confines of gender designation that she suspects Butler derives solely from the linguistic register Butler privileges. Barad argues that the materialist or bodily instrument required in order to produce talk or writing is constitutive of its significance and that it is at the core of the performative nature of the language Butler proposes. It is only on the grounds of materiality that Barad will acknowledge the viability of a linguistic discussion. Her theme is agential realism:

> Agential realism is an epistemological and ontological framework that extends ... its central concerns with the nature of materiality, [and] the relationship between the material and the discursive ... it entails a reformulation of both of its terms 'agency' and 'realism' and provides understanding of the role of human and nonhuman factors in production of knowledge ... moving beyond traditional realism vs social contructivism debates .... (Barad 1998 p. 89)

What Barad calls agential reality offers a new approach in yet familiar ways to consider the feminist issue of grammatical use of *she*. Barad and colleagues like Donna Haraway extend Butler's innovative application of the constitutive nature of the performative aspect of language to include what they call materialist elements, and I would add *somatic* materiality.

Carl Jung's dismissal of pronouns as arbitrary is answered by them even if not directly. The distinction is a particularisation of meaning, and it is demanded by an understanding of feminism and individuation I am proposing here.

Judith Butler's comments in her groundbreaking work *Gender Trouble* (1990) opened up the enquiry in new directions. Butler refers to earlier French writers like Simone de Beauvoir and Monique Wittig in her essays. I will take up discussion of Wittig as Butler did for this chapter because her extreme position is easier to dissect in order to highlight my theme.

## Unspeakable

Jung appreciated the many different modes of communication that derive from the unconscious and frequently worked out effective ways of engagement with inarticulate or illiterate communicants. He was willing to work with symbols his patients used that were so personalised it required all his skills of intuition and study in anthropology to get – what Christopher Bollas would call the *unthought known* in his work *The Shadow of the Object* (Bollas 1987).

Jung recounted the story to his biographer (Jaffé 1984) of what happened with a simple school teacher sent to him by a local doctor. She sidled up to him and

**120** Leslie Gardner

when nothing else worked to reach her, he sang her a lullaby; he had got it right, and intuited what she meant and what she needed to hear. He managed to assuage her insomnia. And in his word association reports, we often note his intuiting meanings from the least literate members, arriving at his interpretations by analysing associations or gestures or in other instances, their art work. From his days working with extreme personalities such as spiritualist mediums, and their often alien personalities and methods of communicating, he was certainly familiar with varieties of statements, articulated or not.

Women find modes of what becomes necessarily deviant communication in ways that Irigaray (Gray 2008), Barbara Cassin and Alcena Davis Rogan explore in their varied ways. I mentioned earlier Rogan's reference in science fiction to alien sexual practices which she uses as a heuristic device (Davis Rogan 2004) in her discussion of Monique Wittig's work. By analysing the futuristic society Wittig creates in her utopian novel, Rogan demonstrates the ripple effects of hierarchical dissolution Wittig outlines, or the disappearance – in another example – of the nuclear family with its dominant paternal structure.

For Barbara Cassin women's communication applies to universal contexts in what we might call archetypal ways or in the rhetorical language she uses, tropical. Later in this essay I will show how she highlights *sophistical* rhetoric as the prime effective prototype for what women's communications resort to when they are unheard or bypassed by listeners or readers. Creating exigency precisely where it may seem not to be applicable, for example in a discussion of ordinary talk about sexual power in Gorgias' *Encomium on Helen* in which the ancient Sophist recommends judgement of Helen be revised. Cassin sees this as an appropriate mode of analysis of women's dialectical talk.

And, naturally it is only when women are aware of being unheard or unnoticed that they resort to other means of transmitting messages.

Cassin and Wittig, and, by resorting to such heuristic as analysis of science fiction, Rogan too, find their means of saying the unspeakable by knowing how to allude to meaning in what is for women a topsy-turvy world. While Irigaray may recommend silence, in fact she finds a means of non-communication that is very loud. The absence of response, as in the Madonna's silence when her son is observed lecturing the sages in the temple at a very young age, yet speaks volumes (Irigaray 2010). All mothers will recognise this message of silent pride in their children's aptitudes.

This paper is about the nature of that *topos* as it is found in our everyday and professional writing. But the discussion will be limited by focusing on the pronoun *she* within a framework of depth psychology as epitomised in Jung's writings.

## Nominalism – conceptualism – realism

In a first move, on a grammatical level, I will take up the philosophical nominalist Nelson Goodman who suggests predication involves the interconnection of extrinsic and interior psyche, a weave that thereby implicates persona (the outward, social presentation of subjectivity).

Explorations in the poetics of the feminine pronoun **121**

Following Abélard, Jung and Ricoeur, I will turn to grammatical exposition to demonstrate the close interconnection of the concrete and the abstract (this is related to discussion of personal/impersonal and universal from earlier material also in *Psychological Types* (Jung 1989): 'Reference is itself a dialectical phenomenon to the extent that discourse refers to a reality, to the world, in sum to the extra-linguistic' (Ricoeur 1975 p. 75).

Discourse and language concern not only inter-personal relations but also intra-personal relations (with assumption of interaction of intra-being with another/oneself as an object of one's own contemplation). The personal pronoun *I* has no significance in itself but takes on meaning in referring to the speaker; and verb tenses – past and future – are anchored by reference to the present. *I* is a metaphor including grammatical functions as agent, but also description of a speaker but also it holds a place in the world. The 'present discourse itself qualifies itself temporally' in what Ricoeur (2003 p. 86) calls an auto-designative tactic. Adverbs and demonstratives too are connected to an instance of discourse (Benveniste 1971) and obtain meaning in that way (p. 77). An instance of discourse links us to the rhetorical work of the pronoun, and to its performative and social aspect.

Personality is implicated. *I* is no one other than the tangible speaker with all her inclinations, emotions, skin textures and economic status, etc. *I* accumulates significance from the speaker. *She* presents other given dilemmas explored further below. The *I* is always particularised; as Foucault says, we are all nominalists.

Jung applies a related nominalist notion to what he sees is Abélard's intellectual reconciliation to the dilemma of collectivity and individuality, which, however, as he complains, is not quite adequate for Jung. It is a move toward an important concept in Jungian psychology, the legitimacy of the symbol taken at manifest value; it is not always reduced to another meaning nor is it always an analogy.

## *I* and *she*; personal and collective unconscious

According to Jung's discussion in *Psychology of Types* Abélard proposes to accommodate the contraries between individual response to the broader category of genus and species. 'It is precisely because he considered none of the accepted standpoints right, but always sought to comprehend and conciliate the contrary view' (1989 para. 68) that draws Jung's admiration.

Abélard's conceptualism weds the concretizing inclination of the nominalist position to the realist's position, by stressing the act of generalising to a 'plurality of perceptions' that we might perform (Cocchiarella 1986).

For Jung Abélard's position is an intermediate one. Conceptualism is a cognitive function which apprehends perceived individual objects, classifies them into their genera and species by reason of their similarities, and thus reduces their absolute multiplicity to a relative unity.

> For anyone who is psychologically so constituted as to perceive chiefly the similarity of things, the inclusive concept is … given from the start; it forcibly

**122**  Leslie Gardner

> obtrudes itself with the undeniable actuality of sense-perception … but for
> one so … constituted as to perceive chiefly the diversity of things, their
> similarity is not clearly given; what he sees is their difference. (Jung 1960
> CW6 para. 70)

In rhetorical terms, medievalist topical logic has prevailed in Abélard's strategy. Cocchiarella's commentary on Abélard's conceptualism underscores the medieval philosopher's analysis and corroborates Jung's reading; both Cocchiarella and Jung's commentaries are based on the biography of Abélard by the French biographer, De Rémusat, so they start from same biographical base line.

Cocchiarella elucidates:

> Conceptualism [is] concerned with the notion of a mental construction …
> and with the construction of concepts … concepts are anything but objects.
> Conceptualism differs from nominalism insofar as it posits universals, namely,
> concepts, as the semantic grounds for the correct or incorrect application of
> predicate expressions … and it differs from logical realism, on the other hand,
> insofar as the universals it posits are not assumed to exist independently of the
> human capacity for thought and representation … concepts are rather cogni-
> tive capacities … Concepts, in other words, are inter-subjectively releasable
> cognitive abilities which may be exercised by different persons at the same
> time as well as by the same person at different times. (Cocchiarella 1986 p. 80)

Reading closely how Jung talks about archetypes which he often sees as mani-festations, this notion of Abélard's conceptualism is close to Jung's idea of archetype and helps us in a step toward the materialism of what grammar might be about, although not quite yet in terms of *soma* which is the feminist move, linked to the unconscious givens of woman-hood. In this case, syntactic rules are the materialist grounding of grammar.

For example, in his essay on archetypes in volume 9ii of his *Collected Works* (1960), Jung characterises meaning itself as an archetype. The intense unspoken and often visceral desire of wanting to find meaning is a *trope* generating cultural and social forms: the figure sitting alone in his study surrounded by papers and books, staring out the window in reverie. Similarly timeless and universal discussion about the active vs. the contemplative life propagates personality elucidated in *Psychologi-cal Types*. But, Jung thought, Abélard needed to take one more step toward Luther's realism in his analysis, but yet not go all the way to sensation – the particular woven in specific ways to the general, as to maintain individuality. (See more discussion of this in my *Rhetorical Investigations* (2010).)

## Exigency and feminism

Jung's attraction to what was Abélard's conceptualism is characterised by cognitive contexts and multi-perspectives and is deepened by the unspeakable that makes the

Explorations in the poetics of the feminine pronoun **123**

grammar of feminine discourse particularly transformative. Urgent action and speech in an extreme moment require appropriate language if the event is to be grasped effectively and if it is to be heard at all. Talking persuasively at a political rally is enabled by heightened or emotive talk; talking in that same way at a tea party may well reposition that tea party from social gathering to political space. Inventing appropriate and astute speech constitutes the moment and is enabled by participants who have an awareness of how contexts and perspectives make that moment. These components make up its exigency.

Medieval discussion about a concept such as *she* had derived from earlier ancient commentary on implied grammar, and predication. There is one classic and famous example of the negative aspect attributed to use of the pronoun *she* and the anomalies of the feminine designation; it is in the sophist Gorgias' work.

Pre-Socratic rhetorician, Gorgias argues that Helen's name is tainted and so is the *she* attached to her, used in referring to her purportedly venal acts. Her name therefore is smeared because it is female, and Cassin points out that Gorgias indicates this adds insult to injury for her, and by extension for all women. It is woman's behaviour. As a mythical figure, her name comes to correlate to its pronominal usage in ancient times and in all times thereafter. 'Helen' comes to mean then and now a woman who caused a war due to her venality.

Helen is a name but also correlative to general female designation as she was never a woman of flesh and blood; it is that altogether woman's name is smeared, tainted by association to her gender. Barbara Cassin points out Gorgias' salience in defending Helen, by picking up on how he extends the personal to collective (not a collection of individuals, but individual as mythic personality) – she is exonerated by the habitual activity of the mythic gods, and the power of sexual allure. Cassin points out his deftness in manipulating inference and emotion. Gorgias criticizes commentators who pilloried Helen as woman, subject to irrational emotion. She is not an individual in her story.

Cassin admires Gorgias' presentation of the pitfalls of nominalism in *Encomium to Helen* as a feminist discussion: does the similar naming solution Wittig uses solve her issues? In Gorgias' famous refutation of Helen's guilt – she was forced unknowingly either by the gods to take up a lover while she was married, and allow herself to be taken away – so how could she be blamed? Or else it was the power of *eros* that overwhelmed her. She was overcome by a passion for Paris. And here's where naming and smearing naming comes into it: Gorgias claims he pursues writing this *Encomium* to 'clear her name': 'the ill omen of her name, which has become a memorial of misfortunes'. This name has inferences to misfortune. Redolent with such primary or objective meanings, her name has been tainted as it is that all women are so smeared.

Cassin argues women communicate by deploying sophistic solutions, operating in a neo-pragmatic world of intentional signage and practical, knowing language – she too emphasises importance of the rhetorical canon of *invention* as primary – shaping what's to come in every statement of being. This is a heuristic that an analyst traces in working with patients daily. We note that Jung senses this in his

**124**  Leslie Gardner

interpretations in the word association tests, finally finding those tests inadequate for just the reason of some contextual blockage whether known or unknown.

This discussion of woman as women, individual as collective, species and genera, has been considered over the centuries, and most recently, themes and tropes developed by feminists in France in the early and late 1960s and through the 1980s and 1990s in the US and throughout Europe are at the core of the consideration. *She* is anathema to writers like Wittig because it implies servitude and sub-humanity, and yet *she* has become a cliché in academic writing when referring to the universal/impersonal position, substituting for *his*. But there is always the residue of the universal disdain in *she* which is hard to ignore. It is tainted by cultural attributes which infects the particular *she*.

## Problems of essentialism

In a sub-section of his essay on 'animus and anima' Jung comments dismissively that

> it seems to me that apart from the influence of woman there is also the man's own femininity to explain the feminine nature of the soul-complex. There is no question here of any linguistic 'accident' of the kind that makes the sun feminine in German and masculine in other languages. (Jung 1960 CW para. xx in 'relations between the ego and the unconscious' 1931)

He goes on to suggest that all that is rational and logical is typical of the masculine animus; i.e. when a woman is rational, she is actually suffused with that male quality, animus: it's not ever a feminine attribute.

A possible response to Jung would be that there is a question around the accidental nature of *she*. However, Jung seems to invoke a notion of a universal essence of femininity that is itself highly problematic.

By not recognising the problematic of that pronoun, Jung misses its contentious nature. As mentioned, grammar becomes a site of exigency in a rhetorical investigation of contexts and personhood. The feminine nature of a man or of a woman is called into question immediately in this inquiry, and transmuted into a matter of register, and of associations and contexts in conceptual ways.

'Essentialism' (i.e. 'the feminine complex' in Jungian parlance is a phrase indicating the essential quality of the female) has strategic purpose. This is therefore not a move to dismiss but rather to propose its appropriate aspect. As Spivak suggests, we can appeal to the rhetorical concept of what she calls 'strategic essentialism': 'The strategic use of an essence as a mobilizing slogan, or master-word like woman or worker or the name of a nation, is a lasting strategy' (Spivak 1993 p. 206). Presenting itself as essential the slogan speaks to the concrete moment in its place and for a purpose.

Essentialism comes paradoxically to be a contingent concept, haunted by what depth psychologists will call pre-consciousness, or pre-verbal unspeakables. Subjectivity is both particular and universal and it is participant in collectivity by way of the unconscious – necessarily imagined to be universal (without boundary or limit).

## Grammar and exigency

To frame the problem more closely in grammatical terms in this section, I will look at Monique Wittig, Eugene Benveniste, and Paul Ricoeur's work. These writers delve into the psychological and metaphorical contexts of pronouns, *she* and *I*. Wittig discusses the appeal of using *elles* (this word form does not exist in English) in her piece 'The Mark of Gender' (1985); it is the feminisation of *they* in the French language which argument of hers I will not tackle here: except to say that it is a solution for her in referring to a group of females that de-essentialises identity yet maintains a distinction, its dialectic strategy.

Weaving our way through these writers' works suggests other ways that elucidate what Jung called the collective unconscious which incorporates primal drives and significance along with potential for transformation. This discussion is part of a larger project to incorporate Jung's theories into the pragmatist fold.

As Cornell argues, the 'recollective imagination', her semiotic-driven concept (Cornell 1993 chapter 2) in which the imagination is utterly transformative but also has a role in extrinsic instrumental practice, conforming to conventional parameters. The recollective imagination offers us a way to think on how a female individual can participate in deviant ways outside the given parameters of operation within familiar contexts. The recollective or also, we might say, the transformative imagination enables participation in the collective as individuated subject/agent by re-engaging outside society, not using tools and modes of existent reality; we operate in an 'as if' world that Jung might well recommend.

Looking at Jung's ideas in this way adjusts the prevailing opinion that Jung's (or any psychologist's for that matter) healing methods recommend adaptive strategies solely for living in a reactionary society. The balance is actually the other way round since the concept of individuation in the case of Jung's work suggests moving toward authentic settlement with personality. Deviancy proposes a satisfactory strategic path for a woman, therefore, because she must inevitably be at odds with society in order to maintain personal subjective cohesiveness and integrity. I believe Jung's strategies accommodate this solution. He too struggles with essentialist language as we note in his willingness to shift perspectives and promote transformation to achieve his goals.

The way deviant signifies here, as manoeuvre, is also paradoxically, congruent with Wittig's argument. However, she rejects the idea that there is accidental use of *she*: i.e. it is not ever indifferent, neutral or arbitrary reference. Both these points are integral to what she claims is the mark of gender: '… grammarians,' Wittig complains, 'think of these marks as a relation of function only and not one of transformation' (Wittig 1985 p. 18).


## Transformation

Here is a further stage in my discussion: the pronoun *she* is the site of what can be a profound instance of metamorphosis. *She* and its uses goes deep into a woman's

**126** Leslie Gardner

heart and soul – how she relates to herself and to others, how she participates in her world, and in her culture (as culture is a sub-set of the world). Knowing how the word *she* is defined in all its epistemological and ontological ways, as contingent and transformative re-shapes cultural functioning and a way of being in the world.

Rogan proposes that women are able to communicate at last within contexts of a utopian future in such works as Ursula Le Guin's novels, and in Wittig's futuristic novel *Les Guerrerios* (Davis Rogan 2004). The dilemmas of using recollective imagination which I explain as a kind of conditional and contingent replay of the future-as-present are clear in the tangle Wittig gets herself into despite the value of her work in signposting the problematic of the grammar of self-referral.

In Wittig's novel, Amazons of the future constitute a female society of lovers (male and female) rather than Oedipal nuclear families of married women. Power relations are horizontal. The futuristic, utopian genre, Rogan argues, allows display of a natural, 'generic capacity to configure cognition as estrangement' (Davis Rogan 2004 p. 65); women's dilemmas speak a language of oppression galvanized into play in this future society. In appreciating contexts of language, the 'as if' interplays with what reality is (there is no escaping the conditional especially for any human being, after all); reality is an interpretation by the populace who have a certain future in mind.

The cognitive manoeuvre of a remembered conditional future that is discovered in the past – i.e. a kind of remembering of the future – offers a configuration of thought which licenses the grammar of reference to the feminine explored in this chapter. The female is conceived as liberated from present oppression in a way formulated over against past repressions and distortions (Cornell 1993).

The word *she* is the mark of a slave for Wittig and, for her, the word cannot be used comfortably. Wittig famously and paradoxically ended a talk concluding she was not a woman. That word woman, she notes, is a demoralised, fetishist word aimed at oppressing a set of people with no phallic appendages. Language universally serves male culture she contended (using herself language which she brands as uncommunicative for a woman!). The use of gender markers for inanimate objects irked her as well by their deep effect on language in its perpetual and damaging insistence on marking erroneous gender distinction.

Wittig feels safer with *I* not only because mostly she thinks she knows who that refers to, but also she supposes that it absorbs a universal attitude: everyone is *I*. (Inevitably, this *I* must include male bodies too, when referring to them.) But we would say to Wittig with knowledge of the unconscious and unknown thought abiding there, that even *I* has its problematic in her terms too, and Ricoeur points out the problem in metaphoric terms, and reveals the incommensurability of this argument.

While *she* is a hostile pronoun given its anomalous inferences for Wittig, and thereby closes down discussion for her, *I*, she finds, is not so hostile. It is an instance of discourse (to use Benveniste's phrase), she contends, that is constituted in the moment, and applies mostly securely to the speaker. This is because (for her) *I* seems to be materially present before the listener; she misses out noting the insecurity of *I* being securely applied to a writer. While Wittig has highlighted the emotive issue

Explorations in the poetics of the feminine pronoun **127**

effectively, we find her self-defeating discussion is countered albeit sympathetically by Butler, which we will come to later when she suggests a way to move on, but also decidedly by male linguistic philosophers.

Benveniste points out that *you* (like *I*) is such another 'instance of discourse' (not of language; to clarify: discourse for my purposes, and as I believe he means it, is a syntactical analysis rather than the contextual, cultural meaning of the word language). The inevitable contingency and particularity of *I* opens up identification in a way that Wittig knows *she* cannot do although only in a future society, where and when Wittig hopes it could. The significance of *she* is rife with oppressive meanings for her and potentially eliminated in socially alien futuristic contexts.

Paradoxically, Wittig might say, *I* is nominative pure and clean. This is contested by many, but especially by Christopher Bollas (2015) who talks about the interior dialogue of *I* and *me* in people suffering from multiple personalities. He further contends that such dialogue is a characteristic and inherent part of subjectivity, and it is especially anomalous turf for the schizophrenic. While this point about a dysfunction of rhetoric, as it might be framed (Vico explained it in terms of a rhetorical framework in his discussion of an incapacity of communication he witnessed when he observed a man unable to refer to himself in first person) is outside the scope of this discussion yet it points to the problem with Wittig's point.

To circumvent the difficulties of identification, Wittig's strategy in her novels is that there is no group designation; names are listed each and every time – names are taken/given thereby controlling and fixing her people as nominative entities. She hopes there is thereby no referencing.

The pronoun is a mode of relationship by analogy between pronoun and its referent. The pronoun attracts significance that may be unintended, as its discursive use has its own rules. These are additional to cultural contexts it attracts. It is in the instrumental dimension of the pronouns, especially *I*, that its subjectivity is revealed, and the transcendence of symbolic analogy evolves into actualisation. This is what worried Wittig of course: she hoped that a nominalist position may do away with such inferences; and indeed in electing to eschew specific pronouns, Wittig also tries to control inferences/analogies but finally without success. As in her novel eschewing *she*, the repetitions of names when pronouns would do, or the use of One for any moment when a nominative position other than the *I* is required is tedious which is not a philosophical problem but a stylistic one.

In a related but perhaps more trenchant comment, we find Spivak alluding to this issue in her discussion of the subaltern: 'naming functions as a form of warfare in taking capacity to rename themselves' (1981 p. 383). It is this aggressive, pre-emptive controlling stance that Wittig hopes the future will afford her and other women as she imagines it might be. The distinction of sexual preference is essential for her too – the lesbian woman is the real woman. That is the *she* if there is to be one – deviant and named.

To understand language's nature and its integral relationship to discourse, depth psychology has answers which respond to the futility of Wittig's solutions and still

**128** Leslie Gardner

maintain feminist clarity. The first stage of this rhetorical move is to recognise the strategic component of language and in her critique of Wittig Judith Butler makes this move in *The Psychic Life of Power* (1997) as well as in other works.

The ground may be the person which Judith Butler nevertheless has trouble identifying with as subject since, as Wittig also proposes, that subject is exigent; the subject is *all* platform of meaning (Butler 1997), all is paradoxically concrete and symbolic at the same time.

It is not that the subject is only a social construct for Butler. Naturally it is that too, but its social construction can be manipulated if the subject is discerning enough to engage in *astute* use of that powerful canon of rhetorical engagement: invention – a careful assessment of arguable action and description with intent (Crowley 1990).

Around the subject, which is this exigent entity of contestation, communication is generated. Its appearance is all in its actualisation. Butler proposes, however, as I would suggest we might say Jung does, that there is a pre-utterance, pre-subject place (to use the prevalent metaphor for primordial or pre-cognitive state). She does not think that Benveniste's pronouncements about the subject's viability in the instance of discourse are the final attribute, or that they are enough.

Butler returns to the notion of the pre-utterance, the pre-actualisation place, a metaphoric construct, a 'fabulation', she says. We might say that the unspeakable – which according to our consigning the subject to exigent appearance is not detectable until a subject communicates – therefore is not there. And such is the pervasiveness of male culture and male discourse and language, that Wittig has even eschewed the unconscious. If unidentifiable subjects are consigned to being unheard, or unheeded, or undetectable, there is no *I* or *you* until a moment of discourse. Certainly there is never a *she*.

But Butler moves on from this point because she commits to a belief in the unconscious. Citing both Hayden White and Jacqueline Rose, she first establishes that there is a trope of the unspeakable the unconscious that has its history as a part of discourse (where she says anyway the nomenclature subject belongs anyway – it has its reality as a symbolic place of communication without which humans could not be human). And, then, citing Jacqueline Rose, Butler proposes that the unspeakable underlay of discourse, which cannot by definition represent or say what this unidentifiable being communicates (and therefore is not), is a twisted utterance, already redolent of failures of communication – and it is the stuff of psychoanalysis.

The word *I* is an instance of discourse and suggests that it is identified with the act or description itself (we may note this distinction clearly when it is called into question as when, in internet exchanges, a message is bracketed by the server as possibly originating from a digital communicator who refers to themselves as *I* – to paraphrase the rubric).

> But this condition is not given in the meaning of the verb, it is the 'subjectivity' of discourse which makes it possible. (Benveniste 1971 p. 230)

It is in the establishment of linguistic contexts that communication is enabled: language is driven by syntactic precepts (discourse).

Ricoeur extends this notion to explore the metaphoric composition of *I* (and by application, perhaps, *she*). Predication is inevitably contingent, anchored as it is in the speaker's personality – reality is inflected by that significance. *I* has meaning by its predication too; it too takes on implicated meaning by reference to the speaker or writer with the caveats mentioned already. Why cannot use of *she* apply here too?

Ricoeur's discussion of pronouns in 'The Rule of Metaphor' moves on from Benveniste, and demonstrates the close interconnection between the concrete and the abstract. In his broad definition of metaphor, Ricoeur includes juxtaposition as a way of metaphoric sequence (or what we might call parataxis, a favourite technique of Jung's who often lists qualities as amplifications to expand meaning, and sometimes paradoxical meaning).

Just as reality implies reference to the extra-linguistic, so it also refers to its speakers by means of procedures that belong to language. Discourse constructions overtake language or, you might say, language is driven by discourse: the concrete is driven by the abstract. *I* has no significance in itself and only takes on meaning in referring to the speaker and its predicates. Temporally, for example, references are anchored to the position of the *I* – the 'instance of discourse'; significance is accumulated from the speaker. Seeing that the unknown thoughts or the unspeakables apply both to *I* and to *she*, the field is levelled for pronominal reference altogether.

Further, it is useful to the discussion here to note the core facility of language that derives from inference and which is the next step: actualisation which Benveniste refers to, which deepens the pronoun. Butler's performative argument constitutes *she* in this way as a possibly generative, potentially transformative pronoun.

To reiterate Jung's position as set out earlier, similarities on the one hand lead to abstractions of traits that could be isolated among features of a group; but also parallel morphologies had similar trajectories, and that is analogy (Cornell 1993). Statistically and also sometimes biologically instilled inferences develop based on observation of repeated similarities, and accommodates contexts to make a complex weave of association. It is at the level of inference that pronouns become sites of contestation for feminists insisting on *she*.

Identified in all sorts of culturally marked ways, Western male/female dichotomous culture inculcates adhesive associations to a discrete entity called female or woman. This is what Wittig despises and seeks to avoid. But there is also an equivalency of *she* to certain biological, somatic, deeply-felt inferences, givens we might say: breasts exuding nurturance for the baby who had been naturally drawn to her body in a way that a male body would not draw the infant seeking nurturance.

Moving on to the level of sign-inference, by applying the word *she* to a specific, named individual, a tactic for inquiry opens up: the dilemma of whether the pronoun leads directly to its referent, enabling us to focus on making a problem of the identity of Jane – a female name appended to a person who is however anatomically identified as male. The *she* is muddled.

**130** Leslie Gardner

Posed this way, the discussion moves us to the universal. It enables us to discuss the difficulties of feminine life without delving into the specific nominalist – that specific is actually arbitrary in the end. Jung moves to conceptualism away from nominalism and by implication, the pronoun gains a universal meaning. He espouses the paradoxical vitality of the symbol as a concrete and material form of abstraction. Wittig chose to eschew the feminine pronoun for its universal, contextual associations, and to circumvent problems by naming individuals. Dilemmas ensue as I have been demonstrating from that position as well because of the deep unspeakable unknown thought.

Similarities on the one hand lead to abstractions of traits that can be isolated among features in a group; but also parallel morphologies are noted from data based on similar trajectories, and that is the objective 'universal' that her name has become in the panoply of the impersonal gods and their interactions with individuals.

The nature of the subjectivity presented here is the capacity of the speaker to position themselves as subject:

> [it is as] the psychic unity that transcends the totality of the actual experience it assembles and that makes the permanence of the consciousness
> … this is the foundation of 'subjectivity' which is determined by the linguistic status of 'person'. (Benveniste 1971 p 228)

To conclude with a few lines from Bollas's *The Shadow of the Object* (1987):

> In the beginning may be the word, but there is also the wordless. The mother-infant dialogue is more an operational and less a representational form of knowledge …. There is in each of us a fundamental split between what we think we know and what we know but may never be able to think … a generative respect towards every representation in thought of the origins of the true self … enables us to face that knowledge we possess but cannot think …. In thinking the unthought known we ponder not simply the kernel of our true self, but elements of our forebears. (p. 283)

## References

Adorno, T. 1992 *Notes to Literature* Vol. 2 New York: Columbia University Press

Barad, Karen 1998 'Getting Real: Technoscientific Practices and the Materialisation of Reality' *Differences: A Journal of Feminist Cultural Studies* Vol. 10 no. 2 pp. 87–128

Barad, Karen 2003 'Posthumanist Performativity: Toward an Understanding of How Matter Comes to Matter' *Signs: Journal of Women in Culture and Society* Vol. 28 no. 3 pp. 801–31

Benveniste, Emile 1971 *Problems in General Linguistics*, trans. Mary Elizabeth Meek Florida: University of Miami Press

Bollas, Christopher 1987 *The Shadow of the Object* London: Free Association Press

Bollas, Christopher 2015 *When the Sun Bursts* New Haven: Yale University Press

Butler, Judith 1990 *Gender Trouble* New York: Routledge

Butler, Judith 1997 *The Psychic Life of Power: Theories in Subjection* Redwood City: Stanford University Press

Cassin, Barbara 2014 *Sophistical Practice: Toward a Consistent Relativism* New York: Fordham University Press

Cocchiarella, Nino B. 1986 'Conceptualism, ramified logic, and nominalised predicates' *Topoi* Vol. 5 pp. 75–87

Cornell, Drucilla 1993 *Transformations: Recollective Imagination and Sexual Difference* New York: Routledge

Crowley, Sharon 1990 *Methodical Memory* Carbondale: Southern Illinois University Press

Davis Rogan, Alcena 2004 'Alien sex acts in feminist science fiction: heuristic models for thinking of a feminist future of desire' *PMLA* Vol. 119 no. 3 pp. 442–56

Gardner, Leslie 2010 *Rhetorical Investigations* London: Routledge

Gorgias 'The Encomium of Helen' 1999 trans. from Greek Brian R. Donovan, downloaded 3 May 2014 http://www.classicpersuasion.org/pw/gorgias/helendonovan.htm

Gray, Frances 2008 *Jung, Irigaray, Individuation: Philosophy, Analytical Psychology and the Question of the Feminine* London: Routledge

Irigaray, Luce 2010 *Il Mistero di Maria* Rome: Paoline Editoriale Libri

Jaffé, Aniella 1984 *Jung's Last Years* New Orleans: Spring Publications

Jung, Carl Gustav 1960 *The Collected Works* ed. Sir Herbert Read, RFC Hull London: Routledge Kegan Paul, esp. Vol. 6 and Vol. 9ii

Jung, Carl Gustav 1989 *Psychological Types* CW 8 London: Routledge

Ricoeur, Paul 1975–1988 *Time and Narrative* (Vol. 1–3) trans. Kathleen McLaughlin and David Pellauer Chicago: University of Chicago Press

Ricoeur, Paul 2003 *The Rule of Metaphor* London: Routledge

Rose, Jacqueline 2006 *Sexuality in the Field of Vision* London: Verso

Spivak, Gayatri 1993 'In a word' Interview in *Outside the Teaching Machine* London: Routledge

Spivak, Gayatri 1981 'Writing and sexual difference' *Critical Inquiry* Vol. 8, no. 2, pp. 381–402

Vico, Giambattista 2011 *On the Most Ancient Wisdom of the Italians* New Haven: Yale University Press

Wittig, Monique 1985 'The Mark of Gender' *Feminist Issues* Vol. 5 pp. 3–12

# APPENDIX

## Voices from the IAJS forum
## October – December 2013

Below, you will find comments, reflections and responses made by various contributors to the IAJS forum seminar held on Feminism in Jungian Studies between October and December in 2013. The voices are clearly from different places and contexts and what they say expresses the flourishing and diverse opinion we find in Jungian and post-Jungian studies around the topic of women and the feminine.

Ginette Paris

Title: Ideas a feminist should dare to leave behind

On top of my list are the ideas about *the* animus and *the* anima, *the* feminine principle and *the* masculine principle. I am bored out of my mind with these abstractions, for two reasons.

The first one is therapeutic evidence that Jung himself would agree with: a crucial aspect of any relationship is the unknown. For evolution to take place, one must cultivate a watchful avoidance of labelling, of jargon, of all theories that have hardened like stale bread. Let's unlearn about animus/anima for a while to refresh our perceptions.

The second reason is a feminist argument. The animus/anima theory was useful for as long as feminist writers (such as Susan Rowland, Lynn Cowan, Pat Berry, and many others) regularly reminded us that theorizing about *the feminine* and *the masculine*, under cover of the anima/animus theory, remains a contribution to an evolving mythology. It never was, and fortunately will never be, a theory to be 'believed in', as one *believes* in the effect of chlorine on bacteria.

The animus/anima theory originally helped psychology move away from gender stereotyping, but it also had adverse results. Many an assertive woman knows what it is to be slapped down as 'animus ridden' while their men, enthralled with their creative anima, left them to fight with the reality principle (matter, money, kids) all the while not getting half the money or the glory.

The animus/anima theory gave way to the neuroscientific notion of brain lateralization (animus bits to the left, anima bits to the right). It comes with the reminder that mental activity is seldom situated on one side only, and the demonstration of how the two sides, the analytical and the intuitive, constantly intermingle.

Although I am grateful for neuroscience's demonstration that Jung wasn't far from guessing the scientific truth about our brains, I am as weary of neuroscientists who try to prove themselves as amateur-philosophers, as I am weary of Jungians who use pseudo scientific notions such as animus/anima. What critics of the neuroscience craze have called neo-bumpology (the claim that consciousness can be located in the brain), neuroredundancy (telling us that if you abuse your child, he/she will have cognitive/affective dysfunctions!) and neurotautology (the 'non-explanation explanation of everything') feels to me like the exact mirror of my weariness about Jungians who *believe* in the mythology of individuation, higher self, animus/anima … as if these notions were equivalent to scientific concepts. I feel like asking: what is wrong with depth psychology being a wonderful narrative (with Jung as our Homer) to imagine the Odyssey of Individuation?

Abandoning the notions of animus/anima does not mean that the basic tension between these two poles cease to exist, but rather that de-genderizing, an intellectual project of our time, demands that we renew the metaphors behind the notions. Using the feminine as symbol of anima and the masculine as symbol of animus does not work anymore, for sociological, historical reasons.

In my classes on mythology, we discuss a whole repertoire of symbols of tensions between opposites: Dionysos/Apollo, Hestia/Hermes, Aphrodite/Ares, Aphrodite/Athena, Zeus/Hermes … but it becomes a soliloquy when the interlocutor is not versed in Greek mythology. Millions of people know more about Star Trek mythology than about Greek mythology, and the animus/anima duo of Spock/Captain Kirk is a great metaphor. Same with Holmes/Watson. And let's not forget some telling gender reversals (i.e. agent Scully/agent Mulder, and many recent others) that deconstruct gender typologies. Cinematographic mythology is great for discovering where we agree and where we don't. I agree with the anima gentleness of the blue humanoids of Avatar, but I am sorry the evil tree killers diabolize bulldozers, which are, for me (it's a personal thing …) wonderful symbols of strength, efficiency and creative power. I expect another story coming out in a cinema near me, where bulldozers, chainsaws and backhoes will be used to plant trees instead of uproot them and will value the strength of bulldozers. That kind of playing with symbols is crucial to keep our mythology fresh and moving. It also makes for a good narrative.

★★★

Nancy Krieger

I'd like to attempt an analysis of a hypothetical case based on the violence in the article you sent around. It is hypothetical, so can be twisted into whatever fits what I am proposing. It is grossly oversimplified, lacking the richness of an actual case.

**134** Feminist Views from Somewhere

I am proposing that this aggression against women could be an acting-out of the aggression felt during the constellation of the negative mother complex. The infant needs aggression to attract attention to get people to supply what it needs for survival. According to various theories (Fordham, Winnicott and others), in the best of cases the infant introjects the good mother, learning to control the anger and wait until the mother (or anyone serving that role) comes and satisfies whatever need is causing the problem.

In less than optimal cases, this anger is then turned against the caregiver who did not come in time, is repressed, but not completely forgotten, implicit memories of the pain are kept.

Years later when something touches on that same anger/frustation the man (or woman) felt as a child, the rage from all of those past experiences now overwhelms the person, but it is experienced no longer in the body of an infant, but in the body with the strength of a grown man (or woman). He (or she) reacts by attacking the carrier of the mother projection.

A classical example of the constellation of an autonomous complex in Jungian theory and certainly over simplified. One we all know, but I think it should be mentioned. (November 29, 2013)

Referring back to the mails I submitted earlier in this discussion about naming: I think we need to consider thinking of the complex in more *specific*, descriptive terms, such as 'abandonment complex' or 'controlling complex' rather than 'mother complex' or 'father complex' *which makes assumptions about what that means*, i.e. leaving unsaid what is actually meant. These terms could refer to many different forms of relationship.

This would also take the blame off of the actual mother or father.

As to calling them 'good' or 'bad', 'negative' or 'positive', this says more about *the speaker or writer's* values and prejudices than about the complex. Good or bad for whom? Certainly negative for the victim of the violence. But bad events can *sometimes* ultimately have good outcomes and the best of intentions can go wrong, as cited with regard to the 'positive mother complex'. (November 2013)

★★★

I am surprised at the extent to which complexes have fallen out of favour with most current Jungian authors. Complexes are what I experience directly in my body when I am happy, sad, angry, hurt, frightened, and all emotions in-between. I run into them every day. I may be ashamed of the way I acted and want to deny it, but if I am honest I must admit they are just common run-of-the-mill complexes. But it is those nagging little everyday complexes that cause me trouble, and I think it is complexes that are causing most of the violence against women (and men). The causes of the complexes probably stem, in part, from very complex socioeconomic conditions.

Granted it was where Jung started, probably supported and maybe even pushed by his then-boss Eugene Bleuler. It was a big topic at the time (1900 to about 1910).

It made his reputation in America. Once he came out with his theory of archetypes in the famous speech in 1919 he almost never went back to 'complexes' except the little paper 'A Review of the Theory of Complexes' in 1934, reviewed in 1948. So through 1948 he had not renounced the theory.

Complexes are what I experience in my body and I am surprised that those Jungians interested in movement and body therapies have not paid them more attention. They are also where we come closest to a scientific and neuro-scientific theory. They are the architects of dreams and what I encounter in my practice.

If we had enough knowledge about the complexes causing the recourse to violence, we could try to identify what archetypes are behind this violence. The sentence I came across most often in the collected works with regard to archetypes: *are they patterns of behaviour?* By studying the patterns, putting them into categories, finding the patterns that connect (as Bateson would say) we might be able to identify the archetypes behind these violent crimes.

I think most who are contributing to this list are trying to identify the archetypes by studying current trends in societies. That is another method, also valuable, but not one that I as a clinical psychoanalyst am competent to speculate on. The social and economic factors are too complex for me to evaluate. I leave it to the others to do.

Hi Nancy,

There has been a debate about the nature of language, within feminist/women's scholarship that goes, roughly: the dominant forms of power and control throughout the world are male, or more specifically they represent and enforce male ideas about how the world is and one way they do this is through language. Thus language becomes a vehicle for power and control, and the reinforcement of masculine-paternal ideas and ideals. So, it is through this masculine-paternal model that boys and girls learn about being a man or a woman. The argument goes that language is never neutral; the voice of the dominant group (in this case male) ongoingly represents its own interests to maintain its position of power and privilege. This does *not* mean that the subordinated group(s) never have a voice.

Rather, it means that any voice produced say as an alternative, has to use the language of the dominating group. And what can happen, then, is that the subordinated groups can mobilise such language to their own ends. Thus Luce Irigaray's important work on mimesis. I spend a lot of time talking about this in my book *Jung, Irigaray, Individuation* if you want to chase it up.

The gendering of terms in langauge and thus the objects they denote/connote is ancient, and might be understood as a way of symbolising the cosmos. Pythagoras schematised this gendering and Aristotle picks up on it in his *Metaphysics*. I hope this is helpful. It's what Leslie is alluding to, I think.

With warm wishes, Fran

Dear Fran,

I've heard the argument, but I don't accept it. We think predominately in language. The language one hears is going to influence how that person thinks. I want

**136** Feminist Views from Somewhere

to stop thinking in terms of male and female and see the thing I am talking about (creativity in my first example, or self-reflection/introverted thinking which is usually considered feminine as another example I happened to come across today) for what it is. If the archetypal image, say of creativity, is formed to a large extent by culture then I understand the movement to change the cultural image from a masculine to a feminine one. But I want to do away with both and try to see the thing for itself.

This may be going against 100 years of Jungian psychology, classifying things as masculine and feminine, and 50 years of feminist theology. I don't see that by replacing the Father God by the Great Goddess we have really changed anything at all. We are still thinking in confining categories. Of course it is always added, 'By masculine and feminine we do not mean "male" and "female"'. Then don't use those terms if that is not what you mean.

Nurturing and caring are usually central characteristics of the Positive Great Mother. I think this is unfair to a lot of men who are very nurturing and caring individuals. Adding a parentheses 'I don't really mean female when I say mother' doesn't make it right in my mind. The instinct, as opposed to the image end of the archetype, is neutral. To care for oneself or another is neutral. Why can't we try to keep it that way by speaking not exclusively of the Great Mother, but of the Archetype of Caring (or Creativity or Self-Reflection …).

I understand the basics/goal of Jungian thinking to be individuation, which involves overcoming categories, whether they come from one side or the other. Whether we clothe it as masculine or feminine, it is still a mask. We can play with the masks as part of the individuation process, as long as we ourselves know that we are playing. I worked in a very male-dominated profession for over 35 years and I've played with a lot of masks. Now that I'm an old lady I want to take them off. Thank you for your efforts to clarify things for me but I'm a bit stubborn.

Warm greetings, Nancy

★★★

Dear Leslie,

I've hesitated to become involved in the discussion up until now because my comments don't really apply to the question of the seminar 'What is feminine in Jungian parlance?' but to what I consider the extreme categorization into masculine and feminine within Analytical Psychology. I found the seminar interesting. Some, as usual, I didn't understand, I am not strong on philosophy but did get some good references … What I found the most useful were the references to individuation and seeing grappling with the feminine as part of the individuation process, independent of the form or direction that that grappling takes, which will be different for each of us. Playing with gender, even to the point of sometimes wearing a mask, I found to be a good idea.

Where I have a problem is with the classification of what seems like every object as either masculine or feminine. A field is a field. Why does it need to be feminine? Creativity is a wonderful, mysterious process. Why does it need to be seen as a property of the Great Mother? Even if it does counterbalance the overly masculine God image we have grown up with. I would like to see the masculine categorization thrown out, not replaced by another, also fragmented image, even if it is the half we have not been seeing. I want to wonder at the mystery of creation, not put it into either a feminine or a masculine jacket. But look it straight in the eye and marvel at it.

I have studied the lists of what is masculine and what is feminine 'in Jungian parlance', but see no reason behind a lot of the classifications. It is the way Jungians speak, and I have learned the language, but it is not mine.

Best wishes, Nancy

★★★

Sulagna Sengupta

The Indian feminist history is old. Its origins are in medieval literature in stories about warrior queens and mystic bards; these are embedded in our minds through popular literature and oral narrative traditions. The mother as an archetypal figure dominated nationalist politics. Gandhi utilized it to mobilize people for the cause of freedom. Gandhi was assassinated by a radical Hindu and the nation never really integrated its Hindu and Muslim citizens. Partition and post-partition communal riots are evidence of a nation's inner split – this is a psychological phenomenon as much as it is religious and social. The Indian women's movement sprung from Gandhian, egalitarian ideology. A notable example is SEWA (Self Employed Women's Association) that has mobilized thousands of women workers to fight oppression and marginalization of poor women. From time to time, the women's movement has intersected with the Dalit movement and used its voice against poverty, illiteracy, gender inequity and has tried to involve men in the dialogue on gender. Although at the national level policy changes are taking place, gender discrimination prevails. Till recently, issues of sexual abuse, rape laws, female infanticide, sex-determination tests did not figure prominently in mainstream news. Now attacks on women, discrimination and abuse get reported in the media and get visibility.

The issues of urban women are different from their rural counterparts, and in different regions of India different levels of women and men's emancipation are seen. Women's concerns figure prominently in Indian alternative cinema, literature and education, even though discrimination persists.

The question about what all this has to do with Jungian psychology is complex. My first full-fledged research project after university was a gender and poverty study in the squatters of Delhi. This early experience with grassroots helped make my early career choices. When I ventured into working on the unconscious I landed in Jungian analysis, in a completely different field from what I had done before. Three experiences from my work in the development sector will highlight the complexity of the issues we face in India sometimes. While attending a gender lab in western India, I met a set of urban, educated, working women who had been sexually abused by their family members. The lab had given them the psychological

**138** Feminist Views from Somewhere

safety to recount their experience, perhaps for the first time. It is a telling statement about women's insidious oppression in India and what lies beneath the outer layers of development. Elsewhere, I had completed a year's fieldwork in several regions of the subcontinent, interviewing marginal women and men farmers from the poorest of households who were using treadle pumps to harvest crops in their homestead farms. These women used a low-end, manual technology to double their incomes and transform their lives. India lives in many worlds and this inspiring image of men and women is another face of the Indian gender scenario. The third experience was a visit to a remote village in South India to review a rehabilitation project of young sex-workers. They had been thrown into prostitution by their families due to poverty and were now being integrated back into mainstream society after rehabilitation. At the entrance of the village where the young girls live, is a temple of Mariamma, the Hindu goddess of fertility and healing. Most men in the village do not work but hand over their sisters or daughters to a life in flesh trade. An entire village stands gripped by forces of unconscious. Social and economic oppression is reinforced by psychological; these experiences show how diverse and challenging the scenario is in a country like India and how important it is therefore to connect various fields of knowledge to find paths of healing and transformation.

The mainstream women's movement does not engage with psychological ideas in a significant way and academic psychology in India does not figure in women's studies. The feminist debate has been more informed by economic and sociological disciplines and Marxist philosophy than by psychology. This gives an idea why any discussion on Jungian psychology is so far-fetched in India. I agree with Andrew on what he brings up about Amartya Sen's work. Sen's studies on famine, gender-inequity, female mortality, women's literacy are read seriously in India even though his ideas do not hold any psychological analysis. It is important to find links between various fields and Jungian psychology offers that in its ties to philosophy, mythology, medicine, literature, history, religion and art. It allows for a deeper understanding of the problem.

★★★

Gretchen Heyer

For so long I have wondered about the absence of rigorous thinking around feminist issues in the Jungian arena. We have a few lights, among them this panel, but this is not anywhere near enough to light a landscape. Jung was something of a universalist thinker, but that was a long time ago with a lot of years between here and there. I myself have turned to Irigary (not Kristeva), Butler, Benjamin and others like Harris and Davies of the relational school, although this has been more out of who I have been compelled towards rather than anything systematic. And it is striking to me that every one of those I just mentioned, including Butler, have connections to Freud's (or Lacan's) branches of the psychoanalytic tree more than Jung's.

Perhaps this is because Jung's style of writing makes it so easy to refer back and say that whatever-is-going-on-now was in some way pre-thought by him, which makes critique a bit difficult. But I also wonder how many of those trying to think things through with a bite to the thought were labelled 'animus ridden' and then ignored? And perhaps the very way Freud wrote enabled people to grab his ideas, rip them up and put them back together ... more permission to use aggression, or not. At least the force of desire was at the forefront, and the academy was more open to him.

At this point, even the word 'feminism' is suspect. It started out as a word to empower women, and to some degree it has done this. Now it is in many ways an exploration of relationship with others within us and without. Yet, clearly we have issues of that old essentialist category of 'women' on a global scale. I do not refer simply to issues of body shape. I live in Houston, one of the top cities in the States for sexual slavery, and the irony is the ethnic diversity of the city makes it possible for both traffickers and trafficked to live anywhere in the city, right in plain sight.

I digress. What I want to say is that this panel has inspired me. I have new books to read and fresh ways of seeing some of the ideas that have become stale, boring, flaccid and useless. I look forward to other thoughts in the seminar, and discovering how this affects my life, and the clinical hour.

Gretchen

Feminisms and desires

Dear Leslie and others,

I have found myself wondering why some would not want to discuss this subject, as if it is not useful. Could it be that in first-world countries women (those with a female body) are seen as integral to the competitive landscape? I heard a recent statistic that 60 percent of college students in the States are now women. Yet, the female college students in my practice cannot go places their male classmates go without 'asking for it'. The limits on their behaviour at times feel to them like limits on their minds. Sure, there can be conversations about archetypes, but these conversations can be prescriptive and restrictive, depending on the moment.

A vignette: Some years ago when working in a hospital on a pediatric floor, I was present as a male doctor came out of a room where a five-year-old girl was hospitalized for brutal sexual abuse. The doctor was visibly shaken and said, 'I can see why they did it to her. She tries to get it'. I felt shocked, as much as hearing him admit his own desire as his blaming her. The little girl in question was seductive with all males, lifting her dress, stroking herself. At five years old the amount of choice she had in this behaviour was none. She had been formed by the perpetrators, by the culture in which she had been born, doing whatever she needed to gain whatever power she could. She 'performed' her gender, and at that time had no other options.

This reduces the conversation to the female body in a very essentialist way. (I am looking forward to reading Frances's book to open my mind on the word.) For me the power of the feminist conversation must go beyond the female body, yet it cannot overlook that body. Feminism is connected to the word Desire in all its forms. Sex is a big piece of this. Power is a big piece of this. How we conceive of and relate to Others within and without is a big piece of this.

**140** Feminist Views from Somewhere

In the clinical hour we are intimately connected to the embodiment of the psyche. What/how we think informs how we practice, a type of cusp between body and theory. There are many Jungs. Many feminisms. Many desires. I am looking forward to thinking more about all of this.

Gretchen

From Susan Rowland

Dear Gretchen,

This is such a powerful post. Your combination of vignette and feminist perspective is so penetrating. And yes, I do mean that word!

One thought about embodiment from me (and it will surprise no one who has ever met me or read anything I have ever written that this is getting to what the typologists would call my inferior functions), so one thought from me on female embodiment inspired by your post is that at the grassroots of where Jungian ideas meet congruent if not cognate therapies, there is a lot of exploratory work going on re the body as an organ of knowing.

And the female body as a knowing organ is on the one hand an ancient resource that has remained rich, partly by virtue of the marginalization of women and the feminine, so that traditions such as herbal medicine; various ritual practices that could attract the term witchcraft; grandmothers' tales; saws; old wives' taboos around menstruation, childbirth, even care of the dead; traditional remedies – this largely unrepresented female tradition we know of, if not know about.

And yet, of course the male body has been *the* body for the mainstream for so long and been woven, even perhaps in largely unacknowledged ways in epistemologies – so that knowing *through and beyond* the female body (you are so right on this!) is still in its infancy. And here I say that as a woman who is not a mother I usually avoid childbirth metaphors but here deliberately use 'infancy' to recall the divine child image of Jungian iconography. And because the point of what I am trying to say here about the body and language is that I don't believe in metaphors any more. 'Infancy' is not a metaphoric description here. Thank you!

Susan

October 10, 2013

Dear Marilyn, [another member IAJS forum]

I have not had the time to follow these posts as closely as I would like over the last days, but wanted to speak to this. I remember your post from the past. I said nothing, in part because I was not sure I agreed but needed to think about why I did not agree, and then the faster minds among us chimed in. It is true (as the one who responded seemed to say) that we have no real way of knowing what any religious or philosophical work of the ages would be if written by a woman. But part of what you are saying is that as women we are always already in a patriarchal culture. It is us as much as it is not, which takes us into Irigaray and Butler. Would there be less killing and death and bloodshed if we were in a matriarchy? I doubt. Would the point of view be different on some of our pivotal texts? Yes, most likely, because the point of view would be coming from a different angle. The story would then change.

But I've been thinking about my own silence with your post and others, and this takes me into consideration of how we silence voices in our trainings … We Jungians are not unique with this, but we may have our special brand of it, our own 'shadow' that rejects voices that disturb us. Although, in our defence, no one really likes being disturbed in ways that matter.

And just a clinical thought on being a woman in the consulting room. Over the years I have noticed that in the more intense and life-changing work with female patients, our monthly cycles often sync up, as if our bodies themselves became the 'third'. But then the question becomes, how to work with this? Do I tell my patients? I have chosen not to; concerned that it would become a kind if pressure, a bond that might foreclose needed anger or separation. This also becomes a kind of silence, although (I hope) a more embodied and considered one than I often have on this list. Thank you for your posts, present and past.

Gretchen

Dear all,

Yes, we have a tension between individual and community, perhaps partially because we are all such characters. Yes, we all have a way of moving away from shadow even as we think we are moving towards it, Gretchen

Dear All,

I am puzzled by much of this exchange. The feminism of the 1960s has evolved in first-world countries. Most women (feminist and otherwise) do not hate men, unless there are deep psychological wounds that need attending to.

Many of us are even rather comfortable with our femininity, our voices, our bodies, our birthing, and yes, our power. Looking over history, some of this has been a rather recent development. And taking less dangerous jobs? Who wants to hire a smaller-stature-curvy-woman on her period to lift a pickaxe?

However, the majority of sexual slaves are women. The majority of those who buy those salves are men. This is not to say that men are poor slobs more visually stimulated. We women are also visually stimulated, also susceptible to abusing power. And just as there are female and male porn stars who enjoy their status and use sex as power, there are many more who find their way into making porn by other paths, and are degraded there. This doesn't even touch on issues of child and adolescent porn, and what happens to those young people. I find the sacred prostitute of little use with these issues. The reason there are more places for women to go who have been abused is because more women are abused.

That aside, the questions of feminism in first-world countries now have more to do with the examination of otherness within and without, the exploration of power dynamics that have been accepted as *is*. We are always already in the mostly-male-created-cultural-and-language-structures in which we live. Blame and victimhood then become irrelevant. It is a matter of what we do.

**142** Feminist Views from Somewhere

Although, there is a stage in growth where blame and speaking out *about* one's victimhood is important. It is the beginning of agency.

Gretchen

★★★

To [member of the IAJS forum],

You raise a lot of points, and I continue to be puzzled. From a larger perspective, we humans are clearly evolving – although at times we Jungians speak of a moment in time as if it is universal – one of our many blind spots. Reptiles evolved physically to fly, but we have evolved mentally to do the same thing. Our minds shift the use of our bodies. Now with the touch of a control panel, a drill rig can be operated. This creates an equal playing field to the bodies of women and men, so job choice becomes a choice of mental acuity.

Before contraception we women were pretty much tied to biology. Of course we then used sex as a primary form of power. Some women may still be using sex as power, although this is usually developmental as they discover their way-in-the-world. In any case, gay or straight, the female sex drive isn't that different than male. We are not biologically any more committed or monogamous. When we don't want to have sex it is because we're exhausted, angry, bored by doing it the same way, thinking of someone else, etc. It is not because of some manipulative power move. Women have other forms of power and no longer need that.

Porn also evolves. In today's world playboy has grown obsolete next to the internet, and internet porn is more and more interactive. A person no longer needs to merely look at a picture in order to amuse himself or herself. People can press a button to meet others with their same sexual proclivities, proclivities that were once thought of as deviant. For men and women, gay and straight, spanking clubs, partner swapping, sexual shavings, group sex and anything else that might be conceived of, has a ready and willing group of people to join in. This is a particular type of relationship, and again, some people get stuck there.

The phrase you used that I find myself repelled by is men wanting a 'willing, loving, adoring partner'. This sounds oppressive. Love is neither willing nor adoring in my book. Love is the ability to tell the truth to one's partner and be terribly unwilling a great deal of the time. Truth is seldom adoring.

I have a practice of about one-third men, two-thirds women, about one-third gay/lesbian, two-thirds straight. In reading your post, I felt as if I couldn't recognize any of the people I see. Sure, some men have porn addictions. This is connected to attachment issues in early life that get played out in adult relationships, not anything biological other than the hit to pleasure centres of the brain that are not limited to gender. For both men and women, it is much easier to have an imagined relationship than a real-life not so willing or adoring one. I have never yet worked with a woman who deliberately used sex as power, although over the years a number of women have felt that the men in their lives withheld sex as power.

As far as the male creation of culture, yes, I am sure women have had some forms of power in past centuries. However, a young woman of today looking for mentors in the writers of ancient philosophy, the old literature, the political leaders, the great inventors, the epic adventuress etc. … she has few to follow. This is changing, but we evolve from what has gone before.

Gretchen

★★★

As I think about it, my puzzlement is due in a large part to my own participation in this conversation. It has been years since I have given much attention to women's 'suffering' or how they are substantially different than men. For me, this is not what feminism is about. Those I read and find compelling are people like Butler, Irigary, and, among the Jungians, Sue Austin. I am looking foreword to reading some of the presenters from the last seminar.

No doubt there are different feminisms. The questions I find interesting have more to do with the ways we have all taken culture into ourselves so it becomes us. This is true for both men and women. Suffering belongs to all of us. This becomes powerful in the clinical hour as people connect to what they have taken in that they can then step aside from, examine, be less compelled by, or not.

This conversation reminds me of ways I have felt boxed up by male Jungians telling me how a female 'individuation' process goes. You are not saying that, and I thank you for this. I have never recognized myself in any of these books, yet they are read as if they are facts. No doubt that is some of my energy here.

That said, I doubt if there are many women on this list or elsewhere who have not been in work or social situations where sex and power are not in some way used oppressively. Most of us have learned to move past this as if it didn't happen, although it may alter our lives. Perhaps men are socialized to move past this type of dynamics at a younger age with locker room banter, etc. All these are interesting things to wonder about, to learn from, and perhaps find some conclusion that will most likely change.

As a last note, my understanding of the rise in sexual slavery in the States has to do with it being a 'reusable commodity' and therefore making economic sense. Drugs get used up. And as far as the words 'willing and adoring'?? They get just a little too close to being compelled by?? But perhaps this is my read of it.

Best, Gretchen

Nathalie Pilard

Dear all,

Thank you very much Ginette for your presentation of Lacan, Beauvoir and Irigaray (that I now definitely want to read).

Your putting it into perspective is necessary when feminism is concerned. Beauvoir's choice is still valid today and is used by many women. It does not solve major inequalities at work. I am personally attached to theory. This is where I start from in order to understand psychologies. I am attached to 'anima' and 'animus' as well as neutral animae. They all work and it is the dream or the situation that makes whether we will use the one better than the other.

**144** Feminist Views from Somewhere

To me, what is absolutely lacking from a theoretical point of view, and that which is also absolutely revelatory in the lack itself, is the gender-ization of the persona rather than the de-genderization of anima and animus. Gendering the persona would correspond to the reality of women at work, and to all the inequalities that they suffer from. I don't want to cut off one of my breasts (a violent de-genderization of my animus). I'd rather want law, for instance, to adapt my being a woman and a mother (Is theory here again?) to external situations. The male persona is very different from the female persona. The palette of the latter is less extended as it is less authorized, less heard and self-censored. Here perhaps could be heard the problematic of the body.

Sincerely, Nathalie

★★★

Dear [addressed to member of IAJS forum],

Your question on pornography in a seminar on feminism is, to me, an illustration of the phenomenology of the reduction (not yours, everybody's) of the female persona *vis-à-vis* the male persona. I hope I can be corrected, that I am wrong.

Sincerely, Nathalie

Dear Nathalie,

I agree with you. But I don't think it's just about the reduction of the female persona *vis-à-vis* the male persona (and you are perhaps not simply saying that). The reduction of women to sexual objects filtered through dominant male paradigms in social practice as the embodiment of temptation and erotic flesh is abhorrent. Such reductionism also operates in the case of abused and prostituted children, male and female!

I really can't see how Jungian readings, interpretations of pornography of any kind can help here: it begs the question of all social phenomena being reducible to psychic matters, and that would include, perhaps, morality and ethics, questions of justice, exploitation, and the Other? Questions of social and personal responsibility can easily be side-stepped it seems to me, once we follow psychic trails that seem to play a causal role in our behaviour. I find this untenable. Women are exploited in ways that undermine and deny our humanity for the satisfaction of male desire. Bring on McKinnon and Dworkin!!!! If there are answers through Jungian imagination, then more's the pity. Careful of conflating explanation and excusing.

Frances

Dear Fran,

Thanks.

Of course. Pornography is much more than a reduction of female persona. And what you clearly articulate is crucial: in this case, we can talk of the dangers of the reduction to psychic matters (at least the description of the female persona? It takes place in the social sphere, but clearly it does not encompass the whole issue).

Sincerely, Nathalie

Dear xxx [member of IAJS forum],
Yes, you get me right when you add 'to be fair to Nathalie'. That *you* feel comfortable associating Aphrodite to pornography (pornography, not sexuality) is a matter of taste. And this is not mine.

Sorry, truly, to all the persons [who find what I am saying, shocking],
Nathalie

★★★

Dear all,
I need to add something having been the target of xxx [member of IAJS forum], and apparently his having been mine. I recognize a pattern …

You write in your email that you rightly got my intention that my criticism was solely addressed generally to our modern patriarchy and clearly then not to you, and yet you start your email by saying that you felt you had been chastised by me.

In other words, you recognize that you sent me the most violent accusation perhaps a little bit too hastily. That, I cannot accept. I understand that it must be more difficult for men to participate in this seminar than it is for women; for men, perhaps should walk on eggs here (and clearly that is not what you did).

With this situation we are embedded in a vicious circle. I can offer you apologies for the matter of taste, which was only a reaction of someone who felt insulted. But I cannot offer you apologies for what you yourself recognize is no offence.
Nathalie

Siona van Dijk
Dear All,
With Gretchen, I too found myself pull back at your "willing, loving, and adoring partner." (The "willing" especially made me wince.) I would like to think that men (and women too) would prefer a confident, competent, and fully realized human being as a (sex) partner, no? Ideally the relationship between these two people would be loving and adoring, of course, but this would be secondary to their mutual autonomy and personhood. "Willing, loving, and adoring" sounds a better description of a devoted dog. (And quite frankly I'd be a little perturbed by anyone who'd settle for someone "willing" to have sex with them. Why not "enthusiastically desiring" instead?)

Also, I think the thing that complicates gender relationships is not the relatively uncomplicated issue of men having higher sex drives (modern pharmacology could no doubt solve this problem quite easily, considering that "diminished libido" is an established side effect of female hormonal birth control), but the fact that women, when it comes to sex and reproduction, shoulder a disproportionate burden (and risk more in general), and not only biologically, but socially, culturally, and professionally. Again, if that burden were relieved, things would likely be very different.

I agree completely that women should be allowed to pursue what interests them. Unfortunately, for much of our known history—and still in much of the world today—any woman with a vocational calling to philosophy, religion, adventure,

**146** Feminist Views from Somewhere

politics, art, or any number of other cultural or intellectual spheres of intellect would have had a seriously difficult time fulfilling that call, and the repercussions of that imbalance still resonate today. What saddens me is the stunted partiality of a field—be it religion or philosophy, philosophy or art—that does not include, and has not been shaped by, the voices and values of both genders.

An earlier post of mine referenced the disparity between men and women in positions of political power. Perhaps it is as you say; perhaps women are simply not interested in participating in the arena of politics and power (at least as they're currently constructed.) But would you mind considering another system in which disproportion representation occurs? African Americans make up 13 percent of the US population. However, only 7 percent of law students are black, and 3 percent of law firm partners. Might it just be that African Americans are not interested in practicing law? Perhaps.

However, considering that, in the United States, the likelihood of black males going to prison over the course of their life is nearly 40 percent (among white males, that likelihood is 4 percent), and considering the blatant disparities of sentencing between black and white men in the US justice system, and knowing the importance of networking and relationships to success in the legal field, it does not seem surprising that young African Americans might struggle with the thought of a career in law. It's difficult to continue to feel passionate about a field that has systematically subjugated the group that you happen to be a part of, especially given that, even if you can maintain that passion, you'll find it difficult to succeed within it. And for much of recent human history, women have found themselves in just this position when it comes to religion, philosophy, law, politics, science, medicine, art, and education.

Of course, power that comes at the expense of another—or that must be enforced with violence—is neither true nor sustainable power, and thus men, too, are disempowered in the patriarchal system. However, it is only in reaching out to each other we stand to gain—and yes, that gain includes more and better sex.

Siona

★★★

Dear all

Don't women, too, experience (both positive and negative) mother complexes? And yet women don't seem to beat up other women in quite the same numbers that that men do. (Admittedly, they do beat themselves up: http://www.hscic.gov.uk/article/3579/Hospital-statistics-on-teenagers-girls-predominate-in-self-harm-cases-boys-in-assaults.)

But I agree [with you both] on the importance of the psychological. "The personal is political" was an early feminist slogan; here, I'd frame it as "The political is personal." Because unless the psychological includes at the very least an awareness of the socio-political, it cannot in good faith be called such. "Until you make the unconscious conscious, it will direct your life and you will call it fate" said Jung; remaining unconscious of socio-political pressures ensures they'll become fate, too.

Appendix **147**

So I appreciate very very much your call for that balancing, and that awareness. It's critical.

Earlier I suggested that one psychological symptom of unconscious socio-political structures was that men would be forced to project the qualities that "masculinity" prevented them from owning (i.e. vulnerability, softness, receptivity) onto women, while women would have to project "unfeminine" qualities, such as aggression and strength, onto men. When this projection is extreme, or fuelled strongly by shame, violence and abuse all too often result.

Of course, owning one's vulnerability and weakness—especially when that weakness might be a tendency toward physical violence—is no more easy than taking responsibility for one's own anger and aggression. So we all have our work cut out for us.

"When the father is absent, we fall more readily into the arms of the mother. And indeed the father is missing; God is dead. The missing father is not your or my personal father. He is the absent father of our culture, the viable senex who provides not daily bread but spirit through meaning and order."

Maybe God the Father went to join the Mother—or at least it seems to me that She's been MIA for longer.

Don't laugh, please! I'm serious. Don't we all—at least if we're lucky—become orphans in the end? Only the unfortunate are survived by their parents. Because of this, both the archetypal father and the archetypal mother must, at some point, die—at least if they are to remain archetypal. Death is the one thing that all fathers and all mothers share, and their passing is something we all (if we're lucky) must come to terms with.

One of the things that tugged me toward Jungian psychology was its emphasis on the developmental experiences of adulthood and old-age—and the death of the father (and the death of the mother) is in many ways its own rite of passage. Still, there must be a way to grieve His passing that doesn't involve scarring and breaking the bodies of women, just as there must be a way to grieve the missing Mother that doesn't involve blaming or attacking men. And I would like to think that Jungian psychology's respect for adulthood and maturation could certainly be useful in floundering through the turmoil of such loss.

Siona

# INDEX

abandonment complex 134
Abélard 121, 122
abstract/concrete interconnection 121, 128, 129, 130
'abstractions of traits' 129, 130
'abundance in a small space' 10, 19
academic disciplines 93, 94
acceptance 21
active/male - passive/female 59, 60
'acts of creation in time' 86, 88, 90
*Addiction to Perfection* 67
Adie, K. 47
adolescent psyche 102
adverbs 121
Aeschylus 97
affect regulation 17
agency 79, 142
agential realism 119
aggression: against women 134
alien inner otherness 41, 47, 52
alignment 14
'aliveness of the world' 10
'amazon' structure (feminine psyche) 25, 26
Ana 75
analyst-patient relationship 16
analytical psychology *see* Jungian psychology
anatomy: as metaphor 78
Anderegg, D. 107
androcentrism 103
Angelou, M. 7
anger/frustration (infant) 134

anima/animus 26, 71, 84, 85, 86, 107, 132–3, 143
animism 86, 87, 88, 91, 95, 97
animus-possessed 100, 110
animus-ridden 132, 139
anti-heroic qualities 71
Antigone 70
anxiety(ies) 21, 49, 58
Apollonian Sky Father 87, 97
appearance (female) 59, 60, 61, 62
archetypal feminism 103
archetypal psychology 84, 101
archetypal theory: Western culture 83
archetype(s): in animistic universe 87; bodily and spiritual pole 96; of caring 136; female warrior 100; feminine structural forms 35; heroes 70, 71; Jung's perspective on 13, 88, 122; masochistic victim 79–80; medial women's meaning-making of 30; mothers 73, 137; as patterns of behaviour 135; of separation 71; symbols derived from 96; 'wild women' 102; of womanhood 66
'area of faith': the potential space as 11
Aristophanes 70
Aristotle 135
art/artists 7, 35, 90, 102
Arya Stark 102
as if 125, 126
*Ashley's War* 112
Athena 97
attachment theory 15, 18
attractiveness (female) 59, 60, 61, 62

## Index

Augustine, Saint 29
Austen, J. 94
Austin, S. 143
authority: clinical 16; inner 15; patriarchal 28, 70, 75; struggle for, in psychoanalysis 14
auto-designative tactic 121
autonomous complex 134
autonomy (heroine's) 79

bad mother 75
Bakhtin, M. 42
Balsam, R. 57, 58, 65, 67
Barad, K. 118, 119
Barbara, Saint 28
bariatric surgery 64
Baring, A. 86, 101
beauty (female) 59, 61, 62, 63
beauty industry 61–2, 65
Beauvoir, S. de 119, 143
Beckett, W. 35
becoming human 9–23
being 15, 18; feminine mode of 88; *Khôra* as a place of 11; love and space 'given' for 20; meaningfulness and continuity of 21
being with 15, 16–17, 18–19
Bella Swan 102, 104–6, 107
belonging 21
Benjamin, J. 51, 138
Benveniste, E. 125, 127, 128, 129
Berger, J. 61
Berry, P. 132
Betty 59, 61
'beyond disciplines' 92
binge eating disorder (clinical vignette) 45–50
biological/corporal bias: of mind and self 17
Bion, W. 12, 20
biosemiotics 91
'blessing of recognition' 21
Bleuler, E. 43, 134
bodily instrument: in communication 119
body: photographic images and changes in relating to 61; as a problem to be solved 65; psyche and tacit knowing 90; as shadow 57, 58, *see also* embodiment; female body; male body; mind/body; right body; wrong body
'bodying forth' 16
Bolen, J.S. 66
Bollas, C. 119, 127, 130
boundedness 21, 22
bourgeois women 61

brain lateralization 133
bringing others undone 41, 49
Bromberg, P. 12, 17–18
Burkett, E. 63, 64
Butler, J. 41, 48, 49, 50, 51, 52, 119, 127, 128, 138, 140, 143

Calypso 25
Caputo, J.D. 11
caring 136
carrier bag: feminism as 84; as feminist space for making and critiquing knowledge 84; as first cultural artifact 84
The Carrier Bag Theory of Fiction 83, 95
Carver, R. 23
Casey, E. 11
Cashford, J. 86, 101
Cassandra 35
Cassin, B. 120, 123
Castillejo, I.C. de 66
cathedrals (medieval) 30
Catherine, Saint 27–8
centrifugal dynamics (of the self) 42–53
centripetal dynamics (of the self) 42, 52
centripetal other 47, 48
*chaos* 11
Christian martyrs 27–8, 35
Christian modernity 87
cinematographic mythology 133
civilization 114n4
Cixous, H. 68
Clairvaud, Bernard of 29
clinical authority 16
*Clouds* 70
Cocchiarella, N.B. 122
*Collected Works* 84, 85, 95, 97, 122
collective psyche 101
collective psychic ground 6
collective unconscious 13, 125; medial women and 26–7, 29, 30, 35, 36; personal and 121–2; symbols and connection of the conscious ego to 96
collectivity 121
Collins, S. 102, 108
combat: power in 109–13
Combat Action Badge 113
coming into being 9–23
coming together 42, 52
coming undone 41, 48, 49–50
communicating subject 118–19
communication: women's 120, 123, 126, *see also* deviant communication; non-communication; unconscious communication

**150** Index

'communing with nature' 5
community: tension between individual and 141
compensatory fiction 106
complex systems 90, 91
complexes 13, 43, 44, 134–5, *see also* cultural complex; feminine complex; inner other(ness); mother complex; trauma complexes
complexity evolution 89
complexity/theory 90, 91, 92, 93, 94, 95, 96
conceptual language 3
conceptualism 121–2, 130
concrete/abstract interconnection 121, 128, 129, 130
conflict (psychic) 26
connectedness 74, 88
consciousness: basic dynamic of history as the movement of higher and deeper 33; Christian martyrs and a new 28; container as founding structure of 84; head as representation of 28; male 85; myths of 86; partial 88; women's primal development task 26, *see also* ego consciousness; pre-consciousness; self-consciousness
constellation 27, 35
container: centripetal other as 47, 48; as first cultural object 83–4; *Khôros* as 11; women's social function as 41, *see also* relation container/contained
containment: by Athena, in detective fiction 97; initialising experience of 20–1; psyche's need for 21; through secondary skin defences 22, *see also* meaningful containment; sheltering containment
continuity of self 12, 21
control: language as a vehicle for 135; paternal 28
controlling complex 134
controlling the land 5
Cornell, D. 125
cosmetic surgeons/surgery 61–2
cosmogenists 14
cosmos 11, 88
Couch 59–60
countertransference 19, 48
Cowan, L. 132
creation: *Khôra/Khôros* as the nursery/basket of 11
Creative surrender 77
creative/destructive tension: between Jung and Freud 14

creativity 14, 77, 90, 91, 94, 95, 136–7
*criatura* 113
Cross, R. 110
cultural complex 101
cultural norms: deviation from as pathology 60
cultural objects 83–4
Cultural Support Teams 112
cultural values 26
culture(s) 4, 26, 86, 90, 91, 94, 136, 143, *see also* male culture; patriarchal culture; popular culture; Western culture

Daenerys Targaryan 102
*daimon* 110
D'Annunzio, G. 32
Darwin, C. 88–9, 90
Davis Rogan, A. 118, 120, 126
De Rémusat 122
death 8
death instinct 13
'deepened state of introversion' 74
defence systems 16, 22
deintegration 77, 79
demonstratives 121
dependence 73, 75, 77, 78, 79
depersonification 33
deprivation 73
depth psychology 3, 14, 51, 57, 96, 118, 127, 133, *see also* psychoanalysis
Derrida, J. 11
desires: feminisms and 139–40
destructive mother 80
detective fiction 97
developmental growth (psychological) 16
deviancy 118, 125
deviant communication 120
devouring mother 73
Dhejne, C. 64
Dieckmann, H. 74
diet industry 62
difference 10, 84
differentiation 15, 71
Dijk, S. van 145–7
Dionysian dismemberment 87–8, 89, 91, 94, 95, 96, 97
Dionysian trickster 97
Dionysus: in Jung's Writings 87–8; transdisciplinarity and 91–5
disconnectedness 4
discourse 121, 126, 127, 128, 129
discrimination 29, 35, 85, 87, 95
disembodied abstraction 90

Index **151**

disembodiment 86, 87
dismemberment 87–8, 89, 91, 94, 95, 96, 97
disorganisation 21
dispossessed/dispossession 6, 49
dissociable psyche 42–4, 53; clinical vignette 45–50
'dissociated not-me self states' 12
dissociated unconscious 12–13, 19, 22, 23
dissociation 13, 14, 18, 43, 107
*Divergent* trilogy 100, 102, 108–9, 111, 114n2
divine 87, 88, 96
Divine, A. 7
divine dismemberment *see* Dionysian dismemberment
divine feminine 30, 101
divinity 30
Dolezal, R. 63–4
domination: power as 99
drama 3, 30
Duse, E. 30–2, 35
'dwelling in them' 90
dyadic systems theory 15, 17
dysregulated affect 18

Earth Mother 86, 87, 88–91, 94, 95, 96, 97
eating disorder: as a symptom of dissociative psyche (clinical vignette) 45–50
ec-static: self as 41, 50–3
*The Ecocritical Psyche* 97
ego consciousness 51
ego-dystonic impressions 43
Ehrenzweig, A. 77
Elizabeth 75–6
Ellenberger, H.F. 45
*elles* 125
embodied knowing 89, 91
embodied unconscious 91
embodiment 140; emotional 'happenings' 11, 12, 16, 19; false sense of 22; psychotherapy and potential for 10; of the unconscious 29, *see also* disembodiment
emotion(s) 85, 121, 123
emotional 'happenings' 11, 12–13, 16
enactments 19
*Encomium on Helen* 120, 123
enigmatic signifiers: unconscious 50, 52–3
Ensler, E. 64
environmental mother 20
epics 83
epistemology 103
Eros 28, 85, 86, 87, 88, 90, 94, 95

*Eros and Psyche* 101
espionage 111
essentialism 85, 103, 124–5, 125
Estrada, N. 112
eternal time 11, 12
ethnic history: and formation of the psyche 5
*The Euminides* 97
evolution theory 88–9, 90
exigency: in relation to feminine pronoun issues 120, 122–4, 125, 128
existential anguish/dreads 17, 21
experience(s): of 'being with another' and implicit procedural memory 18–19; contextualising of women's 103; individuation through military 110; internalization 77; meaning-making out of 9; meaningful containment as continuum of internal/external 10–11; myths of the unconscious as deriving from personal 14; non-recognition of infant 22; of selfhood 41, 50, 51, 53; unformulated 12–13, 22, *see also* lived experience; moments of meeting; patterns of experience

fabulation 128
facial feminization surgery 63, 64
facts: as a source of oppression 34
failure: male gaze and perceptions of women as 61; relational 18
false body 22
fantasy(ies): about a fat woman (Keen's) 62; deriving from anima/animus 84; patriarchal male 59; teleological component in 44
fantasy literature 103; young women and expression of power in 102, 104–9, 110–11
fat female body 58
fat lady (Yalom's) 59, 62
fat studies 57
female beauty 59, 61, 62, 63
female body 3, 139, 140; appropriation for male purposes 5; male gaze 58–9; non-existent ideal conveyed through photographic images 61; separation of land as separation of women from 5; silence about 57–8, 67
Female Engagement Teams (FETs) 100, 112
female identity 59, 63–4
female Marines 112
female mystics (medieval) 29

**152** Index

female soldiers 100, 111–12
female warrior(s) 70, 100, 101, 105, 109, 110, 111, 113
female-centred fiction 109
feminine: animus/anima theory 132, 133; associated qualities 78; first theory of 25; healing of the devaluation of 80; Jung's turn to the 85–7; Jung's valuing of 103; original powers of the ancestral 100
feminine complex 124
feminine pronoun issues 118–30
feminine psyche 25–7
feminism(s) 57; archetypal 103; carrier bag analogy 84; and desires 139–40; in first-world countries 141; and the included middle 95–7; as informing psychology 67
Feminism in Jungian Studies (IAJS Forum 2013) 132–47
feminist novelist: Jung as 84–5, 95
feminists: exploration of linguistic levels of communication 118; Jungian 101; on limited view of women's aptitude for power 99; military recruitment of women 111; popular culture and study of gender and power 102; postmodern 114n1
*femme inspiratrice* 25
fierce young women: expressions of power 99–114
Fisher, B. 7
Flournoy, T. 43, 44
Fordham, M. 77, 134
foreclosure of *Khôra* 21, 22
forest solitude: symbolism of 74, 79
Foucault, M. 119, 121
fragments/fragmentation 43, 44, 47, 88
Frankel, R. 102
Franz, M.-L. von 56, 66, 73
freedom: to become more fully human 10
Freud, S. 13, 14, 17, 43, 103
Frosh, S. 50
fundamental principles: scientific disciplines 92; for transdisciplinarity 92–3
The Furies 97
futuristic utopian genre 120, 126, 127

*Game of Thrones* 102
Gandhi 137
Gaudissart, I. 65, 66–7
gender: communicating subject in enquiry into 118–19; performance 59; popular culture and study of 102; primal division of 83; and psyche 78; relationships 145;

reversals 133; roles 103, 104, 106, *see also* psychic gender; transgenderism
gender markers 126
*Gender Trouble* 119
gender-ization 144
gendered assumptions 60
gendered identities 102
generation theories 89
Genesis 86
Gilligan, C. 101, 106
*The Girl with the Dragon Tattoo* 106
girlhood 101
Girls' Studies 101
God: dualism between nature/matter and 86; perceived as masculine 60
Goldstein, J. 110, 111, 114n5
good mother 74, 134
good poem 10
Goodman, E. 63
Goodman, N. 120
Gorgias 120, 123
Gorris, M. 7
Gourguechon, P. 106
grammar 118, 122, 125
Great Mother 136, 137
Green, S. 59, 60
Greene, A. 57
Greta 60, 61
grief 49–50
Griest, K. 100
Grotstein, J.S. 20, 21
ground 4, 6
guerrilla warfare 111

Hancock, E. 101
The Handless Maiden 71–4, 79–80
happening(s) 11, 12–13, 16, 21
Haraway, D. 119
Harding, E. 66
Harris, A. 101, 102, 138
Hartman, G. 44, 47
Haule, J. 43, 44, 45
Haver, S. 100
head: symbolic meaning 28
'headless woman' sign 67–8
headlessness 28
heart: knowing as a matter of the 34, 35
Hegel, G.W.F. 51
Heidegger, M. 11
Hélène 42, 44–5, 48, 53n4
Hellerstein, D. 59–60, 62
hero(es): archetypal 70, 71; counterbalance between heroine(s) and 79; dynamic relationship between heroine(s) and 73;

independence 78, 79; individuation 71; isolation and dependency 78; moment of glory 77; spear-point stories 83

heroine(s) 70–80; anti-heroic qualities 71; case illustrations 74–7; characteristics 70–1; The Handless Maiden 71–4, 79–80

hetaira 25

Heuer, G. 57, 58

Heyer, G. 138–43

hidden third 93, 94, 96

hierarchical dissolution 120

Hildegard of Bingen 29–30, 35

Hillman, J. 3, 85, 87–8, 94, 97, 99, 101

historical research (Huch) 32–5

historical/developmental time 12

historiography 33

history/myth intersection: as site of psychoanalysis 12, 16, 22

Hogenson, G. 14, 17

Hook, M. 106

hope: loss of 22

horizontal complexity 93

horizontal meaning 93

Huch, R. 32–5

humanisation 16

humus 3

*Hunger Games* trilogy 100, 102, 108, 109, 110, 114n2

hungry ghosts 12

Huskinson, L. 50

hyperdiscipline 92, 96

'I' pronoun 121, 125, 126–7, 128, 129

IAJS Forum (2013) 132–47

ideas 12

identification: with a beautiful appearance 62

identity: dissociation and 12, 53; primary others and 49, *see also* female identity; gendered identities; self-identity

image(s) 14; imprinted in the 'psychological' underground 6; Jung's method of working with 103; medial women's meaning-making of archetypal 30; non-reality of photographic 61; symbols as specific types of 96

imagination 13, 14, 20, 32, 34, 35, 77, 125, 126

immanence 10

immersion 27

impersonal shadow 27

impersonal unconscious 26, 27, 29, 30

implicit knowing 18

implicit procedural memory of 'being with' 18–19

impressions (ego-dystonic) 43

included middle 93, 95–7

independence 71, 78, 79

Indian feminist history 137, 138

individual: tension between community and 141

individual development 52–3

individuality 118, 121, 122

individuation 85, 99, 125, 136; gender differences 78; heroes 71; heroines 71–4; Jung's psychology of 42; through military experience 110; women's 26, 36, 105, 106

infant: anger/frustration 134; relational unconscious 17; unformulated experiences 22, *see also* mother-infant

infant development 15, 17, 21

inferences 123, 126, 127, 129

'initialising experience of containment' 20–1

inner authority 15

inner harmony 33

inner other(ness) 43, 44–5, 46, 47–9, 50, 51, 52

insecurity 26

instance of discourse 121, 126, 127, 128, 129

integration 77, *see also* deintegration; reintegration

intelligences 93, 96

interconnectedness 15, 21, 30, 91

interdependence 93

interiority 41, 43, 46, 51, 88

internal symbolic space 11

internalisation: of anxieties (Jenny) 49; of experience, by heroines 77; of maternal sheltering 21

intersubjectivity 16, 17, 122

introversion 74, 136

invention: in women's communication 123

Irigaray, L. 120, 135, 138, 140, 143

irrationality 85, 118

isolation 78

Ivenes 44

James, C. 10

Janet, P. 43, 44

Jenner, Bruce/Caitlin 63

Jenny (clinical vignette) 45–50

Jensen, G. 101, 102

Jewish people 5, 6

Jones, D. 110

**154** Index

Jung, C.G. 17, 121, 130; appreciation of different modes of unconscious communication 119–20; as cosmogenist 14; dismissal of pronouns as arbitrary 119; essay on animus and anima 124; as feminist novelist 84–5, 95; Hillman on Dionysus in writings of 87–8; interpretation of human experience 14–15; method of working with images 103; powerful aura surrounding 67; tension between Freud and 14; turn to the feminine 85–7; women drawn to 66; writing as proto-transdisciplinary 96, *see also Collected Works*; *Psychological Types*; *Symbols of Transformation*
Jung, E. 56, 60, 65–6, 67
*Jung, Irigaray, Individuation* 135
Jungian feminists 101
Jungian psychology (analytical psychology) 118; archetypal heroes 70, 71; centripetal and centrifugal dynamics in concept of the self 41–53; the founding carrier bag and feminist space for making and critiquing knowledge 84; gendered assumptions 60; need for women's voices 68; obesity in 67; on the perception of power as masculine 99; as rooted in the modernist paradigm 13; silence about the female body 57–8, 67; theoretical ambivalence towards the body 57; trickster in 86; voices from the IAJS forum on women and the feminine 132–47; women drawn to 66; women and the feminine in 103
juxtaposition 129

Katniss Everdeen 102, 104, 108, 109
Keen, S. 62
*Khôra* 11–12, 16, 19, 20, 21, 22
*Khôros* 11
Kimbles, S.L. 101
Klee, P. 9
'know thyself' 13
knowable/unknowable: as site of psychoanalysis 12, 22
knowing(s)/knowledge: complex forms of 96; disembodied abstraction 90; ego-lead enquiry 87; exterior/interior boundary 93, 94; feminine 88, 96; feminine psyche and women's ways of discovering/ creating 26; the founding carrier bag, the novel and the making and critique of 84; implicit 18; incompleteness of 93, 96; Khôra and the development of 12;

medial women's way of 27–35; as 'open' unity 92, *see also* self-knowledge; tacit knowledge; true knowledge; unthought known
Knox, J. 13, 14
Kolmar, G. 8
Krieger, N. 133–7
Kristeva, J. 11
Kugler, P. 50–1, 52

Lacan, J. 50
land: women, and reflections on physicality 3–8
Landau, A. 62
language 42, 91; in feminist/women's scholarship 135–6; gendering of terms in 135; inter-personal and intra-personal relations 121; performative aspects of 119, 129; the psyche and metaphorical 3; as serving male culture 126, 128; understanding nature of 127–8
Laplanche, J. 50, 52, 53
Larsson, S. 106
*Late Fragment* 23
Lauter, E. 103
law of the fathers 14
law of the mothers 14–15
Le Guin, U.K. 83, 84, 95, 126
legitimacy 21, 64
*Les Guerrerios* 126
libido/theory 13, 43
Lioness program 100, 112
Lisbeth Salander 102, 104, 106–7
literal reclamation of women's land/body 7
literature 3, *see also* epics; novel genre; poetry
lived experience 103
Logos 28, 85, 86, 87, 90, 95
'losing one's head' image 28
love 20, 23, 62, 142
*Love and Sacrifice: The Life of Emma Jung* 56
*Love's Executioner* 59
Lyons-Ruth, K. 18

McRobbie, A. 101
male body 140
male consciousness 85
male culture 126, 128
male gaze 58–9, 62, 63, 64
male privilege 59, 60, 63
manhood 114n5
Mann, T. 32
Margaret, Saint 27
Marine Corps programs 100, 111–12

# Index 155

The Mark of Gender 125
Marks, S. 112, 113
martial history (women's) 100, 110, 111
Martin, G.R.R. 102
masculine: animus/anima theory 132, 133; associated qualities 78; God perceived as 60; power perceived as 99
materialism 122
materiality 118, 119
maternal matrix 89
maternal nexus 71, 74
maternal order 14–15
matriarchy 140
mature women: pattern of experience 101
meaning 18, 122
meaning-making 9, 10, 15, 30
meaningful containment 10, 11, 21, 22
Medea 70
media influence 102
medial woman 25–36; Christian/virgin martyrs 27–8, 35; Eleanora Duse 30–2, 35; Hildegard of Bingen 29–30, 35; Ricarda Huch 32–5
mediumistic fantasies (Hélène's) 44–5
Meir, C. 43
memory(ies) 15, 16; implicit procedural 18–19; psychoanalysis and organisation/ reorganisation 18; and reclamation of women's land/body 7
men: appropriation of land/female body 5; idea of women-as-land 6; relationship of feminine structural forms with 26, see also male body; male consciousness; male culture; male gaze; male privilege; patriarchal authority
mental shield 107
Merini, A. 19
metabiography 14, 15, 17
metamorphosis 125
metaphor(s) 3, 5, 78, 91, 121, 129
Metaphysics 135
metapsychology 14, 15, 17
Meyer, S. 102, 105
Miles, R. 110
military recruitment (female) 100, 111, 112
Millennium trilogy 100, 102, 106–7, 111, 114n2
Milner, M. 77
mimesis 135
mind: biological/corporal bias 17, see also mental shield
mind/body: hierarchical division between 86; in psychoanalysis 58; as sheltering containment 20

mind/womb: as space for coming into being 22
mineralisation: of the psychic structural bones 12
misogyny 103, 113
misunderstandings 19
modernist paradigm 13
modernity 83, 85, 87, 95
'moments of meeting' 10–11, 19
monotheism 14, 86
Morrison, T. 7
Moskowitz, C. 64
mother: as an archetypal figure 73, 137; and the feminine psyche 25; impetus of the hero to break free from 71, see also bad mother; Earth Mother; good mother; Great Mother; law of the mothers
mother complex 134, 146
mother-infant: affect regulation 17; attachment 18; facilitation of psychic birth 16; mind/body as sheltering containment 20; mind/womb as space for coming into being 22; potential space between 11; primal recognition 20–1, 22
mother-patient relationship: recognition of toxic elements in 80
Mullholland, J. 113
multiple personality 43, 127
multiple realities 94, 96
multiplicity 10, 88
Mulvey, L. 58–9
muse 25, 32
mutual myth-making 16
mystics (female) 29
The Myth of the Goddess 86
myth(s)/mythology: -history intersection, as site of psychoanalysis 12, 16, 22; cinematographic 133; of consciousness 86; mediality 35; tacit knowledge 89; as universalised patterns of meaning 15, see also mutual myth-making; new mythology
'mythic carpet on the floor of thought' 21
mythic patterns: psychological and spiritual significance 13

Nagy, M. 42
name/naming 123, 127, 129, 134
National Socialism 34
nature: clash of values over 94–5; creativity of 90; Darwin's portrayal 89; dualism between God and 86; experimental science and 87; returning to/communing with 5; unconscious semiotic interconnectedness with 91;

underlying rationality 91
Nazi Germany 33, 34
negative mother complex 134, 146
neo-bumpology 133
neo-Platonists 29
neuropsychoanalysis 15
neuroredundancy 133
neuroscience 15, 133
neurotautology 133
new mythology: privileging of the
    relational 15–16
New Testament 29
Ní Riain, N. 35
Nicolescu, B. 91–5, 96
'no' 6
nominalism 120–1, 122, 123, 127, 130
non-communication 120
non-recognition: of infants' self-experiences
    22
non-representation/void 21
not-I-ness 43, 44, 46, 47
novel genre 84, 88, 95, 97, *see also* detective
    fiction; fantasy literature; futurist utopian
    genre; science fiction
nurturing 136

O – ultimate unknowable reality 20
obesity 67
object relations theorists 43
objectifying male gaze 59
objectivity 92
Old Testament 29
*On Not Being Able to Paint* 77
*On the Origin of Species* 88–9
one-person psychologies 17
ontological doubts 21, 22
ontology 15, 103
opposites/opposition 77, 87–8, 95, 133
orality 74
Orbach, S. 61, 65
other(ness) 11; balance of self with 33; in
    the epic genre 83; primary encounter
    with 51, *see also* bringing others undone;
    centripetal other; inner otherness;
    violent other
outer other(ness) 48, 49
*The Owl Was a Baker's Daughter* 67

the pack: female military recruits' affiliation
    with 112; in female-centred fiction 100,
    102, 104, 108, 109
*The Pack of Lies* 34
Pandora's beauty box 62
parataxis 129

Paris, G. 132–3
Parks, R. 6
partial consciousness 88
particularity 118
partner: heroine as 70–1
passive/female 59, 60, 73, 78
paternal nexus 71, 74
pathology: deviation from cultural
    norms as 60
patriarchal authority 28, 70, 75
patriarchal culture(s) 100, 140
patriarchal male fantasies 59
patriarchal texts 105
patriarchy 67, 107
patterns of behaviour 135
patterns of experience 101
patterns of meaning 15
Penelope (Odysseus) 70–1
perceptual evolution 9, 10
perfect body: pursuit of 57, 61–2, 64–5
performative aspects: of language 119, 129
persona 120, 144
personal experience: myths of the
    unconscious as deriving from 14
personality 43, 44, 51, 121, 122, 123, 125,
    127, 129
Peter 76–7
phenomenological knowledge 89
*The Phenomenology of the Spirit* 51
photographic images 61
physical beauty 59
physicality 3–8, 65, *see also* body
Piaget, J. 91, 92
Pilard, N. 143–4
Pinkola-Estes, C. 66, 102, 109, 113
Pipher, M. 101
place: as meaningful containment 10, *see
    also* Khôra; pre-subject place
placeless 21
Plato 11, 29
pluralism in thinking 10
poetic imagination 32
poetic word: land as a 4
poetry 3; reclamation of women's land/
    body through 7; on 'space hollowed out
    by...love' (Rilke) 20; *Woman Undiscovered*
    8, *see also* good poem
political power 146
Polyani, M. 89, 90
polytheistic psyche 87, 88
popular culture 101–3
pornography 142, 144, 145
Positive Great Mother 136, 137
positive mother complex 134, 146

post-Jungians: engagement with the body 57; nature of the unconscious 13; voices from the IAJS forum on women and the feminine 132–47
post-natal womb 21
postmodernism 9, 13, 114n1
potential space 11–12
power: and appearance 61, 62; in combat 109–13; as domination 99; male as dominant form of 135; of the male gaze 59, 64; perceived as masculine 99; political 146; use of sex as 142; young women's expression of, in fiction 99–114, *see also viriditas*
Powers, J. 101–2, 104
pre-consciousness 124
pre-subject place 128
pre-utterance/pre-verbal 124, 128
predication 120, 123, 129
primal development tasks (women's) 26
primal division of gender 83
primal negation 21
primal recognition 20–1
primal source: nature as 89
projection 14, 19
projective identification 19
property 5
protection: power used as 104, 105
psyche: adolescent 102; body and tacit knowing 90; ethnic history and formation of 5; and gender 78; inside and outside 91, 96, 120; need for containment 21, *see also* collective psyche; dissociable psyche; feminine psyche; polytheistic psyche; Western psyche
*Psyche's Knife* 101
psychic change 22, 23
psychic energy 13, 14, 43
psychic gender 85
psychic integrity 50
*The Psychic Life of Power* 128
psychic rejuvenation 87
psychic retreats 16, 22
psychic skin 16, 21, 22, 48
psychic structures 10, 12, 13, 17, 19
psychical other 52
psychoanalysis: absence of the female body in 57–8; battle for authority in 14; concern/focus of 18, 19; Nicolescu's rejection of attacks on 94; perception of the human project 9; site of 12, 13, 16, *see also* neuropsychoanalysis
psychoanalytic dialogue 19

psychoid unconscious 13
psychological birth(s) 10, 21; analyst-patient relationship and facilitation of 16; *Khôra* as a prerequisite for 12; mismanaged 16, 22
psychological ideal 3–4
psychological reclamation: of women's land/body 7
*Psychological Types* 121, 122
psychology: feminism as informing 67; and need for women's voices 68, *see also* archetypal psychology; depth psychology; Jungian psychology; metapsychology
psychopathology: restructuring of the unconscious 19
psychotherapy: humanising potential of 9–23; perceptual evolution regarding 10, *see also* Jungian psychology
Pythia of the Delphic Oracle 35

quantum physics 92

race 63–4
rage 6, 105
rationality 91, 124
reactive psychological process 79
real 50
realism 122
reality(ies) 92, 93, 94, 95, 96, 126, 129
rebel leaders (female) 108–9
receptivity 78
reclamation of women's land/body 7–8
recollective imagination 125, 126
recovery 49–50
Redfearn, J. 47, 71
reference(s) 121, 129
regression 77
reification 14
reintegration 77, 79
relatedness 85, 88
relation container/contained 20
relational: privileging of 15–16
relational communication (unconscious) 13
relational failure 18
relational matrices 10
relational repair 18
relational trauma 17–18, 20, 22
relational unconscious 16–17, 19, 23
relationships: facilitation of psychic birth in analyst-patient 16; gender 145; recognition of toxic elements in mother-patient 80; structural forms of the feminine psyche 25, *see also* mother-infant

## 158 Index

religions 86, 94, 95
renewal 78
repression/prohibition 14
research methodology: mediality in 35–6
resistance: to patriarchal authority 28
A Review of the Theory of
    Complexes 135
*Revolving House* 9
rhetoric 120, 127
Rhode, E. 12, 13, 16
Rich, A. 35
Ricoeur, P. 121, 125, 126, 129
right body 64
Rilke, R.M. 20
Roman Empire 28
romanticism 4, 32, 34, 95
Rose, J. 118, 128
Roth, V. 102
Rowland, S. 41–2, 103, 132, 140
The Rule of Metaphor 129
Rupprecht, C.S. 103

sacrifice: heroines characterised as 70, 73
Samuels, A. 47, 78
Schapira, L.L. 35
science 87, 94
science fiction 120
scientific disciplines 92
*Scivias* 30
secondary skin defences 22
self: as an ec-static phenomenon 41, 50–3;
    biological/corporal bias 17; centrifugal
    dynamics in Jung's view of 42–53;
    centripetal dynamics in Jung's view of
    42, 52; continuity of 12, 21; Duse's
    elimination of, in acting 31; inner
    harmony and balance with the other 33;
    sense of 16
self-consciousness 51
self-determination 71, 77
self-disgust 21
self-identity 52
self-knowledge 6, 51
self-loss 51
self-possession 6
self-reflection 50, 51, 136
self-silencing 56, 57
selfhood 41, 50, 51, 53
semiotics 91
Sen, A. 138
Sengupta, S. 137–8
sense of self 16
*Sense and Sensibility* 94–5
separation: Dionysian dismemberment 87;

gender and 78; hero as an archetype of
71; of heroine from paternal nexus 71,
74; Sky Father religions 86; of women
from her land/body 5
SEWA 137
sexual reassignment surgery 63, 64
Shachar, H. 105
shadow: the body as 57, 58
*The Shadow of the Object* 119, 130
Shamdasani, S. 43
shame 21, 22
'she' pronoun 119, 123, 125–6, 127, 129
sheltering containment 20, 21
shield: power as a protective 105, 107, 109
Shiffman, M. 108
sign-inference 129
significance (communicative) 121, 127, 129
signs 96
silence 56, 57–8, 67, 120, 141
similarities 121–2, 129, 130
Singer, T. 101
site of psychoanalysis 12, 13, 16
Sky Father 86, 87, 90, 96, 97
Sleeping Beauty 71
social function (women's) 35, 41
social representation 42
*Soldier Girls* 111
*soma* 119, 122
somatic materiality 119
sophistical rhetoric 120, 123
soul in hiding 22
'space hollowed out by ... love' 20
space-time continuum: the opportunity for
    becoming human 10–11, 12
space/interval/site receptacle 11, 12
spear-point stories 83
Spivak, G. 124, 127
splitting: of body from mind 58; of ego-
    alien content into complexes 13; fear
    of recovery from 49–50; from badness/
    bad mother 75; in libido 43; off of
    unconscious pockets of communication
    45, *see also* reintegration
Stack, A. 52
state symbols: heroines as 70
steady state 77
Stern, D. 10
Stewart, J. 63
strategic essentialism 124
*Structural Forms of the Feminine Psyche* 25–7
subject 128
subject/object division 93
subjectivity(ies) 11, 43, 53, 60, 120, 124,
    127, 128, 130

Index **159**

substantive unconscious 13
suicide rates: post sexual and bariatric
 surgery 64
symbols 96–7, 121
*Symbols of Transformation* 102–3
Symington, N. 16
symptoms: unconscious communications 45
synchronicity(ies) 85, 86–7, 88, 89, 90, 91, 95

*The Tacit Dimension* 89
tacit knowledge 89, 90, 91
talk (psychoanalytic) 19
technoscience 94
Teleborian 107
teleology 33, 44
therapeutic worldview (Hildegard's) 30
thought 12
*Timaeus* 11
time: continuity of self over 12, *see also*
 'acts of creation in time'; space-time
 continuum
Todd, L. 7
topos 11
toxic elements: in mother-patient
 relationships 80
traditional values: Christianity and collision
 with Roman 28
*Tragic Beauty: The Dark Side of Venus Aphrodite
 and the Loss and Regeneration of Soul* 62
trans community 64
transdisciplinarity 91–5, 96
transference 13, 19
transformation 125–30
transformative imagination 125
transformative pronoun 129
transgenderism 63, 64
transparency: drama and the elimination of
 self 31
trauma 15; as enigmatic signifiers of the
 unconscious 52, *see also* relational trauma
trauma complexes 16, 22
tribal goal: power as a 104
trickster 85, 86, 88, 95, 97
Tris Prior 102, 104, 108–9
true knowledge 87
truth speaking 118
tsunami: relational trauma as 18, 20
*Twilight* saga 100, 102, 104–6, 107, 110,
 114n2
two-personal relational unconscious
 16–17, 23

Ulanov, A. 66
un-humanised affect 17

unconscious: alien 41, 47, 52; changing
 notions of 13–14; disconnectedness
 from 3–4; dissociated 12–13, 19, 22, 23;
 embodiedness 91; enigmatic signifiers 50,
 52–3; Hildegard's embodiment and living
 of her perceptions of 29; impersonal 26,
 27, 29, 30; psychoid 13; recognition of
 48; relational 16–17, 19, 23; restructuring
 of 19; symptoms as the expression of the
 45, *see also* collective unconscious
'unconscious becoming conscious' 13, 19
unconscious communication 13, 44, 45, 52,
 119–20
unconscious knowing 89
underestimation: of fierce young
 women 104
underground: self knowledge and the need
 to go 'psychologically' 6
unity 42, 92
universal human nature 13, 14
unknowable *see* known/unknowable
unprocessed/unformulated happenings
 12–13, 22
unrelatedness 106
unspeakable(s) 118, 119–20, 122–3, 124,
 128, 129
unthought known 119, 130
urban dwellers: disconnectedness of 4

*The Vagina Monologues* 64
*Vanity Fair* 63
vertical complexity 93
vertical meaning 93
vertical perspective (psychoanalytic) 13
vertical realities 96
Vico, G. 118, 127
victim: heroine as 70, 73, 74, 79–80
violence 135
violent other 50
virgin martyrs 27–8, 35
*viriditas* 30
visions (Hildegards') 29, 30
vitalisation process: *Khôra* as a 12

Wada, E. 35
waiting role (heroine's) 71, 73
Wehr, D. 103, 107
Western culture 28, 83
Western psyche 86
Westwood, V. 35
What Makes a Women 63
Wheeler, W. 89, 90, 91
*When Women Were Birds: Fifty-four Variations
 on Voice* 56

**160** Index

White, A. 112–13
White, H. 128
*The Whole Creation* 89
wholeness 30, 42, 52, 77, 88, 99
Wilchins, R. 65
'wild women' archetype 102
wildness: fierce young women and journey towards 113
Williams, T.T. 56
Winnicott, D. 11, 20, 134
withdrawal 74, 78
Wittig, M. 119, 120, 123, 124, 125, 126–7, 128, 129, 130
Wolff, T. 25–7, 29, 30, 32, 34, 35, 36, 66
woman: as a demoralised, fetishist word 126
women: aggression against 134; collective psychic ground 6; communication 120, 123, 126; Indian urban 137–8; Jungian 66; and land: reflections on physicality 3–8; male gaze 58–9, 62, 63, 64; martial history 100, 110, 111; as observers of themselves 61; pattern of experience in mature 101; perception of power as

masculine 99; primal developmental tasks 26; self-silencing 56, 57, *see also* fierce young women; heroine(s); medial women; mother
*Women Undiscovered* 8
*Women Who Run with the Wolves* 102, 113
*Women's Bodies in Psychoanalysis* 57–8
women's movement (Indian) 137, 138
Woodman, M. 57, 66, 67
word association tests 43, 44, 46, 120, 124
working with the land 5
working the land/body: reclamation through 7–8
wrong body 64

Yalom, I.D. 59, 60, 62
Yingling, S. 106
'you' pronoun 127
Young-Eisendrath, P. 57, 61, 62, 67
Yousafzai, M. 6

Zinkin, L. 42
*zoe* 88, 89, 90, 91, 94, 95, 96, 97